About Island Press

Since 1984, the nonprofit Island Press has been stimulating, shaping, and communicating the ideas that are essential for solving environmental problems worldwide. With more than 800 titles in print and some 40 new releases each year, we are the nation's leading publisher on environmental issues. We identify innovative thinkers and emerging trends in the environmental field. We work with world-renowned experts and authors to develop cross-disciplinary solutions to environmental challenges.

Island Press designs and implements coordinated book publication campaigns in order to communicate our critical messages in print, in person, and online using the latest technologies, programs, and the media. Our goal: to reach targeted audiences—scientists, policymakers, environmental advocates, the media, and concerned citizens—who can and will take action to protect the plants and animals that enrich our world, the ecosystems we need to survive, the water we drink, and the air we breathe.

Island Press gratefully acknowledges the support of its work by the Agua Fund, Inc., The Margaret A. Cargill Foundation, Betsy and Jesse Fink Foundation, The William and Flora Hewlett Foundation, The Kresge Foundation, The Forrest and Frances Lattner Foundation, The Andrew W. Mellon Foundation, The Curtis and Edith Munson Foundation, The Overbrook Foundation, The David and Lucile Packard Foundation, The Summit Foundation, Trust for Architectural Easements, The Winslow Foundation, and other generous donors.

The opinions expressed in this book are those of the author(s) and do not necessarily reflect the views of our donors.

Water Security

Water Security
The Water-Food-Energy-Climate Nexus

"Water sits at the nexus of so many global issues . . . including health, hunger and economic growth. And sadly, water scarcity takes its greatest toll on society's least fortunate. I am absolutely convinced that the only way to measurably and sustainably improve this dire situation is through broad-scale collaborative efforts between government, industry, academia and other stakeholders around the world."

—INDRA NOOYI,
Chairman and CEO of PepsiCo, Inc., Member of International Business Council, World Economic Forum

"To make a difference on the water challenges we all face, governments, civil society and businesses must work together as never before. For business leaders in particular, we need to speak up, stand up and scale up our efforts on water sustainability."

—MUHTAR KENT,
Chairman and CEO, The Coca-Cola Company, Member of International Business Council, World Economic Forum

"In 1911, John Muir observed how, 'When we try to pick out anything by itself in nature, we find it hitched to everything else in the Universe.' A century later, a gathering of the World Economic Forum discovered the same phenomenon. Four hundred top decision-makers listed the myriad looming threats to global stability, including famine, terrorism, inequality, disease, poverty, and climate change. Yet when we tried to address each diverse force, we found them all attached to one universal security risk: fresh water."

—MARGARET CATLEY-CARLSON,
Patron, Global Water Partnership, 2008–2010 Chair of World Economic Forum Global Agenda Council on Water Security

"Over the last few years, the scale and speed of response from a leading group of large companies to the water challenge has been impressive. As this book illustrates, their engagement in partnerships with others to better understand how water works across the economy and how to manage water more efficiently as a result, can offer much potential."

—PROFESSOR TONY ALLAN,
Kings College London, 2008 Recipient of the Stockholm Water Prize, Member of the World Economic Forum Global Agenda Council on Water Security

This publication was prepared by the World Economic Forum Water Initiative to support the Industry Partnership Programme.

Dominic Waughray, Senior Director and Head of Environmental Initiatives at the World Economic Forum, led the development, collation, and editing of this publication, supported by James G. Workman.

Industry Partners are select member companies of the World Economic Forum that are actively involved in the Forum's mission at the industry level.

Partnerships bring visibility and insight to strategic decision-making on the most important industry- and cross-industry-related issues and the opportunity to engage in actions of global corporate citizenship.

The Forum Industry Partners involved in the Water Initiative include

CH2M HILL
Cisco Systems, Inc.
The Coca-Cola Company
The Dow Chemical Company
Halcrow Group Ltd.

Hindustan Construction Company Ltd.
McKinsey & Company
Nestlé SA
PepsiCo, Inc.

Rio Tinto Group
SABMiller plc
Standard Chartered Bank
Syngenta AG
Unilever

With support from
International Finance Corporation
Swiss Agency for Development and Cooperation
United States Agency for International Development
Water Resources Group
World Wide Fund for Nature
World Economic Forum Global Agenda Council on Water Security

And project advisory support from
McKinsey & Company

Water Security

The Water-Food-Energy-Climate Nexus

The World Economic Forum Water Initiative

ISLANDPRESS

Washington | Covelo | London

Library of Congress Cataloging-in-Publication Data

Water security : the water-food-energy-climate nexus : the World Economic Forum water initiative / [edited by] Dominic Waughray.
    p.   cm.
Includes bibliographical references and index.
ISBN-13: 978-1-59726-735-9 (cloth : alk. paper)
ISBN-10: 1-59726-735-X (cloth : alk. paper)
ISBN-13: 978-1-59726-736-6 (pbk. : alk. paper)
ISBN-10: 1-59726-736-8 (pbk. : alk. paper)
    1. Water supply—Management. 2. Water resources development—International cooperation. 3. Water supply—Risk assessment. 4. World Economic Forum. I. Waughray, Dominic.
    HD1691.W365 2011
    333.91—dc22   2010043396

Printed on recycled, acid-free paper ♽

Manufactured in the United States of America
10   9   8   7   6   5   4   3   2   1

Contents

Illustrations

Figures

Tables

Preface

At the World Economic Forum Annual Meeting in Davos-Klosters in 2008, business leaders set out a Call to Action on Water; their goal was to raise awareness—to develop a better understanding of how water is linked to economic growth across a nexus of issues; and to make clear the water security challenge we face to 2030 if a business as usual approach to water management is maintained.

At the same meeting, Ban Ki-moon, UN Secretary-General, sent business a challenge: to use their call to action to help engage governments in the water discussion.

As a result, the last three years have seen an unprecedented level of discussion and analysis on water throughout the World Economic Forum's meetings and elsewhere. These discussions have been underpinned by a multi-company Water Initiative and informed by our Global Agenda Council on Water Security. This publication captures where the debate is now. It is a significant achievement. It sets out the challenge we face if nothing is done to improve water management in the next two decades. It also points to the future, introducing an important institutional initiative on water the World Economic Forum is now engaging in, to move from insight to action with the Water Resources Group.

The data and text contained in this publication are the products of a unique and unprecedented international, public-private-expert alliance to address the water challenge. It represents the multistakeholder ethos of the World Economic Forum: to bring together expertise and insight from all aspects of the economy to further the global, regional, and industry agenda on key issues, in this case water.

A broad network of World Economic Forum constituents has contributed to the ongoing success of this project. In particular, we express sincere appreciation for the foresight shown by the Industry Partners of the Water Initiative Project Board to conceive and develop this publication, and also to members of the Global Agenda Council on Water Security, past and present, for their continuous input to the overall water initiative and this book in particular.

A few special acknowledgments are due. For his vision and determination to grow the Forum's water security agenda, we are indebted to the leadership shown by Peter Brabeck-Letmathe, Chairman of Nestlé SA and Foundation

Board Member of the World Economic Forum. Within the Forum's International Business Council, we are particularly grateful to Indra Nooyi, Chairman and CEO of PepsiCo, Inc., and Muhtar Kent, Chairman and CEO of The Coca-Cola Company, for their extraordinary partnership and commitment to the Forum's work on water. Among our governmental partners we acknowledge with gratitude the long-term support for the Forum's work on water from the Swiss Agency for Development and Cooperation led by Director General Martin Dahinden and his water team at SDC; and our important partnership with the International Finance Corporation, led by Lars Thunell, CEO and his water team at the IFC. Our gratitude and thanks are also given to Margaret Catley-Carlson, Patron of the Global Water Partnership and Chair of the World Economic Forum Water Security Global Agenda Council, 2007-2010. Her contribution to help develop the water agenda through our various convenings and meetings over the past four years has been immeasurable.

This publication also represents the collective input of more than 350 individuals who have engaged in water initiative–related discussions at our various summits and meetings in Africa, China, Europe, India, and the Middle East during 2008–10, as well as in Davos at our Annual Meetings and Dubai at our Annual Meeting of the Global Agenda.

Our thanks to you all.

Finally, for further information, please contact water@weforum.org, or visit www.weforum.org/water.

—Richard Samans, Managing Director, World Economic Forum
—Dominic Waughray, Senior Director, World Economic Forum

Reproduction of Opening Remarks by the United Nations Secretary General Ban Ki-Moon to the Session of the World Economic Forum Water Initiative at the Forum's Annual Meeting in Davos, January 29 2009

Good morning, ladies and gentlemen.

It is a pleasure to see you and pick up the conversation we began here in Davos one year ago.

Lately, I have taken to saying that the past year was one of multiple crises. We have the economic crisis, the food crisis, the energy crisis. To these we can add climate change. All of these crises are still very much with us. They illustrate our world's vulnerability to the shock of diminishing resources. And as you all know only too well, water is very much near the top of the list. Your work is therefore essential and I commend you for it. Over the past year you have come together—academics, business people, government leaders—and put this issue on the global agenda. People are beginning to realize how connected it is to so many challenges—development, peace and security, economic growth. The global public has become increasingly aware how climate change and water scarcity threaten the populations of heavily settled parts of the world. They understand how it breeds conflict. They know how man-made climate change and growing consumption of water are putting unprecedented stress on this dwindling resource. The good news is that we also know how technology can play an important role in mitigating water stress. Many technologies—new and ancient—can improve water, for example, supplying more water from sea-water, harvesting rainfall or deploying new and simple methods of irrigation that save water. Farmers can diversify crops and plant drought-resistant seeds. All this we know. The problem is that we have no coordinated global management authority in the UN system or the world at large. There is no overall responsibility, accountability or vision for how to address the related problems of climate change, agricultural stress and water technology. This is where you come in. Some of you are members of the Global Compact's CEO Water Mandate, which I introduced here last year and has already made substantial progress. I hope many more of you will join. Your work to create a water security Global Agenda Council is essential. So is your effort to develop the economic and geopolitical forecast you are discussing today. For the first time, you are bringing together all the different perspectives and expertise required to define the full dimension of the problem and propose solutions. In doing so, you are creating the framework of a future partnership—bringing together businesses, governments, universities and NGOs. The problem is broad and systemic. Our work to deal with it must be so as well.

I look forward to seeing your work completed. I will help in any way I can.

Foreword

In 1911, John Muir observed how "when we try to pick out anything by itself in nature, we find it hitched to everything else in the universe." A century later, a gathering of the World Economic Forum discovered the same phenomenon. Four hundred top decision-makers listed the myriad looming threats to global stability, including famine, terrorism, inequality, disease, poverty, and climate change. Yet when we tried to address each diverse force, we found them all attached to one universal security risk: fresh water.

To some degree, water stress is as old as time. But in past societies, scarcity found relief through commerce, as parched regions could import from greener pastures. That pressure valve no longer exists on our hot, hungry, crowded, and fast-evaporating planet. A recent McKinsey & Company study found that within two decades, the collective demand of humans for water will exceed foreseen supply by about 40%. That shortage escalates food prices, disrupts energy, constricts trade, creates refugees, and undermines authority. Thirst is now global.

Our collaboration illustrates where and why water is, quite literally, "hitched to everything else in the universe." Water infuses not only our ground beef patty, lettuce, cheese, pickles, onions, ketchup, and sesame seed bun, but also the bag and packaging in which that hamburger is provided, the building in which it was grilled, the energy to cook it, and the financial system that lent the franchise capital. River currents turn turbines or grow fuel or cool plants that generate its electrical currents. On fresh water dangles the life or death of five thousand children each day, the clothing they wear, and whether their weak governing state will grow stable or start to unravel. Water is the single constraint on the expansion of every city, and bankers and corporate executives have cited it as the only natural limit to economic growth. What is striking is that the water nexus has remained on the periphery of priorities for so many for so long. This work seeks to transform our often-willful ignorance into intense interest and informed, pragmatic action.

This volume binds decades of collaborative work by seasoned veterans in the contentious yet fascinating struggle to quench human thirst. Yet this landmark book did not emerge overnight, out of nowhere. It builds on years of debate in dozens of meetings, initially gaining traction in an earlier report prepared for the Davos-Klosters Annual Meeting in 2009 titled *The Bubble Is Close to Bursting*. *Water Security*, however, pushes much further. It presents not only an urgent warning and unique forecast, but also offers positive recommendations; diverse perspectives, profound insights, and pragmatic case studies by public and private authorities confirm the vital role water can and must play over the next two decades to secure the world's economy.

Water is an astonishingly complex and subtle force in that economy, shaping decisions in ways we only now begin to appreciate. But this much is already clear: if "business-as-usual" water management practices continue for another two decades, large parts of the world will face a serious and structural threat to economic growth, human well-being, and national security. Some will feel the heat sooner than others. Indeed, today we see troubling signs of flash points to come. Against various trend lines in agriculture, energy, climate change, urban growth, infrastructure, population, and environmental stress, this book will argue why we simply cannot manage water in the future as we have done in the past.

In 2009, the Forum's Industry Partners and Global Agenda Council on Water Security united to augment, revise, and strengthen the chapters that form this book's thematic backbone. That same year, the Forum persuaded an extraordinary group of CEOs, water experts, NGO heads, scientists, and international officials to provide insights on the various challenges to our common water future and how we must navigate them.

The next phase of the World Economic Forum's Water Initiative will build on the platform, analysis, and decision-making framework inscribed in this book. Yet the work in your hands is neither definitive nor final. Indeed, *Water Security* is by no means is the ultimate word. It merely introduces a fresh tributary into a broad-based and collaborative current, seeking an efficient, productive, and equitable journey towards a natural cycle of rebirth and renewal.

—Margaret Catley-Carlson, Patron,
Global Water Partnership, Canada;
Vice-Chair, World Economic Forum
Global Agenda Council on Water Security

Introduction

The Water-Food-Energy-Climate Nexus: A Facts and Figures Overview

Water security is the gossamer that links together the web of food, energy, climate, economic growth, and human security challenges that the world economy faces over the next two decades.

There is a structural problem in how we manage water across the web of our global economy. Unless it is checked, worsening water security will soon tear into various parts of the global economic system. It will start to emerge as a headline geopolitical issue. The increasing volatility in food prices in 2008, 2009, and again in 2010 should be treated as early warning signs of what is to come. Arguably, it is water that lies at the structural heart of these agricultural challenges: our rapidly accelerating demand for food and fiber is meeting changing rainfall and weather patterns, overlain on land assets with increasingly depleted and polluted rivers and groundwater resources. As economies grow, more of the freshwater there is left available is demanded by energy, industrial, and urban systems. A massive expansion of agricultural land is one option, but this will need to be undertaken in a manner that does not exacerbate greenhouse gas emissions, thereby amplifying the challenge of adapting to changing weather patterns. More crops from much fewer drops is another option. Yet the agricultural sector, particularly in developing countries, often suffers from historically low levels of investment in technology and human capital as well as weak institutions. This means it does not yet have the necessary enabling environment or extraordinary political leadership required to deliver much, much more food and fiber with much, much less water. If we move quickly and together, we can make the needed changes to the system. But a weak international trade regime and a complex arrangement of tariffs and subsidies amplify the cost of crop shortages within the world system.

Why have we got to this state? In many places around the world, we have consistently underpriced water, wasting and overusing it as a result. We have depleted stocks of groundwater at the expense of our future water needs. In effect, we have enjoyed a series of regional water "bubbles" to support economic growth over the past fifty years or so, especially in agriculture. We have not thought through how our global arrangements should reflect water security in their incentives. Trading patterns are out of sync with water resource levels—three of the world's top-ten food exporters are water-scarce countries.[1] For these and myriad other reasons, we are now on the verge of water bankruptcy in many places around the world, with no clear way of repaying the debt. In fact, a number of these regional water bubbles are now bursting in many parts of China, the Gulf States, India, the Middle East, the Mediterranean, the southwestern US, and southern Africa, to name but a few regions. More will follow. The consequences for regional economic and political stability could be serious.

This set of regional challenges becomes a fast-approaching global crisis when placed against future needs for water. As the world economy expands, demand for water will inexorably rise and continue to outpace population growth. This means that there will not be enough water to do all the things we want to do as inefficiently as they are done now. Unlike energy, water has no substitutes or alternatives. We simply cannot manage water in the future as we have in the past, or else the economic web will collapse. Food shortages are a serious possibility. Ban Ki-moon, UN Secretary-General, puts it thus: "As our global economy grows, so will its thirst. . . . Water security is not an issue of rich or poor, North or South. . . . And yet there is still enough water for all of us if we keep it clean, use it more wisely, and share it fairly. . . . Governments must engage—and lead. But we also need private enterprise."[2]

If we are to ensure sustained economic growth, human security, and political stability over the next two decades, how we manage water is fast becoming an urgent political issue. While businesses and nongovernmental organizations do what they can, water has potent social, cultural, and religious dimensions; it can never be viewed only as a pure economic good. Water requires government engagement in its management and reform. An unfettered reliance on markets will not deliver the social, economic, and environmental outcomes needed. Good regulation in water is indispensable.

The recent financial crisis and its aftermath give us a stark warning of what can happen if known economic risks are left to fester. It shows us that, in today's world system, wide collaboration, although difficult, is the only effective way to address a widespread crisis. It also offers us an opportunity: led by government, a multistakeholder effort to improve the management of our future water needs stands out as an urgent, practical, and resolvable issue that, in times of economic austerity, can bring state institutions, business, and civil society together to address commonly (and often locally) felt challenges.

Growing water problems are recognized by rich and poor alike around the world as real issues that affect our businesses, our lives, and our health. In this respect, the effects of water security, with its strong social, cultural, and economic dimensions, can be seen at both very local levels (when a well or river runs dry) and through today's networked and mass media at very global levels (the recent Pakistan floods, for example). Water security issues, whether too little over long periods of time or too much all at once, create emotive reactions from all sectors of society. Water is an environmental issue unlike any other.

Water also lies at the heart of a nexus of social, economic, and political issues—agriculture, energy, cities, trade, finance, national security, and human livelihoods, within rich and poor countries alike. Water is not only the indispensible ingredient for life, seen by many as a right, but also indisputably an economic and social good unlike any other. It is a commodity in its own right with no substitute and no alternative, but it is also a crucial connector between humans, our environment and all aspects of our economic system.

Collected together in this book for the first time, leaders from government, religious groups, businesses, NGOs, academics, entrepreneurs, financial experts, journalists, trade specialists, and many others share their perspectives on the common water challenge we face. Issue by issue, they set out the case for how crucial it is to overhaul our management of freshwater to meet our future social and economic needs.

In chapters 1 through 9, the following sectors are explored:

- Agriculture
- Energy
- Trade
- National Security
- Cities
- People
- Business
- Finance
- Climate

Each of these sections builds on earlier World Economic Forum reports on water[3] and is supported by contributions from leading social, academic, NGO, and business figures or other commentators who have been involved in the Forum's Water Initiative, the Forum's Global Agenda Council on Water, or other related Forum water events over the past few years.[4] Each section is framed within the context of a description of what the situation might be by 2030 if nothing is done, and then an exploration of what options exist for what can be done today.

As you read the following pages, it will become clear that the various commentators place their concerns not in terms of poverty and social justice alone, but also within a wider geopolitical and political-economic context: water security is arguably the arriviste issue in national security and global affairs. Across the contributions, the proposition resonates that water is no longer a niche technical or environmental issue. In the fast-changing world we can see stretching out to 2030, it is increasingly clear that our political, economic, and social stability into the 21st century will depend as much on how we manage our freshwater resources as it will on any of the other well-recognized "hard power," global security issues of the 20th century, such as terrorism, nuclear proliferation, and fossil-fuel security.

In short, the first nine chapters of the book set out the emerging realization of the extent to which water security underpins and connects the food, fiber, fuel, urbanization, migration, climate change, and economic growth challenges the world system faces at least through 2030, if not beyond.

In the final three chapters of the book, attention is turned to what can be done. Happily, and unlike many other issues we seem to face these days, there is the beginning of a good-news story here. These chapters explore breakthroughs in the development of a new economic fact base on water for governments; experiences in developing public-private coalitions that can work with governments to take action on water; and finally, a conclusion that sets out a major next step for the World Economic Forum Water Initiative with the Water Resources Group.

It is clear that governments can (and must) play a leadership role in setting frameworks for improved water management, but many other stakeholders have to also play a role in delivering solutions. This multistakeholder challenge means that coalitions are required—public-private-civil alliances commonly focused on meeting the water security challenge, each leveraging their own comparative advantage within a shared policy framework.

Yet coalition building is not easy. It is beyond the ability of an international agency, an NGO, a think tank, a farmers association, a trade union, or a company to create a "neutral convening" process to build a multistakeholder coalition to address the water security challenge in a properly holistic manner. And even governments find it sometimes difficult to do. Whoever takes the lead, the others suspect (rightly or wrongly) a particular agenda. Power politics dictate that the convener would treat not all stakeholders equally. Transaction costs are high, pace can be slow to start with, and trust takes time to build.

Finding effective ways to help governments take the lead in improving water security must be central in any process that aims to address these difficult issues. Throughout this book, all commentators agree that new arrangements have to be found that allow governments to be confident that citizens, civil society, business experts, and international agencies can work together with them to resolve the accelerating water security challenge in a practical way. We need new approaches. According to Indra Nooyi, Chairman and CEO of PepsiCo: "Water sits at the nexus of so many global issues . . . including health, hunger, and economic growth. And sadly, water scarcity takes its greatest toll on society's least fortunate. I am absolutely convinced that the only way to measurably and sustainably improve this dire situation is through broad-scale collaborative efforts between government, industry, academia, and other stakeholders around the world."[5]

As a result of sustained discussions on this issue over the past five years, such as at the World Economic Forum annual and regional meetings (in particular at the Annual Meeting in Davos-Klosters in 2008 and again in 2010), and through the impact of other significant developments and initiatives (such as the UN CEO Water Mandate[6] and the International Finance Corporation–led 2030 Water Resources Group[7]), several governments are now indicating their readiness to champion such fact-based public-private-expert discussions. Some argue we are now on the cusp of change.

To build on this newfound momentum, proof points or case studies on how to actually make these new coalitions and transformations happen are urgently needed. Confidence needs to be created, especially for governments, that there are practical and fact-based ways of addressing this complex and multifaceted challenge. This is the objective of the next stage of the World Economic Forum's Water Initiative and its partnership with key international analytical initiatives, such as the Water Resources Group.

The following pages are certainly not meant to contain the last word on the water security issue. Instead, by drawing on a range of different viewpoints, and based on the multistakeholder ethos that lies at the heart of the World Economic Forum, the intent of this book is to simply set out for the reader the following:

- first, through a selection of expert perspectives, an exposition of the complex set of challenges we face across our economy in managing our future water needs when looking forward over the next two decades;
- second, what the implications of these challenges to our social, economic, and political well-being may be if we fail to act, based on the best and current thinking on forecasts and growth trends;
- third, some emergent approaches for tackling the problem, including an introduction to a major initiative being undertaken by the World Economic Forum in alignment with many other actors.

As a result, this book should be viewed as the start and not the end of a journey: an opening to a doorway that lets us peep into the forecasted world of 2030 if we fail to address the challenge of water security, and which shines a light on a possible new pathway we might follow in order to avoid this future. Available online on a wiki platform, as well in a hard copy book format, it is our hope that this introduction to the water security issue will encourage you to reflect, research, and then add your thoughts and experiences to the perspectives captured here. The aim is for this text to become a living document that gets added to as the journey towards managing our future water needs progresses over the next few years. The work will be returned to and updated in two years to explore how the issues have developed, hopefully with your contributions captured, too.

The aspiration for this door opener into the water security issue is that when you have finished this book, you will think about water in a rather different way than when you began. To help you start the journey, the remainder of this section gives some facts and figures on water and how it sits at the nexus of food, energy, trade, economic growth, climate change, and other issues.

The Water-Food-Energy-Climate Nexus

Analysis from McKinsey & Company as part of the 2030 Water Resources Group report[8] provides this clear and basic primer to the global water challenge through 2030:

- Globally, agriculture accounts for approximately 3,100 billion m³, or 71% of water withdrawals today, and without efficiency gains this will increase to 4,500 billion m³ by 2030.
- Industrial withdrawals account for 16% of today's global demand, growing to a projected 22% in 2030. The growth will come primarily from China (where industrial water demand in 2030 is projected at 265 billion m³), which alone will account for 40% of the additional industrial demand worldwide.
- Demand for water for domestic use will decrease by 2030 as a percentage of the total water withdrawals, from 14% today to 12% in 2030, although it will grow in specific basins, especially in emerging markets.

A common theme running through this book is how these different but growing demands on water also connect with one another. Based on work developed over the past three years by the World Economic Forum's Global Agenda Council on Water Security, and developed through wider collaboration with other Forum stakeholders, a better understanding of this water-food-energy-climate nexus and the implications it presents for political, civil society, and business decision-makers through 2030 is now beginning to emerge. If water is essential for all the core drivers of economic growth, we cannot afford to have our resources fail.

The vignette below is a first attempt to bring together some of the relevant facts and figures. Much of this information was presented in a paper prepared in August 2010 for the World Economic Forum's International

Business Council (IBC), a group that comprises one hundred of the world's top CEOs.[9] As a result of discussions on the nexus issue, led by the Global Agenda Council on Water Security, within the wider Global Agenda Council network of experts, the IBC and elsewhere, awareness is rising on how interconnected the issues of water, energy, food, and climate actually are.

Deepening our understanding of these interlinkages and developing the new arrangements they will require will likely form a core part of the global, regional, and business agenda in the coming years, if we are to move onto a pathway of sustainable growth. Addressing our water security, so as to manage our future water needs for economic growth, increasingly stands out as a practical place to start.

A Facts and Figures Overview

The world's food, water, and energy resources are already experiencing significant stress or shortfalls—and yet, in the next twenty years, demand for these resources is projected to increase significantly as populations, economies, and consumption rates grow. The world appears ill equipped for the changes, investments, and trade-offs that will be required to meet that demand. Meeting our future food, water, and energy needs therefore presents a very real growth conundrum. The highly interlinked nature of these issues is particularly challenging, as it requires comprehensive solutions coordinated among diverse stakeholders who often lack the incentives or institutional structures required for effective action. A common thread running through this nexus is water.

Rapid Growth Will Intensify Global Demands for Food, Water, and Energy in the Next Twenty Years

In the coming decades, several significant global trends will intensify demand for food, water, and energy resources. These demand drivers include the following:

- Population growth: World population is expected to rise from the current 6.83 billion to 8 billion in the next two decades, largely in the developing world. By 2050, the combined population of Europe, the US, and Canada will account for only 12% of the global total.[10]
- Economic growth: This will be driven largely by emerging markets— the World Bank estimates 6% growth in developing countries in the medium term, compared to up to 2.7% in higher-income countries.

If historic trends continue, the proportion of global GDP produced by Europe, the US, and Canada will be less than 30% by 2050, compared to 68% in 1950.[11]

- Urbanization: More than half the world's population now lives in an urban environment. There are twenty-four megacities with more than ten million people, seventeen of which are in developing countries. China already has more than one hundred cities with more than one million inhabitants; India has thirty-five; and the US has nine. By 2050, China's cities will house 73% of its population (up from 46% today), and Indian cities will encompass 55% of its people (up from 30% today).[12]

A growing, increasingly prosperous, and rapidly urbanizing global population will demand more food, energy, and water resources to meet its needs. Expected trends will include:

- Increased food demand and changing diets: The world's growing population, much of it more prosperous and more urban, will demand more quantities and different types of food. To meet growing demand in the next twenty years, farmers will need to increase production by 70–100% and reduce postharvest loss. Changing diets—driven by rising incomes and other shifts—will increase demand for resource-intensive products such as meat. Global demand for meat will increase 50% by 2025, helping to drive a foreseen increase of 42% in grain demand.[13] In a world where nearly one billion people suffer from hunger or malnutrition, existing food and agriculture systems seem ill prepared to meet these challenges. Increased production alone will not solve the problem of hunger, which also results from lack of access or purchasing power by the poor.
- Increased demand for energy: The International Energy Agency forecasts that the world economy will demand at least 40% more energy by 2030 compared to today.[14] McKinsey & Company in its work for Project Catalyst estimate that 77% of the requisite energy infrastructure has yet to be built. By 2030, China will need to expand its power-generating capacity by more than 1,300 GW (1.5 times the current level of the US), and India by 400 GW (equal to the current combined power generation of Japan, South Korea, and Australia).[15] Increasing access to energy is a priority for many countries—1.5 billion people in the developing world lack access to electricity, and more than 3 billion rely on biomass for heating and cooking.[16]

- Accelerating rates of water use: As we get richer, we get thirstier. Between 1990 and 2000, the world's population grew by a factor of four, but freshwater withdrawals grew by a factor of nine.[17] This means that withdrawals of water through 2030 will increase much more quickly than does global population, as people get wealthier and consumption patterns rise. Recent analysis suggests the world could face a 40% shortfall between water demand and available freshwater supply by 2030.[18] Many countries are already extracting groundwater faster than it can be replenished (Mexico by 20%, China by 25%, and India by 56%).[19] If current trends continue, by 2030 two-thirds of the world's population will live in areas of high water stress.[20]

The Pressure On Water Resources as the World Economy Grows Will Be Particularly Intense

Increasing water scarcity could cause annual grain losses equivalent to 30% of current world consumption (recall, this is at the same time as we want to increase food production by 70–100%). It may be difficult to augment more surface water to overcome these challenges.[21] The amount of water impounded behind dams has quadrupled since 1960, with recent estimates placing the volume of water trapped behind (documented) dams at 6,000–7,000 cubic kilometers. At the same time, water withdrawals from rivers and lakes have doubled since 1960.[22] Related to this, cross-border water management issues have become geopolitical flash points in numerous regions. Yet, as demand continues to grow, competition for water will inexorably intensify between economic sectors, as well as between geographies. Where regional economies are growing fastest, demand for water for energy and industrial use is projected to rise sharply between 2000 and 2030 (56% in Latin America, 63% in West Asia, 65% in Africa, 78% in Asia).[23] Recall that across these regions, on average, 70% of water is already allocated to agriculture. How to square these seemingly impossible circles?

The effects of climate change—and the potential for poorly constructed policy responses to it—will accelerate the pressure on these challenges. Even the most conservative models predict that climate change will likely impose additional pressures on water demand, availability, and accessibility, tightening the margin between average water supply and demand. Climate change threatens major mountain glaciers, which act as the world's largest freshwater banks, feeding principal rivers and providing water to more than two billion people in Asia alone. In the 1990s, the Himalayan glacial mass shrank at three times the rate of the previous decade; given current trends, these freshwater glacial banks may largely disappear by the end of this century.[24] While estimates vary and predictions are difficult, climate change may reduce agricultural yields in developing countries as a whole by 10–25%, including up to 40% in India alone—affecting not only food supplies but also employment and income.[25] The sector employs up to 65% of the global labor force and contributes up to 29% of GDP; significant losses in agriculture are likely to have substantial economic effects, particularly for the poor, which in turn may fuel further resource degradation.[26]

These Issues Are Highly Interlinked, and Thus Must Be Addressed in Tandem

More complicated still, these various issues are all highly interlinked, and solutions to one can in fact worsen another. Currently, 70% of the world's freshwater withdrawals are used for agriculture,[27] and it takes one liter of water to grow one calorie.[28] This means that a near doubling in food production will not be sustainable without significant—perhaps radical—changes in agricultural water use. Yet energy production is the largest industrial user of water, and expanding energy production requires more access to freshwater. For example, in the US, energy demand is forecast to increase 40% by 2030.[29] The US Geological Survey estimates that to produce and burn the one billion tons of coal Americans use each year, the mining and utility industries withdraw between 208 and 284 trillion liters of water annually. That's equal to about half of all freshwater withdrawals in the US today.[30] An increase in energy demand by 40% using current energy systems could translate to an increase in freshwater access needs by 165% according to some estimates.[31] How will this be achieved under business-as-usual approaches? Department of Energy officials have told the US Congress that future energy production will be dependent on water access.

The International Energy Agency forecasts that more than 75% of the increase in energy use from 2007 to 2030 will be met through fossil fuels, especially coal. By 2050, the resulting carbon emissions could lead to a concentration of carbon in the atmosphere (one thousand parts per million) that is more than double that which international negotiations are currently struggling (and failing) to achieve.[32] The resulting rate of global warming would exacerbate water scarcity and affect food production.

By 2030, hydropower will become the world's dominant renewable energy source, providing more than twice the amount of its nearest rival, onshore wind power. About 170 GW of hydropower is currently under construction, 76% of this across Asia.[33] But as hydropower is estimated to evaporate about seventeen cubic meters of water per megawatt hour[34] (compared to between 0.7 and 2.7 cubic meters of water per megawatt hour in closed loop cooling thermal electric power plants), the new hydropower capacity in Asia alone could lead to the evaporation of thousands of kilometers cubed of water from its reservoirs.

When water use is taken into account together with carbon emissions, some renewable energy sources begin to look less sustainable. It is not just hydropower. In the case of shale gas extraction, which is water-intensive and can pose a risk to water quality, US legislators and regulators are already expressing concern. Similar concerns are arising over the water requirements for concentrated solar thermal plants. In fact, thirty-five such plants in the California/Nevada desert are currently in negotiations with state regulators to try and get the water they need for cooling. One plant alone requested 4.9 billion liters, or 20% of the water in the local valley.[35]

Policy decisions can help, but in some cases they can make matters worse. Due to policy incentives designed to reduce vehicle emissions, by 2030 the International Energy Agency predicts that at least 5% of global road transport will be powered by biofuel—more than 3.2 million barrels per day.[36] But producing those fuels could consume between 20% and 100% of the total quantity of water now used worldwide for agriculture.[37] This is clearly an unsustainable trade-off in terms of both water consumption and land use, as fields are converted to grow fuel rather than much-needed food crops.

This difficult reality is fast complicating the standard definition of "sustainable" energy. Do governments pursue increased energy access at the expense of decreased water access, or zero-carbon or zero-water energy policies, or must all be pursued simultaneously? Energy security and water security thinking are not yet aligned. But such multiple goals will become a necessity—raising the prospect of a future in which we may track both energy and water intensity per unit of GDP with equal vigor.

Cross-border Trade and Investment Can Help in Theory, but Are Problematic in Practice

For countries facing water resource shortages, trade—in theory—should be a viable solution. For example, countries can import "virtual water"—buying one kilogram of wheat from abroad rather than using 1,300 kilograms of water to grow it at home.[38] Trade in virtual water would then allow domestic water to be allocated away from irrigation and towards higher-value industrial and energy uses to help the economy grow. Some estimate that by trading in virtual water, Asia could reduce its water use for irrigation by up to 12% through increased cereal imports.[39]

But by 2030, due to the growth of their industrial and energy sectors, all countries in South Asia, the Middle East, and North Africa will be facing such trade-offs for domestic water use. Ideally, the 2.5 billion inhabitants of these regions would be able to turn to the world trade system to meet their food and fiber needs, so that they could allocate more domestic water to energy and industry. The international trading regime is, however, ill prepared for such a spike in demand for agricultural trade. In fact, agricultural exports had declined to just 9% of international trade in 2001;[40] staples in particular are thinly traded, as seen in the price volatility of wheat, sugar, rice, and other commodities during between 2008 and 2010. As mentioned above, trading patterns are also out of sync with water resource levels, as three of the world's top-ten food exporters are actually water scarce, and three of the top-ten food importers are water rich.[41] While climate change may increase productivity in northern regions, some irrational and historically more protectionist trade regimes may limit other countries' access to those gains.

Without Effective Policy Frameworks, the Scramble for Resources May Drive a Retreat from Globalization

Unable to rely on trade to ensure their food security, fast-growing economies that need to secure food supplies are increasingly striking land-lease deals with poorer nations that have fertile, well-watered land. Between 2006 and 2009, the media reported deals totaling more than twenty million hectares in developing countries.[42] Most are government-to-government deals with state-owned enterprises or investment companies acting as agents. Japan now has three times more land abroad than at home. Saudi Arabia, Kuwait, South Korea, and China have secured deals in Sudan, Ethiopia, DRC, and Pakistan. Libya has secured an oil-for-land deal with Ukraine.[43] Some NGOs report that countries such as Cambodia, Laos, and Sudan are leasing significant amounts of land to external investors while still receiving food aid.[44] In effect, one could better view these so-called land grabs as water grabs. The purchasing countries have plenty of land; what they are short of is water.

Regional and international organizations are trying to address the issue and define acceptable frameworks for such investments. But given forecasted resource trends, the scale and volume of such deals may well increase rapidly in the next two decades, with water-rich areas capturing significant investment from water-scarce countries. The growth in these bilateral arrangements could diminish the influence of many multilateral organizations with responsibilities for managing water and the environment. Further, as more deals like this occur, wider implications about securing and sustaining equitable water access for others (such as local society, business, ecosystems, etc.) who may share the river basin with these new arrangements could emerge, creating flash points in times of water scarcity.

The scramble for resources will generate new geopolitical dynamics, potentially coalescing around national interests and alliances, thereby bringing a retreat from multilateral globalization. The roles of international organizations may be thrown into question. Global companies, too, may face a baffling new landscape where the rules have significantly changed—or where there are no rules at all.

The challenges of natural resource scarcity—food, water, and energy—are closely interlinked, and policy and other attempted solutions must take this into account. But taking an integrated view of such issues is highly challenging to most institutions, given the complexity and cross-sectoral approach required. The political commitment necessary to take bold action is often hard to muster.

A Bold Shift Is Required to Transform Crisis into Opportunity

Finding sustainable growth models that can work across these issue areas while sustaining a global economic recovery will be challenging, but it is possible. Technical investigation, economic analysis, and policy formulation need to become much more interlinked. It is becoming clear that pursuing a low-carbon development path, for example, while crucial, must also be set in a wider context for sustainable growth, including water security. Growth strategies must accommodate the interrelated environmental constraints as well as meet the aspirations of countries and individuals for social and economic development. This means the new models must also generate more and better jobs and income opportunities if social cohesion is to be maintained in an ever more crowded and interconnected world. The new Green Growth paradigm, championed by South Korea, offers a useful new approach.

While the transition in political, economic, and business thinking is just beginning, the challenge of this water-food-energy-climate nexus is arguably larger and more systemic than any one business or government can deal with on its own; a wholesale shift is required. Coherent policies across a range of portfolios, as well as socially buttressed, stable policy frameworks and investment climates, will be crucial for a successful transition. The creation of multistakeholder platforms can help to generate the necessary consensus and also engage the wide range of expertise and implementation capacities that effective responses will require. Designing them to move from analysis to convening to transformational reforms ("ACT") can help focus such diverse groups on making an impact. These are the kinds of "new normative approaches" that will be required,

This is a difficult agenda for governments to lead by themselves. In this challenging and complex landscape, civil society and business leaders can play an important and constructive role to support governments in a comprehensive water-food-energy-climate reform process by driving progress along several tracks:

- sharing and developing knowledge among relevant stakeholders to access the best available data and developing common frames of reference on the need for solutions;
- innovating new business models that address resource challenges through new technologies, investments, or efficiency gains;
- initiating or engaging in policy dialogue with other stakeholders to develop broad-based support for effective policy frameworks and incentives;
- demonstrating leadership commitment to develop market-based solutions and forming partnerships and collaborations with other relevant stakeholders to implement them.

Notes

1. See "World Grain Exporters and Importers," *RiaNovosti*, http://en.rian.ru/infographics/20100812/160171412.html, based on statistics from the US Department of Agriculture for 2009–10.

2. Quote taken from United Nations Secretary General Ban Ki-Moon's speech at the World Economic Forum Annual Meeting in Davos-Kloster to a private session on Managing Our Future Water Needs—A Call to Action. January 24, 2008.

3. See "Water Initiative Publications," http://www.weforum.org/en/initiatives/water/Publications/index.htm. Water Initiative Publications include "Innovative Water Partnerships," January 2010; "The Bubble Is Close to Bursting," January 2009; "Thirsty Water: Water and Energy in the 21st Century," January 2009; "Managing Our Future Water Needs," January 2008; and "Realizing the Potential for Public-Private-Partnerships in Water," January 2008.

4. See the acknowledgements for the full list of contributors.

5. World Economic Forum Water Initiative, *The Bubble Is Close to Bursting*, 2009.

6. See "The CEO Water Mandate," http://www.unglobalcompact.org/issues/Environment/CEO_Water_Mandate/.

7. See McKinsey & Company, *Charting Our Water Future*, 2009.

8. Ibid.

9. For more information on the IBC, see http://www.weforum.org/en/Communities/InternationalBusinessCouncil/index.htm.

10. United Nations, *UN World Population Prospects*, 2008 revision; and Food and Agriculture Organization of the United Nations, *World Agriculture: Towards 2015/2030*, 2007.

11. World Bank, *Global Economic Prospects, 2010: Fiscal Headwinds and Recovery*, 2010.

12. UN-HABITAT, *State of the World's Cities, 2008/2009,* 2009; and Jack Goldstone, "The New Population Bomb: Four Megatrends That Will Change the World," *Foreign Affairs,* January/February 2010, http://www.foreignaffairs.com/articles/65735/jack-a-goldstone/the-new-population-bomb.

13. United Nations Environment Programme, *The Environmental Food Crisis,* 2009.

14. International Energy Agency, *World Energy Outlook, 2008,* 2009. BLUE Map scenario illustrates reductions of emissions to 14 Gt by 2050.

15. Project Catalyst, *Project Catalyst Brief,* 2009.

16. The Secretary-General's Advisory Group on Energy and Climate Change, *Energy for a Sustainable Future,* 2010.

17. J. R. McNeill, *Something New under the Sun: An Environmental History of the Twentieth-Century World,* 2000. If these figures are accurate, the same data set suggests that total freshwater use in 1990 was about forty times that of 1700.

18. McKinsey & Company, *Charting Our Water Future,* 2009.

19. United Nations Development Programme, *Human Development Report, 2007/2008: Fighting Climate Change,* 2007.

20. Food and Agriculture Organization of the United Nations, *Coping with Water Scarcity,* 2007.

21. International Water Management Institute, *Water for Food, Water for Life: A Comprehensive Assessment of Water Management in Agriculture,* 2007.

22. Millennium Ecosystem Assessment, 2005. *Ecosystems and Human Well-Being: Wetlands and Water Synthesis.* World Resources Institute, Washington, DC.

23. World Economic Forum Water Initiative, *The Bubble Is Close to Bursting,* 2009.

24. United Nations Development Programme, *Human Development Report, 2007/2008: Fighting Climate Change,* 2007.

25. William Cline, *Global Warming and Agriculture: Impact Estimates by Country,* 2009.

26. World Bank, *World Development Report, 2008: Agriculture for Development,* 2008.

27. Ibid.

28. Food and Agriculture Organization of the United Nations, *Growing More Food—Using Less Water,* 2009.

29. International Energy Agency, *World Energy Outlook, 2009,* 2009.

30. Keith Schneider, "Will There Be Enough Water to Power the Future?," *Ecomagination,* http://www.ecomagination.com/will-there-be-enough-water-to-power-the-future/.

31. Danish Hydraulic Institute, *A Water for Energy Crisis?,* 2007.

32. International Energy Agency, *World Energy Outlook, 2009,* 2009.

33. Ibid.

34. World Economic Forum Water Initiative, *Thirsty Energy: Water and Energy in the 21st Century,* 2009. See also chapter 2 of this volume, where the data are reproduced.

35. Geoff Schumacher, "Solar, Water Don't Mix," *Las Vegas Review-Journal,* October 2, 2009, http://www.lvrj.com/opinion/solar-water-dont-mix-63234432.html.

36. International Energy Agency, *From 1st- to 2nd-Generation Biofuel Technologies*, 2008.

37. International Water Management Institute, *Water for Food, Water for Life: A Comprehensive Assessment of Water Management in Agriculture*, 2007; and Danish Hydraulic Institute, *A Water for Energy Crisis?*, 2007.

38. See "The Concepts of Water Footprint and Virtual Water," http://www.gdrc .org/uem/footprints/water-footprint.html.

39. Tony Allan, King's College; member, World Economic Forum Global Agenda Council on Water Security, personal communication.

40. Food and Agriculture Organization of the United Nations, *The State of Food and Agriculture*, 2008.

41. See "World Grain Exporters and Importers," *RiaNovosti*, http://en.rian.ru/ infographics/20100812/160171412.html, based on statistics from the US Department of Agriculture for 2009/10.

42. International Food and Policy Research Institute, *"Land Grabbing" by Foreign Investors in Developing Countries*, 2009.

43. John Vidal, "How Food and Water Are Driving a 21st-Century African Land Grab," *Observer*, March 7, 2010, http://www.guardian.co.uk/environment/2010/ mar/07/food-water-africa-land-grab; and Dominic Waughray, "The Pending Scramble for Water," *BBC News*, February 2, 2009, http://news.bbc.co.uk/2/hi/busi ness/7790711.stm.

44. For example, see Thin Lei Win, "Cambodia Faces Land Rights 'Crisis,'" *TrustLaw*, http://www.trust.org/trustlaw/news/cambodia-faces-land-rights-crisis-campaigners/.

CHAPTER I

Agriculture

This chapter explores the water-food nexus. It benefits greatly from the perspectives of many public, private, academic, and NGO representatives who have taken part in various Forum sessions and workshops on water issues over the last three years. Some personal perspectives from specific leaders close to the water and food agenda appear at the end of the chapter.

Background

In 1972, the Club of Rome released a report titled *The Limits to Growth*. Using state-of-the-art economic modeling, the Club of Rome report drew rather startling conclusions that warned of the food shortages and environmental consequences that could come with unfettered population and economic expansion into the 21st century.

In general, *The Limits to Growth* was stereotyped as either a neo-Malthusian projection of population collapse caused by global shortages of food and other natural resources, or a critique of economic growth suggesting that the world should shift to a steady but much poorer state.

Since 1972, the earth's human population has increased by more than two billion people. Global wealth has increased dramatically. We have witnessed a Green Revolution in agriculture across the developing world. Many people now eat much better diets than they did forty years ago.

So was *Limits to Growth* wrong?

In fact, it had something slightly different to say than is more popularly thought. Writing in 2010, Professor Jorgen Randers, one of the study's original authors, pointed out that "very few seem to know that *Limits to Growth* was in fact a scenario analysis of 12 possible futures from 1972 to 2100. And that the main scientific conclusion of the study was that delays in global decision-making would cause the human economy to overshoot planetary limits before the growth in the human ecological footprint slowed. Once in unsustainable territory, human society would be forced to reduce its rate of resource use and its rate of emissions."[1]

Professor Randers reflected that if only they had the words back in 1972, they could have called the report "Limits to Our Environmental Footprint." The intent was not to recommend a limit to economic growth per se, but to recommend a lowering of the environmental impact per unit of GDP, and a simultaneous step change in the efficiency per unit of natural resource used.

The need for human society to make such a step change in resource-use efficiency—in order to get the same utility, if not more, from a smaller stock of natural resources—is the technician's way of expressing what has now become something of a mantra in agricultural hydrology circles: how to get more "crop per drop." Thus the challenge the Club of Rome identified in 1972 is very close to the challenge our global agriculture sector now faces with regard to water: how to get much more crop with many fewer drops?

Another feature worth noting in the Club of Rome's report is how the economic warning that something needed to change might play out. As growth under business-as-usual conditions "overshot" planetary limits, they predicted shocks to the system arising from the collapse of resource stocks, perhaps in the early 21st century, which in turn would be reflected in the market.

Arguably, the early stages of these signals are now starting to be seen. As this book goes to press in the autumn of 2010, there has been a summer heat wave across the Northern Hemisphere, creating unprecedented and prolonged hot spells from Russia through to India; erratic weather patterns, causing catastrophic floods in Pakistan; floods and mud slides in Brazil, China, and Europe; and the worst drought in more than one hundred years in southwest China, the worst drought in twenty years in Thailand, continued drought in North and West Australia, and unprecedented droughts in Afghanistan, across the Caribbean, and in Kenya. There have also been recent and unprecedented price spikes in wheat and coco prices, sustained high prices in sugar as supply tightens, and a soaring cotton price "heralding the end of cheap clothes," according to some commentators. This amalgam of headlines could have been one of Professor Janders's scenarios back in 1972.

As predicted, the market now seems to be sending us early signals about challenges to our food security. The question is, should we be concerned, and if so, how should we respond?

Published by the International Water Management Institute in 2007, *Water for Food, Water for Life: A Comprehensive Assessment of Water Management in Agriculture* sought to address these exact issues. Seven hundred leading scientists collaborated to produce the report, and its 645 pages were peer reviewed by fifty experts. It is the best scientific sourcebook available on the global challenge of water for agriculture. It concluded that we should indeed be concerned. Specifically the study asked is there enough land, water, and human capacity to produce food for a growing population over the next fifty years. Its sobering answer is no, unless we act to improve water use in agriculture.

The report expresses in evocative terms the pressure agriculture exerts on our freshwater supplies: "Imagine a canal 10 meters deep, 100 meters wide, and 7.1 million kilometers long (enough to go around the world 180 times). That is the amount of water it takes each year to produce food for today's 6.5 billion people. Add 2–3 billion more people and accommodate their changing diets, from cereals to more meat and vegetables, and that could add another 5 million kilometers to the channel of water needed to feed the world's people."[2]

Josette Sheeran, Executive Director of the World Food Programme, agrees. As she wrote in a summary of the 2008 World Economic Forum Global Agenda Council discussions on the environment and sustainability:

> To feed ourselves the world will need to double food production in the next 40 years to meet projected demand. Among the middle classes, global demand for meat alone is expected to increase by 50% between now and 2025. Among the poorest today, over one billion people—one-sixth of the world's population—do not have access to adequate food and nutrition. And an increase in two billion people is expected by 2025, with population growth highest in the poorest parts of the world. In contrast, an estimated 33% of food in richer countries gets wasted. Still, we will have to produce even more food in the future and food of higher protein content. But our ability to meet current and future production needs is seriously challenged by increasing water scarcity, climate change, and volatile energy costs and supplies. Unless we change how we do it, we will not be able to supply our future food needs.[3]

But the issue of agriculture and water availability is not straightforward. It has several facets, including the provision of the right quantity of water at the right time and at the right level of quality. This complexity introduces different risks to farmers across the globe and thus requires specifically tailored solutions to the farmers' needs, based on the water availability, climatic conditions, agriculture practices, soil, economics, policies, regulation, and so on. Water is local.

Examples of such tailored solutions to local conditions include the use of drought-tolerant crops to mitigate drought risks, salinity-resistant crops (as required in many parts of India), and drainage and other tools to address flooding or too much moisture (as in the case of the 2010 Pakistan flood). More efficient irrigation, measurement, and integrated stress management (both "biotic"—to manage insects, weeds, fungi, etc.—and "abiotic"—to manage water, heat, cold, etc.) is also crucial. This can help optimize the utilization of water on a field, combating challenges such as weeds, which compete with the crops for nutrition and water, and pests damaging the crop and yield, thus reducing growth and the effectiveness of the applied water.

Incentives for proper field and crop management are also important, not only to manage water more effectively and efficiently on the farm, but also beyond. Pollution from excess fertilizer and chemicals degrades water, and careless cultivation and erosion can muddy it up. The US Environmental Protection Agency blames agriculture as the country's leading cause of water quality impairment. When agriculture loses excessive nitrate, phosphorous, pesticides, and mineral salts in the water, these pollutants may have a social and environmental cost.

Thus, unless the world's agricultural system rapidly adapts to improved practices and incentives such as those mentioned above, unless it develops and deploys new crops and implements more efficient technologies to improve water use efficiency and resilience to drought in agriculture, future levels of agricultural production won't keep up with the trends that await it.

Trends

Overall, about 70% of global freshwater withdrawals are currently used for agriculture (reaching up to 90% in some fast-growing economies). But inefficiencies in agricultural water use are generally extremely high. Traditional irrigation, in most water-scarce countries consumes only about half the water it withdraws; the rest is lost, leaks back to the land or simply evaporates.

Our human population is expected to expand from 6.38 to 8 billion over the next fifteen years.[4] This growing population will contain a much larger and more urban middle class than today, who will demand more quantities and different types of foodstuff from world agriculture. To meet these new demands, a doubling of food production will likely be required in the next forty years. Consequently, total world cereal demand is projected to grow from 585 million tonnes today to 828 million tonnes by 2025. This is a rise of 42%. This means that in the next twenty years, farmers will need to increase production on aggregate by 70–100% and reduce postharvest loss. The speed and scale of these productivity improvements that will be demanded of the world's agriculture are unprecedented. Interestingly, more than 25% of the increase in grain demand will actually be due to changes in consumer diets (more grain for more livestock) rather than to population growth alone.[5]

The rise in demand for livestock has significant implications for the water-agriculture nexus. Meat, on average, requires about ten times the water per calorie than plants. As a result, the average daily diet in California requires some six thousand liters of water in agriculture, compared to three thousand liters in countries such as Tunisia and Egypt.[6]

Global demand for meat is expected to increase by 50% between now and 2025, doubling from 229 million tons in 1999–2001 to 465 million tons in 2050. While high proportions of meat in European and American diets have been the case for many years now, this trend is also catching on in emerging markets.[7] In China, consumption of meat has increased from fewer than 20 grams per capita per day to 150 grams.[8] This is still far behind the 350 to 400 grams consumed per capita per day in the US. Demand for dairy products from livestock will also grow, again increasing the pressure on agricultural water sources. Milk demand is expected to nearly double, from 580 million tons today to 1,043 million tons by 2025.[9] Consequently, growth in the livestock sector will place upward pressure on agricultural water use, accounting for about 8% of total global human water use, mostly for the irrigation of feed crops. This is approximately the same as total human use of freshwater withdrawals for washing and domestic uses.[10]

Another recent upward pressure on water use in agriculture is the switch to growing feedstock as first-generation biofuels, often with generous government subsidies. To combat greenhouse gas emissions, countries around the world have set ambitious targets to replace a significant part of their fossil-fuel energy consumption with biofuels. For example, the European Union has set a target of a 20% blend of biofuel in the road transport mix by 2020. But the water intensity of biofuel feedstocks is of concern. While it can vary greatly depending on the feedstock used and where and how it is grown (irrigated biofuel crops, for example, are much more water-intensive than nonirrigated ones), the production of grain and oilseed crops grown for biofuels is more water-intensive than the production of petroleum (corn can take between 9,000 and 100,000 liters per gigajoule (GJ) of energy, soy 50,000–270,000 liters/GJ, whereas petroleum takes between 28 and 72 liters per GJ).[11] Sugarcane is generally not irrigated. It is also important to note that feedstocks that could be used for second-generation biofuel production, including grasses and crop wastes, are likely to use less water than today's feedstocks. But good information is not available on the water use per unit of energy for these crops, because they are not yet in commercial production. Nevertheless, since the energy market, measured in calories, is twenty times the size of the food market, replacing 5–6% of energy consumption by first-generation biofuels would risk doubling water withdrawals for agriculture. This clearly is an impossible trade-off, and it seems that many policy makers have not yet fully thought it through.

In many parts of the world, water withdrawals for agriculture are already greater than natural replenishment levels. In Yemen, parts of India, and northern China, water tables are falling by more than 1 meter per year. In Mexico, extraction rates in a quarter of the country's 459 aquifers exceed long-term recharge by more than 20%. One-tenth of India's grain is already watered by the unsustainable, overpumping aquifers. National groundwater overdrafts exceed 25% in China and 56% in India.[12]

As discussed, the development and deployment of new agricultural technologies will be critical to address the water challenge facing agriculture. But ironically, while more investment in agricultural technology and research is urgently required, until very recently international aid to improve agricultural productivity in developing countries has fallen. Official development assistance to agriculture fell one-third since the early 1990s, from 12% to 3.5%.[13] Initiatives to revitalize the productivity of agriculture, such as those promoted by the Gates Foundation and others, are overdue and extremely welcome. To take forward the important findings of *Water for Food, Water for Life*, however, it will be critical for these initiatives to focus on the water-agriculture nexus in their work.

The other important trend with regard to the water-agriculture nexus is of course the impact that worsening water security has on global agricultural commodity markets and food prices. For 50 years or so, we have enjoyed steadily falling food prices, especially in developed economies. This has been due in part to technological advances, but, arguably, due mostly to our failure to internalize environmental and energy costs into food prices. However, since 2007 there has been continued price volatility across the global economy. The increasing water security challenges facing agriculture have been a significant contributor to food price volatility. The symptoms of this problem can be seen in three related areas: in global food and commodity prices themselves; in the changing volumes of trade and price trends for other food and agricultural commodities across water-stressed areas; and through knock-on effects in other markets for various crops and foodstuffs, which in and of themselves are not necessarily water-stressed.

A useful recent example to illustrate each of these points is the 2010 wheat price rise, due to the heat wave, drought, and subsequent water stress that crops in Russia were exposed to during the summer months. Wheat prices rose gradually to begin with, as concern about potential yields slowly grew. They then suddenly spiked by approximately 70%, following the announcement of a wheat export ban by the Russian government. Prices then leveled in the following months, but remained approximately 50% higher than they were prior to the drought.[14] But the effects of this weather impact were further amplified as corn prices initially rallied in reaction to wheat. Then, as a result of unfavorable weather conditions in the US, they also followed a continued upward price trend similar to wheat. Other commodities, such as cotton, suffered similar effects, driven by weather events on the opposite side of the planet when floods in Pakistan created a supply risk in Asia. The market reaction among commodity speculators was to allow each effect to feed off the other, amplifying the overall trend of food and agricultural commodity price rises worldwide. The trigger for them all, however, was water insecurity—too little for long periods of time or too much all at once. This has led the food and agricultural commodity markets back to earlier price bubble ranges of recent times, particularly when analysts start to add into their thinking the chronic long-term surface and groundwater challenges and increasing climatic variability that many agricultural regions of the world now face. The issue is then amplified through the wider context of general market uncertainty arising in the aftermath of economic crises.[15]

This narrative shows how the water-agriculture nexus now sits within our interlinked world economy, and how local weather and subsequent water effects on crops can have very global effects very quickly, even if they might not be related to long-term climate change.

Forecast

Projected water withdrawals in developing countries will be 27% higher in 2025 than in 1995.[16] But overall consumption of *irrigated* water as part of this increase will likely rise more slowly (much of the rise will be due to a rapid

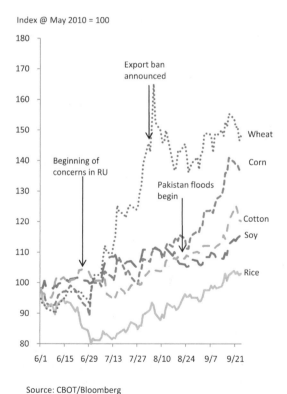

Source: CBOT/Bloomberg

Figure 1.1 Commodity Price Evolution Since June 2010.

Index @ May 2010 = 100

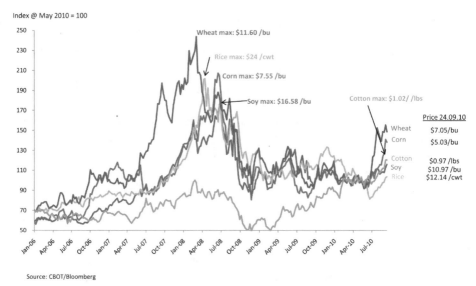

Source: CBOT/Bloomberg

Figure 1.2 Commodity Price Evolution Since January 2006.

expansion in energy and industry). Under a business-as-usual scenario, projections to 2025 show that potential irrigation demand may grow by about 12% in developing countries, while it may actually decline in developed countries by about 1.5%.[17]

Much of the increase in food production in major developing countries (including in India and China) will still come from the continued unsustainable use of groundwater. Rains can potentially replenish aquifers, but this is not a long-term solution, particularly as increased environmental variability (changing weather patterns, heat waves, floods, etc.) will likely narrow the margin between supply refreshments of reasonable water quality and increased demand.

Due largely to depleted groundwater, the irrigation water supply reliability index for developing countries will likely decline by almost 10% by 2025, falling from 0.81 in 1995 to 0.75 in 2025.[18] By then, up to a quarter of India's harvest could be at risk as groundwater is depleted beyond recovery. At some stage, ongoing problems from overabstraction of groundwater, such as saline intrusion, subsidence, or pollution, could create a tipping point. The world could face annual losses equivalent to the entire grain crops of India and the US combined by 2025 (30% of global cereal consumption).[19] Recall that this could happen at the same time as global demand for cereals is projected to *rise* by 42%. In combination, these two trends could cause major shortfalls in food supply, fueling further uncertainty in the global agricultural commodity markets and amplifying potential price volatilities. An unprecedented series of reactions from the markets could ensue.

According to Pasquale Steduto, Chief, Water Development and Management Unit, Food and Agriculture Organization, United Nations, Rome, "The first signs of water stress are experienced through environmental degradation of natural ecosystems that depend substantially on the availability of freshwater. The second sector that will feel the effects of water stress is the agricultural sector." Some dampening effect could be achieved as economic development helps to reduce waste in the food supply chain within currently developing economies. Today, 40–50% of crops are lost due to unpacked food in traditional agricultural supply chains; this can be reduced to less than 3% by investing in more modern supply chains. But economic growth may also lead to many more new middle-class consumers in developing countries also throwing away more of the food they purchase than before, similar to the current behavior of consumers in developed countries, who throw away up to 33% of their food purchases.[20]

Implications

Agriculture is still central to the economy for most developing countries, especially in sub-Saharan Africa. It can employ up to 70% of the labor force, and its share of GDP can be up to 33%. If present trends continue, however, the United Nations Development Programme fears that the livelihoods of one-third of world's population will be affected by water scarcity by 2025.

Another key political implication of these trends will be the greater reliance on agricultural trade. Almost 55% of the world's population will be dependent on food imports to an increasing extent by 2030 as a result of insufficient domestic water to grow all the food the country will need. But as recent events illustrate, and as the chapter on trade in this book explains, it may not be a sound bet, at least in the short term, for governments simply to rely on the international trade system for their food.

Whichever way one looks at the problem, unless there is a radical improvement in how agricultural water is managed and used, there will simply not be enough water to grow the food needed to adequately meet the demands of an increased population and changing diets by 2030. When set against expected increases in environmental variability and the secondary economic and political effects that are created when the markets react to food shortage and supply uncertainties, business-as-usual water use practices in agriculture cannot be an option for governments to contemplate.

Although the global economic effects can be sudden and profound, the political effects of water scarcity can be both gradual and local. Historically, this has meant that government willingness to respond to the agricultural water challenge has generally been weak and fragmented. Due to the economically invisible and politically silent trade in virtual water to date, there is indeed no obvious crisis event for national governments to react to. The World Wide Fund for Nature describes water scarcity as an "invisible event."[21]

Nevertheless, in a world where nearly one billion people already suffer from hunger or malnutrition, our existing food and agriculture systems seem ill prepared to meet these dramatic challenges that lie ahead during the next two decades.

The Way Forward

All these trends point in one direction: we must grow much, much more using much less water. And we must create the incentives for farmers to do so. According to Michael Mack, CEO of Syngenta, Switzerland, "Every decision, including no decision, will have an impact on the future. Freshwater is limited; we have to value it accordingly! Food security will need an efficient use of land and water resources and free trade of agricultural produce to better share the embedded water. Farmers need incentives to invest in water efficiency and they need access to technologies that increase productivity."[22]

In terms of growing more crops with fewer drops, modern agricultural technology can be a big part of the solution. Individual farmers and large multinational corporations alike have long been experimenting with the development of crop varieties, crop protection, and modern crop-enhancement solutions to help mitigate water and weather risks. Many resource-efficient crop technologies are already available, and many more are expected to become commercially available within the next five years. Certain breakthroughs will reduce yield variation or improve crops to be grown in water-stressed regions (such as corn).

Modern agricultural solutions can bring about exponential improvements in efficiency in many developing countries. Brazil, for example, has already doubled soybean production over the past ten years on the same amount of hectares. But the challenge of embarking on a new Green Revolution is not just about increasing yield; it is about increasing yield while reducing the amount of water that agriculture demands. To meet our future food needs while managing our future water needs, a Blue-Green (or Turquoise) Revolution is required 21st-century agriculture. Technologies *can* be deployed to further optimize each drop of water in new solutions, which *can* stretch agricultural water resources as never before. But a transformation in the sector is required.

New technologies in agriculture are not blunt instruments. Companies at the forefront of agricultural technology innovation are taking a precise approach to improving water efficiency by creating tailored solutions for different regions, crops, and farmer needs. Not only can crops be made more water-efficient through modern breeding and genetic modification, but a host of new applications can help plants withstand drought and heat. These technologies can increase water productivity and optimize production while helping farmers manage different water-related risks specific to their particular crop, soil, climate, land, and regional conditions.

For example, improving traditional rice-growing methods, such as flooding paddies, could dramatically reduce the amount of water needed to grow more crops. Changing such traditional growing methods, however, will require using all the modern tools available, including crop protection and enhancement, and the development of new rice varieties, coupled with education and supporting regulations.

Other water savings can come from seed treatment, crop protection, and crop-enhancement products that can help farmers grow healthy and strong crops even during periods of water stress. Modern herbicides also have an added benefit by replacing an ancient technology—the plough—enabling minimum-tillage agriculture, which keeps the soil structure more intact and therefore keeps more water stored in the soil and reduces surface runoff. Crop-enhancement products such as plant-growth regulators can enable much more robust and efficient crops while reducing the water required by greatly expanding its root growth, while other technologies reduce the plant's loss of moisture through the surface of leaves.

There is also plenty of diagnostic work to show that a dedicated focus must be given to the efficiency gains to be achieved in irrigated agriculture through the implementation of modern technologies. These can drastically reduce the amount of water used in farming by efficiently delivering water with greater precision directly to plants. Irrigation combined with optimum delivery of fertilizers and crop-enhancement and -protection products holds significant promise for increasing productivity and water efficiency while reducing runoff.

An integrated approach, using the technologies outlined above and tailored to the local conditions, local crops, and particular farmer needs, can optimize production and maximize water use efficiency in agriculture. As a result, farmers can not only produce more food but also become more effective stewards of their land, protecting against rain runoff, soil erosion, water or heat stress on plants, flooding, and desertification of arable land.

Debates will likely continue about the ethics and politics of "genetically modified organisms." Yet as the climate changes, as volatility increases, and as the cost of water and food security escalates, the value and necessity of these engineered crops will likely rise accordingly. Investments in modern technology in agriculture will likely have to play a key role in meeting the future water-food-energy-climate challenge.

With regard to creating the incentives for farmers to embrace a "Turquoise Revolution" in agriculture, it is clear that policy reforms as well as technology deployments are vital. Alongside technology, reforms to agricultural water rights and price incentives lie at the heart of the agricultural reform agenda. Agricultural water is in general hugely underpriced, free, or sometimes even subsidized explicitly or implicitly. Consequently, it can often have little value attached to it as an input, and therefore wasteful practices ensue.

Given that it will be simply impossible to manage water for agriculture in the coming decades as inefficiently as it has been done in the past, reforms to agricultural water rights and water prices must be explored and pursued as part of the reform toolkit. The search for and development of good case studies and pilot projects is crucial. Approaches that potentially hold merit include those that change the incentive structures for water management so that AAA-grade water is able to go to high-value uses and users, and that those who give up their highest quality water also win, such as in the Murray-Darling basin in Australia. Conversely, other approaches that merit wider investigation and uptake include those systems that incentivize the purchase and reuse of gray water safely and efficiently for agriculture, as is being done in Israel. Israel has become a world leader in maximizing agricultural output per drop of water; the government strictly regulates how much water farmers can use and requires many of them to irrigate with treated sewer water. Incentive approaches can also be developed that limit the non-beneficial use of water in irrigation, including, for example, deficit irrigation, where crops are watered only in critical periods. There are also case studies from history to be examined; one can be found in the Aflaj in Oman, where tradable water rights among farmers have led to efficient and sustainable agricultural irrigation systems for more than 4,500 years.

No government and no industry alone can tackle the monumental task of scaling up technologies and overhauling water resource management practices for agriculture. Yet if the forecasts are even halfway accurate for the coming two decades, substantial reform is imperative. How to start? By working together to support government reform agendas, those in private industry, farmers, NGOs, and other experts and stakeholders can create coalitions so the journey can begin. Co-designed public-private partnerships and policy frameworks have the potential to transform cash-poor rural areas, delivering the resources required to develop the infrastructure and knowledge that farmers need to enhance agricultural productivity and therefore water efficiency.

A key component of change, therefore, is to stimulate innovation within the water-agriculture nexus, creating new infrastructures for knowledge sharing, accessing technology, and piloting scalable projects. By taking new approaches to resolving the challenge, governments, farmers, NGOs, domestic and international companies, local entrepreneurs, development agencies, and international finance institutions can be aligned to work in concert on the water and agriculture challenge. Their joint incentive is the benefit they will each gain through developing, financing, and engaging in new arrangements that facilitate the implementation of technology and policies within the agricultural sector, whereby better water management delivers enhanced food production and improved environmental conditions. Such arrangements and innovations need not be limited to agricultural technology alone. They can also include access to affordable micro-finance, credit, and financial risk-management mechanisms, such as insurance for weather-related crop losses.

Empirical studies from the US and Italy suggest that agricultural innovation and breakthroughs respond to price signals both locally and globally. By removing government policies that distort global food production and by encouraging trade, crop production could be refocused towards those locations that are best suited to grow the world's food. Such a profound transformation in world agriculture will take time. But the role of such public-private coalitions to help educate, enable, and incentivize individuals, communities, and governments could be the way to start transforming the way the world uses its limited water resources in agriculture.

If this is the ideal solution, then, to conclude, we return to the realities of where we began: *Water for Food, Water for Life: A Comprehensive Assessment of Water Management in Agriculture.* How do we actually and in a practical sense start to begin the necessary journey of agricultural water reform? The *Water for Food, Water for Life* report recommends that reforms in water for agriculture, while vital, cannot follow a blueprint. They are specific to local institutional and political contexts, and therefore require negotiation and coalition building. The state is the critical driver, but civil society and the private sector are important actors. Informed multistakeholder negotiations are essential. Working with farmers within new public-private coalitions in specific locations, with the support of government to prove that change can happen—this then seems to be how to start the urgently required "Turquoise Revolution" for agriculture.

Perspectives

The following personal perspectives amplify the main themes touched on by this chapter. They help to illustrate the range of current viewpoints on the water-food nexus. The views expressed do not necessarily represent those of the World Economic Forum, nor do they necessarily represent the views of the other individual contributors or the various contributing companies or institutions.

- Pasquale Steduto, Chief, Water Development and Management Unit of the Food and Agriculture Organization of the United Nations in Rome, also a Global Agenda Council on Water Security member, reminds us of the overall challenge facing the agricultural sector in the next two decade if future food security is to be assured.
- Juan Gonzalez-Valero, Head of Public Policy and Partnerships at Syngenta; and Peleg Chevion, Head of Business Development Water at Syngenta, draw attention to a wider set of technological and institutional ways to improve water use in agriculture: through modern breeding technologies, through ways to decrease water loss in agriculture, through improved water delivery and no-till methods, and through improving postharvest crop protection, among others.
- Daniel Bena, Director of Sustainable Development at PepsiCo, illustrates a specific rice-seeding innovation introduced by PepsiCo that is saving significant amounts water in rice cultivation in India.
- Ajay Vashee of the International Federation of Agricultural Producers reminds us of the centrality of the farmer to this debate. He sets out some pointers on what the specific needs of farmers are from new technology and improved water management systems, as well as the necessary elements of a farmer-focused water reform policy framework, which includes the balanced use of water rights for farmers as one element among many within an integrated water resource management system.
- Sir Mohammad Jaafar, Chairman and Managing Director of the Kuwaiti Danish Dairy Company, provides a compelling perspective of the water-food challenge facing the Arabian Gulf region
- Peter Brabeck-Letmathe, Chairman of Nestlé, focuses on farmer incentives, drawing our attention to the ancient water rights scheme in Oman called Aflaj mentioned above. Drawing from lessons in history, he suggests that flexible, specific, and locally administered systems of water management among farmers can be found and do work.

Responding to the Increase in Land and Water Demand to Guarantee Future Food Security

PASQUALE STEDUTO, CHIEF, WATER DEVELOPMENT AND MANAGEMENT UNIT, FOOD AND AGRICULTURE ORGANIZATION, UNITED NATIONS, ROME

To appreciate the challenge of food security, one must first grasp how and where demand will change over the next four decades. By 2050, humankind will swell to nine billion people, with most of the increase coming in cities of developing countries, where income levels rise proportionally.

This increase of global population from six to nine billion will demand 70% more food: annual cereal production must rise from 2.1 to 3 billion tons, and meat production must rise from 200 million to 470 million tons. However sobering, these projected figures are actually conservative, excluding crops diverted and biofuels, as well as climate change uncertainty. They simply represent the food we are asking agriculture to produce for human consumption.

So was Malthus right after all? Is the world running out of land and water resources to the point where agriculture fails to produce enough food for a still-growing population at levels sufficient to lead a healthy and active life? Let's unpack this question to address each underlying concern.

How Much Will Arable Land Expand?

The world's considerable unused reserves could in theory be turned into arable land. After all, only a third of the planet's 4.2 billion hectares of suitable cropland is being farmed. In reality, the potential to convert these remaining lands is limited. Many uncultivated lands play vital ecological roles that can't be sacrificed without risk of larger effects. Half of the remaining lands are concentrated in just seven countries (Brazil, Democratic Republic of the Congo, Angola, Sudan, Argentina, Colombia, and Bolivia). At the other extreme, there is South Asia and the Near East/North Africa, which have virtually no spare land considered suitable for agricultural expansion. Human settlements and urban sprawl will cover prime arable land with homes, malls, apartment

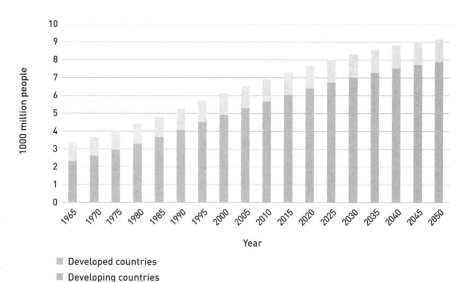

Figure 1.3 World Population, 1965–2050. *Source:* United Nations Population Division, UN-DESA, UN Revision 2008.

blocks, roads, and parking lots. The remaining marginal land can support only a few staple crops. As developing countries cultivate more cropland, developed countries will contract. Overall, by 2050 the world's net amount of arable land will expand an additional seventy million hectares, or 5%.

How Much More Water Will Be Required?

Developing regions, where renewable water resources have not been exploited, will likely expand their irrigated farmland by 14%, requiring the withdrawal of an additional three hundred cubic kilometers of water. In the developed world, cultivation contracts by 2%, reducing agricultural water withdrawals by twelve cubic kilometers. Assuming that agricultural water demand will not exceed available water resources by 2050, the world will withdraw 11% more freshwater for farms.

But there's more to the picture than quantity. Over the next four years, this 11% increase in irrigation water will expand the world's harvested irrigated area by 17%, thanks to expected improvements in water use efficiency. Changes in cropping patterns—for example, much of China will shift from rice to maize—will help farmers grow more crop per drop.

Like the world's supply of arable land, global freshwater reserves are unevenly distributed. The Near East/North Africa region uses about 58% of its water resources in irrigation, while Latin America barely uses 1%. Three year average data on production and land use from 2005–2007 shows that eleven countries used more than 40% of their renewable water resources for irrigation, a critical situation. Eight more countries consumed more than a fifth of their renewable water resources, the threshold of impending water scarcity. By 2050, the situation will worsen.

Irrigated lands have been expanding rapidly and continuously, especially in the developing world, but this trend is now starting to slow down. By 2050, some 60% of all land with irrigation potential will be in use; three-quarters of the world's irrigated lands will be in developing countries. Annual growth of developed countries' irrigated area peaked at 3% in the 1970s, dropping to 1.1% in the 1980s and to only 0.2% over the last decade.

Are Land and Water the Only Source of Food Growth in the Future?

Agricultural harvest productivity rises through a combination of various dynamics: higher crop yields, expanded arable cropland, and increased cropping intensities. In developing countries, where innovation boosts harvested cropland area by an additional 17%, yield increases and crop intensities will account for 80% projected growth in crop production.

In South Asia, where land is scarce, crop intensification will rise by 95%; in North Africa, where water is scarce, crop intensity doubles. Sub-Saharan

Africa and Latin America will continue to expand arable land for agricultural growth, but even there intensification will play a bigger role.

Higher crop intensification will increasingly depend on irrigation. Yield increases will rely on technology. And due to variability in production, many countries will rely more on trade. Over the next four decades, developing countries will more than double their net imports of cereals to three hundred million metric tons. In exchange, developed countries will import other food commodities like vegetable oils and sugar. Two volatile wildcards in these projections involve biofuel expansion and climate change.

FURTHER CONSIDERATIONS

The potential for investments in agricultural research and development—which yield a 30–75% rate of return—has been neglected in most low-income countries. In these areas, hunger persists due to the lack of income opportunities and the absence of effective social safety nets. Growth, by itself, does not eradicate hunger and malnutrition; only food does that. Food security demands a system of fair trade, one that provides support and greater market access to farmers in developing countries.

Through political will and judicious institutions, we can ensure that key decisions are taken and implemented effectively, so that all men and women will have the opportunity to farm on an equal footing.[23]

Water Scarcity: Agriculture Provides Solutions

JUAN GONZALEZ-VALERO, HEAD OF PUBLIC POLICY AND PARTNERSHIPS, SYNGENTA; AND PELEG CHEVION, HEAD OF BUSINESS DEVELOPMENT WATER, SYNGENTA

Water is the biggest limiting factor in the world's ability to feed a growing population and reach food security. Already agriculture uses about 70% of freshwater withdrawal. By 2050, we will need to double agricultural production to feed an expected nine billion people. This means with current water management practices, in 2050 we will need to double the amount of water used today to feed the world.[24]

Increasing urbanization, industrialization, and affluence around the world—which is shifting diets towards more water-intensive foods such as meat—are exacerbating water shortage. It is clear that we need better water management strategies to close the gap between supply and demand.

It's time to take the broadest perspective on water management and food security. Three key issues must be addressed if we are to feed the world without depleting this finite resource:

- we need to unlock plant potential to use water more efficiently with better yields;
- we need to reduce unproductive loss of rain and irrigation water on farms,
- we need to decrease crop loss in the food chain—less waste saves water.

The good news is that water scarcity can be mitigated affordably and sustainably through cost-effective measures using existing technologies.[25] And savings in the agricultural sector can make a significant difference, resulting in more water for other needs.

AGRICULTURE IS PART OF THE SOLUTION

Solutions have to focus on the vital role of water management in agriculture. By tailoring solutions to the specific needs of farmers around the world, natural resources can be used effectively to achieve food security and protect the environment.

Investments in new agricultural technologies have created a "toolkit for farmers" based on three integrated solutions. First, modern technologies are enabling us to grow more from less. Better seeds developed through modern breeding and biotechnology are able to withstand heat and drought and preserve yield. For example, Syngenta has developed a new corn seed that can use available moisture more efficiently, resulting in higher yields in water-stressed acres. Such corn hybrids not only have the potential to reduce water use in irrigated farming, but also will provide a critical hedge against drought. Modern crop-protection products and plant regulators can also help plants to handle the stress of periodic drought or to use water more efficiently. Some grow shorter, more robust plants, while others grow more roots or reduce the plant's loss of moisture through the surface of leaves, thereby protecting yield even when plants get less than optimal water.

Second, reducing water loss in agriculture requires full implementation of improved water delivery and no-till methods. About 40% of water used in irrigation is wasted through unsustainable practices such as field flooding. Efficient irrigation systems that deliver water, combined with crop-protection and crop-enhancement products ("chemigation"), have great potential to save water and increase productivity. Modern herbicides allow no-till and minimum tillage so plowing isn't necessary and soil structure is preserved. As a result, soil is able to receive and retain water more effectively and reduce runoff.

Finally, about 40% of the food grown is never used—part is lost when harvested crops spoil during transport, storage, processing, and packaging. Another portion is wasted when consumers, food companies, and retailers throw food away. We need to increase postharvest crop protection and infrastructure, especially in developing regions where poor farmers have to rely on inefficient harvesting, storage, and transportation. To successfully address losses in the food chain, a combination of policy measures will be necessary: continued science-based regulation of crop-protection products, investment support in postharvest technologies, scrutiny of the role of the food-processing industry and supermarkets, and pricing mechanisms and strategic efforts to visualize and educate the public on reducing food waste.[26] Decreasing this food loss would save water without affecting food security.

Charting a sustainable future for water resources and food security will require the concerted effort of governments, industries, and nongovernmental and humanitarian organizations. Public-private collaborations and cross-industry partnerships can optimize water allocation, provide the necessary frameworks to invest in efficient technologies and infrastructure, and create incentives to reduce food waste throughout the food chain. Water is everybody's business.

Improving, Water, Food, and Climate Security: A Novel Approach to Direct Seeding of Rice

DANIEL BENA, DIRECTOR OF SUSTAINABLE DEVELOPMENT, PEPSICO, US

Of all the freshwater consumed in India, 85% is for agriculture, with the remainder used by industry and domestic consumers. Agriculture is a key sector in the Indian economy, as more than 60% of the population depend on it for their livelihood. About 50% of the 85% total freshwater consumed in agriculture in India is used for rice cultivation, which in India lags behind the water efficiency of other major countries.

In line with PepsiCo's commitment to improve agricultural sustainability and farmer earnings, a new initiative was developed to promote direct seeding of rice (DSR). DSR helps conserve roughly 30% of the water (0.9 million liters of water per acre) used over traditional methods of puddling. To put this in context, if only 25% of the Indian rice cultivation can be shifted to direct seeding, the water savings that result would be equal to the total water consumed by Indian industry.

Traditionally, in India rice is cultivated by sowing seeds in a small nursery, where the seeds germinate into saplings. The saplings are then transferred manually into the main field and grow with 2–3 inches of water at the base of the crop for the first 4–6 weeks, mainly to prevent weed growth. In DSR, the seeds are planted directly in the main field using a tractor-driven direct seeding machine developed by PepsiCo. The crop is grown without standing water at the crop base.

DSR avoids three basic operations: (1) puddling (a process where flood irrigation is used to compact soil and reduce water seepage), (2) manual transplanting, and (3) standing water, which may serve as a vector for water-borne diseases, like malaria.

As farmers are realizing the great benefits of DSR, this innovative process is becoming extremely popular. During 2009, PepsiCo carried out direct seeding on over 6,500 acres across five states in India, comprising different agro-climatic and soil conditions and with various varieties of rice.

Benefits of DSR include:

- water savings exceeding nine hundred kiloliters per acre;
- energy savings of 30%, as less water requires less energy to pump it;
- labor savings of 53%, since there is no need for manual transplanting;
- reduction in emission of greenhouse gases by 75%, as there is no biomass immersed in water at the crop base, and therefore little to no methanogenic emission activity;
- reduction in cultivation costs to the farmer of $US 30 per acre, due to reduced labor and energy costs;
- farmers having observed an increase in system productivity as the yield of succeeding crops improves (further data are currently being collected to better quantify this benefit);
- improvement in soil quality available to the plants, as avoidance of puddling leads to lesser soil compaction, thereby allowing the roots to reach deeper zones, which enables extraction of leached nutrients.

Farmers Facing the Water Challenge

AJAY VASHEE, INTERNATIONAL FEDERATION OF AGRICULTURAL PRODUCERS

Agriculture, through its multiple services including food, feed, fuel, and fiber, is dependent on water as one of its key strategic resources. Yet it will receive a declining share of the available freshwater supplies, which will become increasingly variable under climate change.

Farmers, who are called on to feed an additional 2.7 billion people by 2050 and sustain livelihoods, are the first victims of water problems in terms of quantity, quality, and access. Lower yields and higher food prices continue to plunge millions into hunger and poverty. Farmers, and with them the entire international community, face a huge challenge in maintaining and increasing environmentally sustainable agricultural production. To tackle this challenge, investments in sustainable agriculture and the involvement of farmers in long-term strategies for water management are prerequisites. Farmers should be recognized as essential allies in facing water challenges.

Farmers needs for sustainable water management arise from the following areas:

- The combination of climate change, water stress, and new agricultural demands require adaptation at the farm level for food and energy security.
- Climate change in particular has severe effects on water availability, especially in dry regions. Changing weather patterns adversely affects food production, and consequently food commodity prices, as was shown in the summers of 2008 and 2010 when world commodity prices rose sharply due to drought.
- An integrated approach to the sustainable management of natural resources (water, land, biodiversity): farmers must be supported to effectively adapt to climate change, including through programs to enhance adaptation and resilience among the poorest farmer populations, the improved management of water in food, energy, and other policies, combined with better risk-management tools.
- The water-food-energy-climate nexus and the compatibility of policies: More research is needed to better understand this nexus at all administrative levels and its effects on stakeholders, including farmers. Agriculture is central in this complex interrelation.
- A shift in focus to more crops per drop: Research for crops that increase yields per land unit with less water and arable land use is crucial.
- Bio-energy for rural development and income diversification: More research is needed to determine the favorable conditions for bio-energy production in relation to the conservation of natural resources and water use, completed with well-documented, successful agricultural experiences and practices in this field.
- Irrigation agriculture and technology transfer to farmers: Irrigation techniques must comply with high water efficiency and precision levels to increase yields while decreasing water demand. Investment in appropriate technology and the involvement of farmers' organizations, to successfully carry out technology transfer to farmers and to accelerate their adoption, is essential.
- Unlocking the potential of rain-fed agriculture: Improved water productivity (soil-water management), as well as improved capacities for water harvesting and storage, will make the production in rain-fed crop lands more efficient and directly improve the livelihoods of smallholder farmers and poor rural communities.
- Risk-management tools for farmers to cope with extreme weather events: The development of appropriate national risk-management response strategies and precautionary measures are crucial to enable farmers to deal with extreme weather events, pests, and diseases and to avoid heavy losses.

- Research for farm-level adaptation to climate change: Farmers have to be able to improve the efficiency in water use and adapt farming practices and water infrastructures to variations in precipitation, including droughts and floods.
- Involving farmers' organizations in capacity building: Good practices and new farm techniques should be replicated and upscaled through farmer-to-farmer exchange visits with the help of famers' organizations. Their role should be recognized in the follow-up on research and scientific programs.
- Farmers should be rewarded for ecosystem services: For long-term positive effects, incentives must encourage and enable farmers to continue providing ecosystem services through the adoption of environmentally friendly practices. Stewardship programs offer the necessary positive incentives to recognize and reward the positive role of farmers in adopting these practices to enhance water quality and ensure its efficient use.

But what are the policy framework needs for the involvement of farmers in sustainable water management? Integrated water resource management strategies should recognize farmers, especially women, as key players, including:

- the recognition of multiple use and functions of water services in farming, benefiting poor rural communities in terms of water quantity and quality, erosion control, and water infrastructure;
- a shift from supply- to demand-driven water management, which will make water use communities more responsible and proactive in managing and sharing water in a socially and environmentally responsible way;
- balancing water resources between water user communities through effective property rights and water-planning frameworks to help ensure the water needs of rural communities. The struggle against poverty must be addressed through agriculture and rural development.

Farmers should be involved in water management policies through consultation frameworks, including public-private partnerships. Farmers should benefit from fair water pricing policies, taking into account a range of factors, including farmers' capacity to pay. Smartly designed policies can help achieve rational water use and a mix of crops better suited to the water resources in terms of profitability and water availability.

Farmers need investments and funding to develop technologies adapted at the farm and local level, which are accessible and affordable to the producers, complying with their specific needs. This is essential to sustain future levels of food production in harmony with the environment. A water rights–based approach should ensure an equitable access to water, a condition for farmers to be able and willing to invest in new practices or improved and efficient infrastructure. A global vision is necessary to ensure coherence in trade policies, markets, and sustainable water management, environmental protection, and food security worldwide.

Water Challenges in the Arabian Gulf

Sir Mohammad Jaafar, Chairman and Managing Director, Kuwaiti Danish Dairy Company

The Gulf Cooperation Countries (GCC) sometimes has the reputation of being indifferent to global environmental challenges. What can a region that is the world's major producer of hydrocarbons hope to contribute to the debate?

The Kuwait Danish Dairy Company (KDD) is a fast-growing food company that is headquartered in Kuwait, a country that happens to have the lowest per capita water availability in the world.[27] Kuwaitis have always been conscious of water as a precious asset. Much of the world is only now realizing what this means. When water availability drops below 1,500 cubic meters per capita per year, countries begin to import food, as this book shows. The figure for our country for natural renewable water resources is ten cubic meters per capita per year, and the figure for total withdrawals including desalination is 306.

According to 2007 World Bank data,[28] per capita availability will fall by half across the Middle East and North Africa region by 2050 based on current trends. Twenty-one countries fell below that threshold in 2000. Fourteen more will join them by 2030. More than half the world's population will depend on food imports as a result of insufficient domestic water.

We understand water scarcity. We prosper because we are rich in hydrocarbons, but we cannot afford to leave water out of our thinking. Yet that is what the world did in the era of apparently limitless natural resources. By failing to think about water when using biofuels to solve a carbon problem, the world exacerbated a water problem that affects food production.

The recent volatility in raw material prices has had a serious impact on businesses like ours, which depend on sourcing raw materials from world markets. Carbon-footprint measurement alone is not an adequate ecological metric. Kuwait's only natural water resource is its groundwater. It provides part of our supply of drinking water and all the water for our agriculture. It isn't only finite. It's vulnerable to pollution from oil exploration and from landfills. We know about ecological disasters, too: our aquifers suffered serious damage from the oil fires of 1991 at the end of the first Gulf War. Nearly all our tap water and water used for industry has to be desalinated. This is a necessary, but expensive and carbon-intensive, technology. Desalination can have a role in helping to achieve food security and to grow high-value crops in coastal areas if there are government subsidies for capital costs, but in general it is cost-ineffective for agriculture.

So our local agriculture, aside from marine and hydroponic farming, remains limited. Gray water, or recycled wastewater, is the final water resource we have, and the only one that can actually grow. Kuwait operates the largest membrane-based wastewater treatment station in the world at Sulaibiya, which produces water for agriculture and for recharging aquifers. Kuwait has not experimented in large-scale grain farming. Saudi Arabia was recently forced to abandon a wheat-farming program because of dangerous depletion of its groundwater reserves. Wheat-farming proved to be unsustainable in the desert. Saudi Arabia continues to support the world's largest dairy farms. Will they prove to be sustainable in the long term?

KDD's dairy processes involve recombining milk from powder. Our dairy products contain "embedded water" exclusively from sustainable sources. Kuwait recognizes that it is the steward of a local desert ecosystem that has value. Agriculture, fishing, and groundwater management require continuous research. We are growing mangroves in the intertidal areas of our coastline in order to enrich our coastal ecosystem. But for our part of the Middle East, large-scale sustainable agriculture will mean outsourced agriculture. Conducted responsibly, this can benefit all parties. Outsourcing our agriculture can help us to improve our own food security while providing investment to a sector that is woefully underinvested and competes directly with energy investment.

The immediate issue of water, in the GCC as elsewhere, is demand management. This entails a thorough, consistent program of public education, a process we support. Our own industries need to become more water-efficient. As investors outside Kuwait, proper risk management will require us to be responsible citizens in the water that we source.

When making investments, water security, regulation, and supply chain risks must all be considered. Water governance and management must operate effectively at local and regional levels. Each region has different needs, but many best practices can be adopted globally. Like all other regions, GCC countries will need more intensive dialogue between industry, governments, and research bodies in an effort to find solutions and to define these best practices and bring water to the head of the political agenda.

Governance and management require strong local institutions. We need more intensive educational programs, starting in schools. Business as well as government has a role to play here. Public health education in the Middle East is needed to help us improve our own health, and it can also raise awareness of the water that is embedded in the food that we import (e.g., in red meat products).

New tools for sustainable water management are emerging: water neutrality, water offsets, fair "water stewardship," measurement of "virtual" or embedded water, water labeling, and pollution offsetting. Their benefits need to be understood: immediate cost savings, future cost savings, indirect cost savings, reduced risk, improved stakeholder perception, consumer preference, first mover advantage, and so forth.

Successful water pricing policies will present some of the most complex political challenges that governments will face in the coming decades. It is not surprising that most still shy away from the issue. Pricing models will differ. But without pricing, there can be no meaningful policy. It is still unclear how, if at all, this will play out in our region, where water subsidies are heavily masked by hydrocarbon subsidies. Yet successful pricing and taxation models do already exist in different parts of the world, and tradable water rights have been made to work in poor rural areas. We will need national plans, regional bodies and a global water forum.

The High Cost of Priceless Water and Oman's Ancient Alternative

PETER BRABECK-LETMATHE, CHAIRMAN, NESTLÉ SA, SWITZERLAND

Put bluntly, water has no price. Or the price is suppressed below what it is worth.

Oman's farmers might beg to differ. For 4,500 years, in a hot and arid land, that desert society has developed a continuously functioning system of tradable water rights, within a scheme of freshwater supply and irrigation known as Aflaj. The basis is full recovery for the infrastructure cost, with the farmers building the irrigation system on their own. Using gravity, water is channeled over as much as seventeen kilometers from underground sources up to twenty meters deep or springs in the nearby mountains. These resources support both agriculture and domestic use. The irrigation network is maintained by its joint owners (i.e., the individual shareholders). This is still very much the exception when compared with water systems in other regions in the world, and full cost recovery for the infrastructure is only a first step.

Once the water arrives at the village, everyone—villagers, guests, and travelers—gets free access to enough water to drink. The canal then goes to the mosque, where water is also free for ceremonial washing, but other quantities are set aside and sold to finance the mosque and the school. Beyond that, the water becomes private property. Water is defined in shares—days, hours, or minutes of rights—to use for irrigation. Water rights are inherited and, even more important, they are tradable. In frequent auctions, parts of the water rights can be sold and purchased or leased within the village community. If a farmer does not need water temporarily, he leases it to another farmer who has additional land available to grow crops. If a farmer wants to invest in more efficient irrigation, he can finance this investment by selling some water rights permanently. Thus water gets a market price, set by those who know best: the farmers. And since farmers trade among themselves, the cash exchange remains within the community and is no additional financial burden overall.

Aflaj is also an illustration of the heterogeneity of water prices paid in auctions—they differ between five and twenty-two US cents per cubic meter, depending both on the time of the year (i.e., the temperature and the crops grown) and also on the particular year and the specific watershed. Interestingly, in Japan and Korea there is a discussion about a negative price—that is, compensating farmers for withdrawing water at certain points in time, because of positive externalities, such as flood alleviation.[29] As can be seen, the complexity of water use, coupled with the local context, is such that it probably cannot be managed by centrally administered prices; rather, it requires some form of market mechanism like the one developed by the Omani farmers.

Notes

1. "What Was the Message of *The Limits to Growth*? What Did This Little Book from 1972 Really Say about the Global Future?," Jorgen Randers, Professor, Norwegian School of Management BI, Oslo, Norway, April 2010, paper written for the Club of Rome.

2. International Water Management Institute, *Water for Food, Water for Life: A Comprehensive Assessment of Water Management in Agriculture*, 2007, p. 5.

3. World Economic Forum, *Summit on the Global Agenda*, http://www.weforum .org/pdf/summitreports/globalagenda.pdf. Network of Global Agenda Councils, *Environmental and Sustainability Cluster*. A report from Josette Sheeran, the Chair of the Environment and Sustainability Cluster of Agenda Councils, which met at the Summit on Global Agenda, Dubai, United Arab Emirates, November 7–9, 2008; December 1, 2008.

4. United Nations, *UN World Population Prospects*, 2008 revision; and Food and Agriculture Organization of the United Nations, *World Agriculture: Towards 2015/2030*, 2007.

5. United Nations Environment Programme, *The Environmental Food Crisis*, 2009.

6. International Water Management Institute, *Water for Food, Water for Life: A Comprehensive Assessment of Water Management in Agriculture*, 2007.

7. Steinfeld, H., Gerber, P., Wassenaar, T., Castel, V., Rosales, M., Haan, C. de. "Livestock's Long Shadow: Environmental Issues and Options," FAO, 2006. http:// www.fao.org/docrep/010/a0701e/a0701e00.htm

8. Food and Agriculture Organization of the United Nations online database, http://faostat.fao.org/.

9. Food and Agriculture Organization of the United Nations, *Long Shadow: Environmental Issues and Options*, 2006.

10. International Water Management Institute, *Water for Food, Water for Life: A Comprehensive Assessment of Water Management in Agriculture*, 2007.

11. For corn and soy, the higher numbers represent crops that are irrigated, while the lower numbers represent nonirrigated crops; for petroleum, the variation depends mainly on the refining process

12. United Nations Development Programme, *Human Development Report, 2006: Beyond Scarcity*, 2006.

13. Ibid.

14. CBOT/Bloomberg, Commodity price evolution since January 2006.

15. Ibid.

16. United Nations Development Programme, *Human Development Report, 2006: Beyond Scarcity*, 2006.

17. International Water Management Institute, *Water for Food, Water for Life: A Comprehensive Assessment of Water Management in Agriculture*, 2007.

18. International Food Policy Research Institute, *Global Water Outlook to 2025: Averting an Impending Crisis*, 2002.

19. Ibid.

20. Pasquale Steduto, personal communication.

21. World Wildlife Fund for Nature (WWF), *Living Planet Report 2008*, 2008.

22. World Economic Forum Water Initiative, *The Bubble Is Close to Bursting*, 2009.

23. References for contribution: Nikos Alexandratos, "World Food and Agriculture to 2030/2050: Highlights and Views from Mid-2009," in Food and Agriculture Organization of the United Nations, *Expert Meeting on How to Feed the World in 2050*, 2009; Food and Agriculture Organization of the United Nations, Natural Resources Management and Environment Department, http://www.fao.org/nr/water; Food and Agriculture Organization of the United Nations, *World Agriculture: Towards 2015/2030*, 2007; and Jelle Bruinsma, "The Resource Outlook to 2050: By How Much Do Land, Water, and Crop Yields Need to Increase by 2050?," in Food and Agriculture Organization of the United Nations, *Expert Meeting on How to Feed the World in 2050*, 2009.

24. International Water Management Institute, *Water for Food, Water for Life: A Comprehensive Assessment of Water*, 2007.

25. McKinsey & Company, *Charting Our Water Future*, 2009.

26. International Water Management Institute, *Saving Water: From Field to Fork: Curbing Losses and Wastage in the Food Chain*, 2008.

27. Kuwait Institute for Scientific Research, Water Resources Division. www.waterkuwait.com/KISR_WRD_brochure_Mar_2008.pdf.

28. http://siteresources.worldbank.org/EXTMETAP/Resources/Sardinia-METAP-Climate-Change-AdaptationMENA.pdf.

29. Organisation for Economic Co-operation and Development, *Asian Water and Resources Institute: Agricultural Water Pricing in Japan and Korea*, 2008.

CHAPTER 2

Energy

This chapter explores the water-energy nexus. It benefits greatly from the perspectives of many public, private, academic, and NGO representatives who have taken part in various Forum sessions and workshops on water issues over the last three years. In particular, in 2009 the World Economic Forum in partnership with IHS Cambridge Energy Research Associates (IHS CERA) created a report titled *Thirsty Energy: Water and Energy in the 21st Century*. Much of the text in this section has benefited from excerpts from this earlier report and from a review by IHS CERA. Some personal perspectives from those close to the water and energy agenda appear at the end of the chapter.

Background

We might not think about it, but there is a strong link between water and energy. The intersection of water and energy is ancient—water wheels have been used since the Middle Ages to provide mechanical energy as an alternative to human or animal power, and the first oil wells in the US used drilling technology that was developed to drill for water. But the relationship between water and energy has taken on a new urgency as concerns have grown about the competing pressures for multiple uses of water, as highlighted by the introduction to this book. Today, energy uses about 8% of all freshwater withdrawn worldwide and as much as 40% of freshwater withdrawn in some developed countries. Energy and water are linked in two primary ways—water is used in the production of nearly all types of energy, and energy is used in the provision of water and the treatment of wastewater.

When discussing how energy uses water, the distinction between the volume of water withdrawn and the volume consumed is very important. Water withdrawn is the total volume removed from the water source. Water consumed is the amount removed for use and not returned to its source. Water withdrawal for energy is much larger than water consumption, by as much as twenty-five times in the US, primarily because many power plants use water for cooling and then return it to the water body. But water amounts withdrawn are also important because energy production relies on water availability for smooth operation and because the water withdrawn is not always returned to the ecosystem in the same state in which it was withdrawn. In many countries, the quality of returned water is highly regulated, although this is not the case everywhere.

Trends

Water's role in the energy value chain varies depending on the type of energy in question. The energy value chain is divided into three components: production of energy raw materials, transformation of the raw materials into a form usable by consumers, and delivery to the final consumer. In some cases, the primary use of water is in production of the energy raw material, while in others transformation to a usable form is the primary water use. But in each case, delivery of the final energy product to the consumer uses minimal water.

Water Used to Produce Natural Gas and Liquid Fuels

Figure 2.1 depicts the natural gas and liquid fuels value chain, including liquid transportation fuels. It describes the amount of water consumed (not withdrawn) at each stage of the value chain. For most processes in this value chain, the figure shows how the majority of water use occurs at the raw materials stage.

As an example of how to read this figure, compare the water used to produce gasoline from different raw materials. Producing traditional oil uses three to seven liters of water per gigajoule (GJ) and refining that oil uses an additional twenty-five to sixty-five liters of water, for a total of twenty-eight to eighty-two liters of water per GJ of finished gasoline. Since one liter of gasoline contains 0.034 GJ of energy, production of each liter of gasoline from traditional oil uses approximately one to three liters of water. A similar calculation for gasoline made from oil sands results in water use of around three to fifty-five liters of water per liter of gasoline.

More background on how water is used in the gas and liquid fuels value chain can be found in the World Economic Forum/IHS CERA report *Thirsty Energy: Water and Energy in the 21st Century*. The key takeaways from figure 2.1, however, are the following:

- Minimal water is used in the production of traditional oil and gas resources, between three and seven liters of water per GJ. In fact, water is produced from the underground formation along with the oil and gas. While the quality of this water can range widely, the vast majority

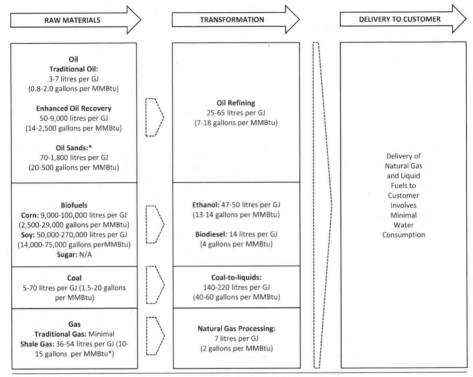

Source: Adapted from US Department of Energy, Energy Demand on Water Resources.
Report to Congress on the Interdependence of Energy and Water, December 2006 (except where noted).
*CERA estimate.
Note: MMBtu = million British thermal units; GJ = gigajoules.

Figure 2.1   Gas and Liquid Fuels Value Chain—Water Consumption.

is at least as salty as seawater.[1] As wells mature, the amount of water produced along with the oil often increases, reaching as much as forty times the amount of oil produced as the well reaches the end of its useful life. As much as 75% of this produced water is r-injected into the oil reservoirs to enhance oil recovery, as described below.[2] Disposal of water not reused can be a problem, however, particularly when this water is salty or contains metals or other contaminants.

• Enhanced oil recovery (EOR) techniques and unconventional oil resources are often net users of water, sometimes of large quantities (50–9,000 liters/GJ). EOR involves injecting water or gas into a reservoir to maintain pressure in the reservoir and ultimately recover more of the underground oil. Often, water recovered along with the produced oil is reinjected to enhance recovery. At other locations, the produced water is not of sufficient quality, and another water source must be found, particularly for steam injection methods of oil recovery.

- Oil sands are another resource that involves the use of large amounts of water, between 70 and 1,800 liters per GJ. When the oil sands are mined and oil is removed at the surface, steam is used to strip the bitumen from the surrounding clay and sand. When oil sands are produced in situ, steam is pumped underground to strip the bitumen and allow it to be moved to the surface in a process known as steam-assisted gravity drainage. Either way, a high-quality water source is necessary to make the steam.
- Regardless of whether the oil comes from traditional or unconventional sources, petroleum refining requires another twenty-five to sixty-five liters per GJ, the variation depending on the complexity and types of processes used in the facility. Refineries use water mostly for process cooling, and some refinery processes also generate water contaminated with a variety of substances, including oil, suspended solids, ammonia, sulfides, and chromium. This water is usually treated at wastewater facilities at the refinery and then discharged to public sewer systems or directly to surface waters, depending on the degree of treatment.[3]
- While traditional gas resources require minimal water in their production, unconventional natural gas resources are generally net users of water, between thirty-six and fifty-six liters of water per GJ. Most natural gas resources considered "unconventional" today involve gas trapped in tight formations underground, including shale or sandstone. Producing gas from these reservoirs requires fracturing the underground formation with water to allow gas to flow to the production well. The estimates in the figure are for the initial phase of production. Water use is likely to decrease as the well matures, and some older wells will produce water rather than consume it.
- The water required for the transformation of gas into a form used by consumers is minimal, seven liters per GJ.
- The water intensity of biofuel feedstocks can vary greatly, as the figure shows, depending on the feedstock used and where and how it is grown. Irrigated crops are much more water-intensive than nonirrigated ones. The higher numbers shown in the figure represent crops that are irrigated, while the lower numbers represent nonirrigated crops. Grain and oilseed crops grown for biofuels are much more water-intensive than the petroleum (corn, 9,000–100,000 liters/GJ, soy 50,000–270,000 liters/GJ). Sugarcane is an exception to this rule, as it is generally not irrigated. In fact, a period of drought during its growing phase is needed to concentrate the sugar.[4] It is also important to note that feedstocks that could be used for second-generation biofuel production, including grasses and crop wastes, are

likely to use less water than today's feedstocks. But good information is not available on the water use per unit of energy for these crops, because they are not yet in commercial production.

• As with many energy raw materials, water pollution from biofuel production is as important an issue as water use. Fertilizers used on crops, including those grown for biofuels, run off into surface water bodies. The excessive levels of nutrients that result have caused algae blooms, anoxic conditions in surface water, and even contributed to a "dead zone" in the Gulf of Mexico of approximately 22,800 square kilometers (8,800 square miles), where there is inadequate oxygen to support aquatic life. Nitrates from fertilizer runoff can also cause human health problems, especially in rural agricultural areas where nitrates are most often found in drinking water.[5] "Blue baby syndrome" can occur in infants fed formula made with water high in nitrates, because the nitrates limit the blood's ability to carry oxygen throughout the body.[6]

• To transform raw material feedstocks into a biofuel form usable by consumers also requires water, albeit much less than at the raw material stage (47–50 liters/GJ for ethanol, and 14 liters/GJ for bio-diesel). Ethanol is produced by a biological fermentation process involving a slurry of ground grain and water. Future technologies for cellulosic ethanol production will involve the same water-phase fermentation process, with application of enzymes to break cellulose into sugars preceding the fermentation. Thus, at the transformation phase, second-generation biofuels are unlikely to use less water than current technologies. Bio-diesel production is much less water-intensive, since the chemical reactions involved do not take place in a water phase. Vegetable oils are reacted with an alcohol, usually methanol, to produce alkyl esters or bio-diesel.

• The water required for use in coal mining depends on the method of mining, varying from five to seventy liters per GJ. For example, underground coal mines use water for cooling the cutting surfaces of mining machinery and inhibiting friction-induced ignition of coal dust or gas. Surface mines often use water to suppress dust from the mining process and on roads entering the mines.[7] The majority of bituminous coal in most parts of the world is cleaned before it is burned, in order to reduce the ash and sulfur content and increase the coal's heating value, using more water.[8] But water contamination, rather than use, is the primary issue in coal mining. Drainage from mines and from piles of mining waste can become acidic when sulfur-containing minerals are exposed to water and oxygen. The acidic water dissolves some metals that may be present in the rock and soil, frequently including lead, zinc, copper, arsenic, and selenium. These metals are then carried with the water throughout the affected watershed and can be absorbed by plant and animal life in the food chain.[9] Water contamination is an issue in many areas where coal is mined, from the US and Canada to China and Australia.

- The water intensity required to transform coal to liquids is higher, ranging from 140 to 220 liters per GJ. Coal-to-liquids plants use water in three primary ways. The largest need is for water to cool process streams. Water is also used to feed steam-producing boilers and in the liquefaction process itself. The amount of water used in liquefaction depends on the design of the plant. In some plants, water reacts with carbon in the coal to form carbon monoxide and hydrogen. Water can also be used in scrubbers to remove ammonia and hydrogen chloride from intermediate gas streams.[10]

- Almost no water is consumed in the delivery of natural gas and liquid fuels to customers.

Water Used to Produce Electricity

Figure 2.2 depicts the value chain for electricity provision. Unlike liquid and gaseous fuels, the majority of water use in electricity occurs at the transformation stage, mostly for cooling of thermal electric generation plants. As in the previous figure, the data describe the amount of water consumed, not withdrawn.

Two types of water cooling technology, as well as dry cooling, can be used in thermal electric power plants. Once-through cooling systems withdraw large quantities of water but return the majority of this water to the source, generally at a higher temperature, after one trip through the condensers. The mechanism used to withdraw the large quantity of water needed and the higher-temperature water returned to the source has the potential to harm aquatic life near the plant. Closed-loop systems recirculate cooling water and reject excess heat through a cooling tower or pond. These plants withdraw only enough water from the source during steady state operation to make up for water lost due to evaporation. Although closed-loop systems withdraw 95% less water than once-through systems, closed-loop systems actually consume more water, since the water withdrawn is all lost to evaporation. Dry cooling systems rely on air rather than water for cooling. But since air is a less efficient heat sink than water, dry cooling systems are less efficient, particularly in hot weather. Table 2.1 presents water consumption in thermal electric power plants per unit of net power produced with closed-loop cooling.

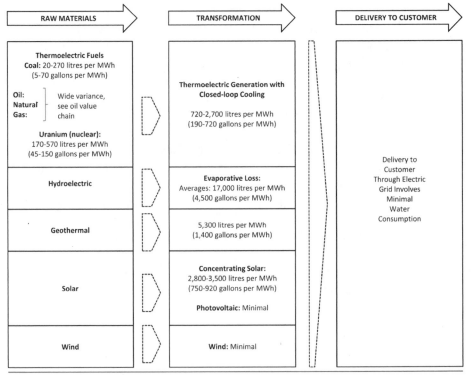

Source: Adapted from US Department of Energy, Energy Demand on Water Resources.
Report to Congress on the Interdependence of Energy and Water, December 2006
Note: MWh = megawatt-hours

Figure 2.2 Electricity Industry Value Chain—Water Consumption.

To illuminate the data in the table, compare the water use of different forms of electricity generation. A megawatt hour (MWh) of electricity from coal uses 20 to 270 liters of water at the coal mining stage and an additional 1,200 to 2,000 liters when the energy in the coal is converted to electricity, totaling 1,220 to 2,270 liters of water consumed per MWh. In comparison, nuclear energy uses 170 to 570 liters of water per MWh during the mining of uranium and production of the reactor fuel, and an additional 2,700 liters per MWh as the energy from nuclear fission is converted to electricity, for a total of 2,870 to 3,270 liters of water consumed per MWh.

Again, much more background on how water is used in the electricity value chain can be found in the Forum/IHS CERA report *Thirsty Energy: Water and Energy in the 21st Century*. But the key takeaways from the figure are the following:

- Renewable forms of raw material, including hydroelectricity, geothermal, solar, and wind, require little or no water at the raw

	Litres per MWh	Gallons per MWh
Nuclear	2,700	720
Sub critical Pulverized Coal	2,000	520
Supercritical Pulverized Coal	1,700	450
Integrated Gasification Combined-cycle, slurry fed	1,200	310
Natural Gas Combined-cycle	700	190

Source: Water Requirements for Existing and Emerging Thermoelectric Plant Technologies. US Department of Energy, National Energy Technology Laboratory, August 2008

Table 2.1   Water Consumption in Thermoelectric Power Plants per unit of Net Power Produced Closed-loop Cooling.

materials stage. Further, wind and solar power generation use virtually no water during the production of power, except for minimal and occasional use for washing turbine blades or solar cells.

- In the transformation of the raw material into a form usable by consumers, concentrating solar can be relatively water-intensive, consuming between 2,800 and 3,500 liters of water per MWh.
- Within the nuclear energy production process, the amount of water used in uranium mining is similar to that used in coal mining, and the problems of water pollution are also similar. But uranium requires much more processing than coal to become a usable fuel for electricity production. The process of converting uranium ore to finished reactor fuel involves several steps that use water, including milling, enrichment, and fuel fabrication, using up to two thousand liters per MWh. These additional processing steps make uranium a much more water-intensive fuel than coal per unit of electricity produced.
- Thermoelectric forms of electricity generation, including coal, natural gas, oil, and nuclear, constitute 78% of world electricity generation capacity.[11] All thermal electric plants that use steam turbines require cooling to condense the steam when it exits the turbine, and water is by far the most common source of cooling, using between 720 and 2,700 liters per MWh for closed-loop cooling. In fact, cooling uses 80% to 90% of the water consumed in thermal power plants, regardless of the fuel source. Table 2.1 shows the wide range of water use for thermoelectric cooling in plants with closed-loop cooling systems. The amount of water needed for cooling depends on the type and efficiency of the power plant. Natural gas combined-cycle plants use the least water per unit of power produced, whereas nuclear plants use the most.[12]
- Hydroelectric power currently makes up 20% of world electricity generation capacity; its evaporative loss is the equivalent water use of seventeen thousand liters per MWh. Water consumption through

evaporation occurs because more water evaporates from reservoirs than from naturally flowing river systems. Estimating consumption for hydroelectric generation is thus particularly difficult because it relies on modeling rather than measurement. Water consumption of hydroelectric systems varies widely based on the surface area of the reservoir and the local climate. Run-of-the-river projects without storage result in much less water consumption than reservoirs with large surface areas.

Energy Used in the Provision of Water and Wastewater Services

In addition to the use of water in energy production, energy is a significant input to modern water provision and wastewater treatment systems. Figure 2.3 shows energy consumption in the domestic water industry value chain.

The figure shows how energy is used to move water from its source, treat it, pump it to end users, and treat it after its use. In fact, electricity accounts for approximately 80% of municipal water processing and distribution costs.[13] Municipal and industrial water supply and wastewater treatment systems in the US consumed an estimated 138 terawatt hours of electricity in 2005, just over 3.5% of the total consumed,[14] which is equivalent to the amount of electricity used to run all the refrigerators in the US.[15]

These rolled-up numbers hide the differences in energy use for drinking-water provision based on the water source. On average, groundwater supply requires about 30% more electricity on a unit basis than does surface water, because of the expense of raw water pumping.[16] But high-quality groundwater requires little energy for treatment. Pumping water over long distances or great elevations is very energy-intensive. For example, water supplied to Southern California from the state water project travels 610 meters (2,000 feet) over the Tehachapi Mountains, the largest lift of any water system in the world, and requires about 2,400 kilowatt hours (kWh) per million liters (9,200 kWh per million gallons). The electricity used to deliver water to customers in Southern California is equal to one-third of the average total household electricity use.[17] Water can travel long distances for agricultural use as well, also resulting in large energy costs.

Desalination is one of the most energy-intensive water provision mechanisms, as the figure shows. The amount of energy used depends on the salinity of the source water. Desalting brackish groundwater (200–1,400 kWh/million liters) is less energy-intensive than turning seawater into fresh drinking water (3.600–4,500 kWh/million liters). Disposal of brine created during the desalination process is an additional problem for desalination plants. Brine is typically twice as salty as the intake water for the plant, and also contains higher concentrations of unwanted constituents found in the intake water,

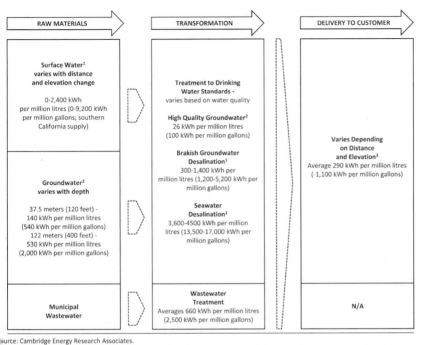

Source: Cambridge Energy Research Associates.
Energy Down the Drain: The Hidden Costs of California's Water Supply. Natural Resourse Defense Counci and Pacific Institute, August 2004.
Energy Demand on Water Resources: Report to Congress on the Interdependence of Energy and Water US Department of Energy, December 2006.
Electric Power Research Institute: *Water and Sustainability (Volume 4): US Electricity Consumption for Water Supply and Treatment - The Next Half Century,* 2000.
Note: kWh= kilowatt-hour.

Figure 2.3 Domestic Water Industry Value Chain—Energy Consumption

including manganese, lead, and iodine. Ocean disposal is the most common and least expensive option, but it can have significant effects on the marine environment. Evaporation ponds and deep well injection are other options.[18]

Forecast

According to Nestlé Chairman Peter Brabeck-Letmathe, ". . . under present conditions and considering the way water is being currently managed, we will run out of water long before we run out of fuel."[19] A fast-developing, increasingly prosperous, urban global population will demand more resources to meet its energy needs. Aging capacity needs to be replaced and basic energy access also needs to be improved. Currently, in the developing world more than 3 billion people still rely on traditional biomass for heating and cooking and 1.5 billion people lack access to electricity.[20] Tackling energy poverty is a developmental priority for many countries.

Consequently, the International Energy Agency (IEA) forecasts that the world economy will demand at least 40% more energy by 2030 compared to today.[21] McKinsey & Company in its work for Project Catalyst estimates that 77% of the requisite energy infrastructure has yet to be built. By 2030, China will need to expand its power-generating capacity by more than 1,300 GW (1.5 times the current level of the US), and India by 400 GW (equal to the current combined total power generation of Japan, South Korea, and Australia).[22]

Under the IEA's reference scenario, more than 75% of the global increase in energy use from 2007 to 2030 is expected to be met through fossil fuels, especially coal. By 2050, the resulting carbon emissions could lead to a concentration of carbon in the atmosphere (one thousand parts per million) that is more than double that which international negotiations are currently struggling (and failing) to achieve.[23] Transforming coal into electricity requires relatively large amounts of water, as Figure 2.2 illustrates. But the resulting rate of warming would exacerbate water scarcity still further.

As economies grow, different sectors will increasingly compete for scarce resources, and policy makers will be confronted with difficult trade-offs. Across the world, where regional economies are growing fastest and where agricultural water use is already high, demand for water for energy and industrial use is projected to rise sharply between 2000 and 2030 (56% in Latin America, 63% in West Asia, 65% in Africa, 78% in Asia).[24] In the US, where energy now accounts for 40% of all freshwater withdrawals, some have estimated that water use for energy would have to increase by 165% to meet demand in 2025.[25]

When set against a broader context of water and energy interlinkage, the low carbon growth challenge for energy seems doubly hard to meet: how to meet the world's growing energy needs with both low greenhouse gas emitting energy and with much greater water use efficiency, all within the next two decades? If much of the energy mix through 2030 is still to be coal, it is worth noting how water-intensive such generation of electric power really is. Are energy policies promoting low carbon and low water use really possible?

As the information above sets out, the low carbon, low water use energy challenge is not only something to consider in relation to coal. Several "clean" energy sources are also rather thirsty. The IEA estimates that by 2030 hydropower will strengthen its role as the world's dominant renewable energy source, providing about 1,100 TW hours of electricity, more than twice the amount of its nearest rival, onshore wind power.[26] They estimate that about 170 GW of hydropower is currently under construction, 77% of this across Asia (55% in China, 9% in India, and 13% in other parts of Asia). Yet when set against an average evaporation loss equivalent to 17,000 liters per MWh, the volumes of water evaporation from this new hydropower capacity will be unprecedented.

Biofuels are another clean energy source with high water requirements. As the above data show, production of biofuels from corn or soybeans can use orders of magnitude more water than the petroleum fuels that they replace. Demand for biofuels as a low-carbon fossil-fuel alternative is increasing quickly. By 2030, the IEA predicts that at least 5% of global road transport will be powered by biofuel—more than 3.2 million barrels per day.[27] But producing those fuels could consume, according to some estimates, between 20% and 100% of the total quantity of water now used worldwide for agriculture.[28] This is clearly an impossible trade-off.

Implications

This difficult reality is fast complicating the standard definition of "sustainable" energy. Do governments pursue increased energy access at the expense of decreased water access, or must low carbon and low water use energy policies be pursued simultaneously? If so, how?

There are real trade-offs at work here. For example, one form of solar-energy generation, the concentrated solar thermal plant, uses relatively large quantities of water in relation to other renewable alternatives, as Figure 2.2 shows. A recent *New York Times* article drew attention to this fact with the headline "Alternative Energy Projects Stumble on a Need for Water."[29] In fact, plans for thirty-five solar thermal plants in the California/Nevada desert are currently in negotiations with state regulators to try and get the water they need for cooling. One plant alone requested access to 4.9 billion liters of the water in the local valley.[30] Does this mean that concentrated solar thermal plants should be planned in relation to a water policy as well as a low-carbon energy policy? The US Department of Energy seems to thinks so: in July 2010 it issued a report to Congress that explores a number of strategies to reduce the water consumption of concentrating solar power electricity generation.[31]

Nuclear power plants are also particularly vulnerable to water scarcity. In the southeastern US, the Tennessee Valley Authority shut down one of three reactors at its Browns Ferry Nuclear Plant for several days to avoid heating the Tennessee River to levels dangerous to aquatic life. Due to a drought that reduced the river level during the hottest temperatures of the last fifty years, the plant could not discharge the cooling water since it would have exceeded the permissible temperature limit.[32] During Europe's record hot summer of 2003, river levels became too low for some of France's nuclear reactor plants to operate. As energy demand soared for air conditioners, total electricity generation was forced downward due to a lack of water for cooling. France cut its power exports in half to make up for the difference. These kinds of hot weather events are predicted to become increasingly frequent as the climate changes.[33]

The emergence of shale gas as another potential source of cleaner energy, especially in the US, also possesses significant water resource implications. Shale gas development raises concerns about the volume of water needed for the process of hydraulic fracturing, or "fracking," and the potential for water contamination during fracking and gas production. The US Environmental Protection Agency is conducting a study on the impact of hydraulic fracturing on drinking water resources. This study is estimated to cost roughly $US 6 million and is expected to be ready by 2012. The results of the study could clarify the debate about the environmental effects of shale gas and how to regulate the fracking process. These are just some examples of the implications arising from an emerging understanding of the links between energy and water, which is becoming more apparent as demands for both resources escalate.

Under drought conditions, a generating plant may have to shut down or severely curtail its operations if water levels are too low for cooling water withdrawal or if the temperature of cooling water discharge would exceed permitted limits. Conversely, plans to switch from gasoline to electricity or biofuels to increase national energy security can result in a switch from dependence on foreign oil to a dependence on domestic water. Consideration of water resources when setting policy for energy security and climate change is crucial to avoid aggravating another serious problem—water shortages. In the US, the interdependence of energy and water has become so tightly interlinked that the US Department of Energy reported to Congress that energy production is very much at the mercy of water availability.[34] As energy policy and investment programmes are developed across the world, especially in fast-growing economies to meet energy access, economic growth, and low-carbon challenges, it is clear that the energy-water nexus will also emerge as a crucial part of the decision-makers' trade-offs.

This nexus works in both directions, of course. As well as the water security implications for energy, Figure 2.3 highlights the amounts of energy required for water provision. Looking forward to 2030, the issue of desalination stands out in this regard. Worldwide, 52% of desalination capacity is in the Middle East, largely in Saudi Arabia, where thirty desalination plants meet 70% of the kingdom's present drinking water needs. North America has 16%, Europe 13%, Asia 12%, Africa 4%, Central America 3%, and Australia 0.3%.[35] Across all these regions, the forecast is for widespread growth in desalination plants. *Global Water Intelligence*, a United Kingdom–based industry publication, recently estimated that the global desalination market will grow 12% annually through 2015—and then accelerate. Predictions are for 20% or more growth in China, India, Australia, and the US. Total investment in new plants could top $US 56 billion.[36]

Yet, as noted, energy intensity remains the principal barrier to greater use of desalination (3,600–4,500 kWh/million liters). It would be ironic indeed if water-intensive energy sources such as coal or nuclear were installed to provide the power for desalination plants. Are these interconnected policy issues being considered?

The exploration of linkages between water and energy is still in its infancy. Water and energy are tightly linked, but these links are still rarely considered in policy making. It is clear that decision-makers and corporations will need to better integrate energy issues into water policy, and water issues into energy policy, given future water constraints. Considering water and energy together can offer substantial economic and environmental benefits.

The Way Forward

According to Peter Gleick, President and Co-Founder of the Pacific Institute in the United States, "We are intelligent human beings: we've decoded the human genome; manipulated substances at the subatomic level; eliminated some diseases permanently. We have the intellectual resources to tackle the water problem."[37] Approaching the energy-water nexus in an integrated manner is challenging, but there are examples of effective strategies. Ideas include the following:

- Water consumption by power plants can be reduced by switching from water cooling to air cooling, or by other new technologies, such as integrated gasification combined cycle generation plants. Air cooling reduces plant efficiency, however, so the water saved must be traded against additional greenhouse gas emissions.
- Clean energy and clean water can go hand in hand—the city of Perth has recently constructed the world's first large-scale desalination plant using renewable energy. It will be important to explore new types of renewable energy (solar, wind, and wave) to fuel the new energy demands for desalination, as energy costs are the principal barrier to the greater use of desalination.
- Wind power firms are now marketing wind as a zero-water, rather than just a low-carbon, power alternative.
- Combining water and energy efficiency efforts can save substantial water and energy at lower cost and can, when tackled in concert, improve the provision of both services. Can the tackling of water and energy efficiency together provide a strategy to address both the mitigation and adaptation issues of climate change together, in one bundle?

It is clear that solving the energy and water security challenge will require new policies that integrate energy and water solutions and innovative technologies that help to boost one resource without draining the other. Discussions between water and energy professionals and decision-makers need to be encouraged with some urgency, so that a mutual understanding of the water and energy security issues the world faces can be achieved and low-carbon solutions sought.

The 2009 IHS CERA report for the World Economic Forum on water ended with the following five questions, which remain potent for both the energy sector and the wider decision-making community:

- How will the energy sector's share of water use change in the future?
- How can energy companies measure and monitor their water use, given the local nature of water resources and the differing value of water from place to place?
- What role will water markets play in allocating future resources? How might water markets change the economics of various energy technologies?
- How can the industry best engage with the other stakeholders, including agriculture, other industries, and government to shape future water policy?
- What technologies can improve the water efficiency of the energy industry? How can the energy industry become better integrated with other industries, agriculture and municipal water, and wastewater operations to optimize water use and reuse?

Perspectives

The following personal perspectives amplify the main themes touched on by this chapter. They help to illustrate the range of current viewpoints on the water-energy nexus. The views expressed do not necessarily represent those of the World Economic Forum, nor do they necessarily represent the views of the other individual contributors or the various contributing companies or institutions.

- Peter Gleick, President and Co-Founder of the Pacific Institute in the United States, provides his perspectives on the tight link between water and energy and how poorly these linkages continue to be understood or used in policy.
- Peter Brabeck-Letmathe, Chairman of Nestlé, focuses on the first-generation biofuel issue and the competing demands on water for food crops they create.
- J. Carl Ganter, Cofounder and Managing Director of the Circle of Blue, provides some perspectives on how clean energy solutions in the US affect water.

- The Dow Chemical Company illustrates how desalination technologies are fast becoming more energy-, and therefore cost-, efficient.

Water and Energy: New Thinking

PETER GLEICK, PRESIDENT AND CO-FOUNDER OF THE PACIFIC INSTITUTE IN THE UNITED STATES

Water use and energy use are closely linked.[38] Moving, treating, and using water require substantial amounts of energy. Producing energy takes substantial amounts of water, especially with traditional fossil and nuclear systems. Yet rarely are these energy connections adequately evaluated. And they are even more infrequently addressed by policy-makers, or energy and water managers. Limits to energy are beginning to affect water systems, and limits to water are beginning to affect energy systems. Considering these two resources together offers substantial economic and environmental benefits. Additionally, a new problem that must be addressed is the challenge of global climate change, which affects policies in both areas.

THE ENERGY CYCLE

The entire energy cycle requires water, from mining to generation to distribution of energy. Energy end use and waste disposal also use and contaminate water resources. For example, the largest withdrawal of water in the US and most other industrialized countries is for power plant cooling. Most cooling water is not "consumed" but is returned to a river or lake after a rise in temperature. Yet in arid and semiarid regions, power plant water demand can be substantial compared with the water resource available, causing problems for other users and natural ecosystems. Nuclear and fossil-fuel energy systems require far more water per unit of energy produced than most renewables, depending on cooling system type. As water resources become increasingly scarce due to human demands and changes in supplies, we have begun to see examples of energy production constrained by lack of water. Nuclear and fossil-fuel plants have been either derated or temporarily shut down when water is short. New cooling technologies have been required to reduce water demands that threaten fisheries or other aquatic ecosystems. And finding additional water to cool new power plants is increasingly difficult in some regions where water supplies are constrained. More such problems are likely to develop in coming years.

WATER SUPPLY, USE, AND TREATMENT ALL REQUIRE ENERGY

Our water systems all require substantial energy, from collecting water at a source, to conveyance, treatment, distribution, end use, and waste treatment.

The energy intensity of water provided depends on the source of water and how it is used. For example, Southern California relies on a wide range of water sources. The energy intensity of providing that water ranges from fewer than five hundred kWh per acre-foot for local sources and reclaimed wastewater to more than four thousand kWh per acre-foot for desalinated seawater from reverse osmosis systems. (An acre-foot of water is equal to 1,233 cubic meters, or 326,000 gallons.) Different choices about the source of water thus have different implications for energy requirements and hence greenhouse gas emissions. The California Energy Commission recently estimated that as much as 20% of California's energy use went to some aspect of water supply or use. Water efficiency efforts can save substantial water (and energy) at lower cost, often more quickly than new "supply." Water efficiency should be given a higher priority by resource planners, and water-efficiency programmes at all levels should be designed to capture multiple benefits. More science and analysis are needed, but some suggestions include:

- Phase out irrigation, energy, and crop subsidies that promote wasteful use of water and energy.
- Pursue new standards and smart labeling of water-efficient appliances that also save energy.

CLIMATE-WATER-ENERGY LINKS

Water and energy are also linked to climate change through the emission of greenhouse gases. Some climate change—perhaps significant climate change—is already unavoidable. We must both move to avoid those consequences we cannot manage and learn to manage those effects we cannot avoid. A key element to any climate strategy will thus be to reduce the greenhouse gas emissions associated with our water systems by developing non-carbon energy sources for water and to figure out how to adapt to unavoidable effects on water availability and infrastructure.

CONCLUSIONS

Water and energy are tightly linked, but these links are poorly understood and rarely used in policy. Decision-makers and corporations should better integrate energy issues into water policy and water issues into energy policy. Failure to link these issues will inevitably lead to disruptions in the supply of both water and power, while thoughtful, integrated policies will provide important advantages.

Burning Up Food as Fuel: The Role of Water

PETER BRABECK-LETMATHE, CHAIRMAN, NESTLÉ SA, SWITZERLAND

Back-to-back years, 2007 and 2008, brought the world to a major food crisis that is far from over. The prices for staple cereals—the major source of calories and proteins for the poor—remain 60% higher than five years earlier, and in the second half of 2010 went up even higher.[39] And the underlying imbalances and expectations that caused the crisis have only grown worse.

Biofuel policies, and the both open and hidden subsidies fueling them, play a central role in causing this situation. For example, in 1959 Switzerland's Parliament decided that all roads should be financed with a tax on fuels. But five decades later, it exempted biofuels from the tax, thus encouraging drivers using biofuels to use the roads for free. Other countries mandate a certain, ever-larger percentage of biofuels in gasoline.[40] In the larger US and the EU economies, annual biofuel subsidies add up to US$ 5 billion.

But biofuel boosters ignore the hungry side of the equation. The additional grain calories, transformed into fuel, could have fed 250,000 people with cereal staples for one full year.

Moreover, policy statements have influenced expectations and, as a result, prices. Markets for staple foods were already strained before governments pushed the conversion of food into fuel. One reason for this stress was the lack of water.[41]

Agricultural water is typically free or heavily subsidized. That often leads to waste, and worldwide falling groundwater tables increasingly put food production at risk. On average, it takes a half liter of water to grow one calorie of grain. Calories are a unit measuring energy—energy in food burned by a person, or, in biofuels, burned by a machine. In other words, a thousand liters could grow enough calories to feed one person per day or fuel the drive to your local bakery to buy croissants.[42]

Sure, that's "only" a thousand liters and two thousand calories. But consider the relative size of the global food and energy markets. When measured in calories, the energy market is twenty times the food market. So if governments would replace only 10% of global energy consumption with first-generation biofuels, they in the same stroke would double agricultural water withdrawals.

Today, the biofuel bandwagon seems almost unstoppable, and annual targets rise ever more ambitious. The Intergovernmental Panel on Climate Change mitigation report suggests that 25–80% of today's total global energy consumption by 2050 should be biofuels.[43] The result would be an eightfold increase in agricultural water withdrawals for biofuels alone. Nor are biofuels emissions-free, as often claimed.[44] Measured in lifecycle analysis of agricultural production—a complex process that generates significant amounts of methane and nitrous oxide[45]—some perform worse than fossil fuels.[46]

Perhaps, promoters concede, but second-generation biofuels will be better. We'll pick up waste from plants in fields and fallen wood in forests, and convert this "cellulostic" material into biofuel. The small print of these brochures[47] reveals that the main and probably most efficient source would be specifically grown plants, such as the whole plant of a new variety of energy corn, growing twice as high as normal corn. This "new and improved" version would still, alas, allocate orders of magnitude more water to global biofuel crops, with a devastating impact on the food market.

Ambitious biofuel policies must consider how they affect actual water withdrawals at a time when naturally renewed water accessible for human use is in increasingly short supply. Unchanged policies will first affect the expectations and prices of staple foods, and then, due to risks related to water shortage, lead to actual food shortages.

Choke Points: The Collision Between Water and Energy

J. CARL GANTER, MANAGING DIRECTOR, CIRCLE OF BLUE

Two unmistakable global resource trends—rising energy demand and diminishing reserves of freshwater—are drawing ever nearer to a historic confrontation that is getting more difficult and costly to avoid. Regardless of whether the world perpetuates the fossil fuel economy with unconventional fuels or moves to clean energy, both require much more water than we are using today. Unless new technologies are developed and much more energy and water conserving practices are embraced, world economies face a limit on resources that puts prosperity and the health of the planet in even more peril.

Circle of Blue's team of journalists and researchers are exploring this emerging global "choke point" as part of an ongoing worldwide project to understand the place where water supply and energy demand converge.

In the report, "Choke Point: U.S.," Circle of Blue concluded that meeting higher energy demands has put energy production and water supply at odds in the places where growth is highest and water resources are under the most stress, such as California, the Southwest, the Rocky Mountain West and the Southeast. Despite the high consequences, this resource conflict—and its potential stranglehold on growth and investment—lies under the radar in critical decisions, from identifying the locations of thermoelectric plants and smart grids to issuing municipal bond ratings.

Perhaps most stunning and relevant are the probable consequences to clean energy investment: Unless the U.S. plans more carefully, generating energy from more sustainable alternatives is almost certain to consume much more water than the fossil fuels they are meant to replace.

Other key findings:

- The region that is confronting the energy–water choke point first and most dramatically is the American Southwest, where climate change is steadily diminishing snowmelt in the Rocky Mountains. The Colorado River transports less water than it did a decade ago and soon may not provide enough water to power the Hoover Dam's electric generators.
- Tapping the "unconventional" oil sands of Canada, the oil shales of the northern Great Plains, and the gas shales of the Northeast, Texas, Oklahoma and the Upper Midwest uses three to four times as much water than the conventional oil and gas reserves they are replacing.
- Developers in North Dakota will produce one hundred million barrels of oil and one hundred billion cubic feet of gas this year from the Bakken Shale. However, concern about the amount of water required for fracturing the shale and releasing the hydrocarbons is generating civic pushback from farmers and rural residents.
- Carbon capture and storage technology, which is a favored potential tool to reduce carbon emissions from fossil-fueled electric generating plants, is undergoing a handful of tests, including at a new electric generating plant just permitted and partially financed by the Energy Department in arid Kern County, California. But the technology also increases water consumption at coal-fired utilities by 40 percent to 90 percent, according to the Energy Department.
- Roughly US$ 100 billion was invested in 2010 in North American unconventional oil and gas development, according to industry reports and estimates. Some US$ 18 billion was invested in wind, solar, bio-fuels, geothermal, and other clean energy production and research. In both sectors, scant attention was paid to whether new sources of energy can be developed without severely damaging the nation's freshwater reserves. In "Choke Point: U.S." we make an airtight case that this resource collision, which has keen implications for the American economy, environment, and quality of life, is too important to go unaddressed any longer.

Solutions from the Sea

THE DOW CHEMICAL COMPANY

In "The Rime of the Ancient Mariner," Samuel Taylor Coleridge wrote, "Water, water everywhere, nor any drop to drink." The centuries-old poem—in which a thirsty sailor curses the surrounding sea in vain—reveals a tragic irony that still rings true. Millions of people live on the coast and yet remain unable to access the most basic of human requirements: clean, potable water. The pressure to secure freshwater will increase over the coming decades.

For these reasons, in 2008 Dow Chemical's Chairman and CEO Andrew Liveris joined UN Secretary-General Ban Ki-moon and eleven other multinational organization leaders to launch the UN Water Call to Action. In terms of solutions, Dow believes that seawater desalination holds great promise to bring potable water to large cities and small villages alike—hence, Dow's efforts in purification technologies, striving to purify some of the 97% of the world's water locked in salinity. Today, seawater reverse osmosis (SWRO) technology produces nearly 2% of the world's drinking water. Each day, desalination plants with Dow technology unlock 218 million gallons from places like Tampa Bay, Florida, to Ashkelon, Israel, to Perth, Australia.

Now coastal Africa has tapped into this increasingly affordable solution. Ghana's growing population and dwindling, unreliable potable water supplies led the country's water authority to plan one of the continent's largest desalination plants. The start-up marks a significant shift in thinking of "appropriate technology" for developing countries. Why? Because water production costs have fallen due to more efficient membrane technology and reduced energy consumption. Funded partly through international financing, the plant will not only provide a supply of potable water for Ghana, it will also help protect against the further depletion of the country's valuable natural wetlands and aquifers. The desalination plant will use Dow technology to produce freshwater that will meet World Health Organization drinkable water standards and help ensure the lowest possible capital and operating costs.

Reducing the overall energy consumption is the key to desalinating more water with fewer effects and at less cost. New pressure-reducing technology has brought down the cost of producing freshwater from seawater from an average of US$ 2.43 per cubic meter in 1980 to US$ 0.65 per cubic meter in 2007. Compared to 1985, today's SWRO membranes produce twice the freshwater, sell for half the cost, and reject 99.8% of the salt. Other factors are energy-recovery devices that are able to use some of the pressure energy contained in the brine.

Advancements in membrane technology also address environmental concerns. Modern desalination plants require much less energy than twenty years ago and can be powered by alternative technologies such as wind turbines. Today, modern desalination uses less energy and produces in a more environmentally friendly way than pumps lifting, treating, and transporting conventional supplies of water. From Ghana to Tampa Bay, desalination helps protect high-quality groundwater and reduce the pumping of aquifers. Over the next five years, Dow is committed to further reducing the cost of desalination and water reuse by 35%.

Coleridge's Ancient Mariner might delight in the new technology. But despite desalination's promise, there is, of course, no one panacea—or one sector—to quench the world's growing thirst. More aggressive conservation, installation of decentralized water systems, and increased deployment of water reuse plans will all play an important part in a comprehensive response to global water scarcity. And these solutions require a collaborative approach from government, business, humanitarian organizations, and other stakeholders. It is Dow's belief that industry's key role in this is to continue to innovate.

Notes

1. US Department of Energy, *Energy Demands on Water Resources: Report to Congress on the Interdependency of Energy and Water*, 2006.

2. US Department of Energy and the National Energy Technology Laboratory, *Addressing the Critical Link between Fossil Energy and Water*, 2005.

3. Energetics, *Energy and Environmental Profile of the U.S. Petroleum Refining Industry*, 2007.

4. Luiz A. Martinelli and Solange Filoso, "Expansion of Sugarcane Ethanol Production in Brazil: Environmental and Social Challenges," *Ecological Applications*, June 2008, http://www.esajournals.org/doi/abs/10.1890/07-1813.1?journalCode=ecap.

5. National Oceanic and Atmospheric Administration (NOAA), "NOAA and Louisiana Scientists Predict Largest Gulf of Mexico 'Dead Zone' on Record This Summer," July 15, 2008, http://www.noaanews.noaa.gov/ stories2008/20080715 _deadzone.html.

6. World Health Organization, "Water-Related Diseases: Methaemoglobinemia," 2010, http://www.who.int/water_sanitation_health/diseases/methaemoglob/en/.

7. Center for Waste Reduction Technologies, *Industrial Water Management: A Systems Approach, Second Edition*, 2002.

8. US Department of Energy and the National Energy Technology Laboratory, *Addressing the Critical Link between Fossil Energy and Water*, 2005.

9. Environmental Mining Council of British Columbia, *Acid Mine Drainage: Mining and Water Pollution,* 2000.

10. US National Energy Technology Laboratory, *Emerging Issues for Fossil Energy and Water: Investigation of Water Issues Related to Coal Mining, Coal to Liquids, Oil Shale, and Carbon Capture and Sequestration*, June 2006.

11. US Energy Information Administration, *Annual Energy Review, 2007,* 2008.

12. US Department of Energy, National Energy Technology Laboratory, *Water Requirements for Existing and Emerging Thermoelectric Plant Technologies*, 2008.

13. Electronic Power Research Institute, *Water and Sustainability: U.S. Electricity Consumption for Water Supply and Treatment—The Next Half Century*, 2000.

14. Ibid.

15. US Energy Information Administration, *U.S. Household Electricity Report*, 2005.

16. Ibid.

17. R. Cohen, B. Nelson, G. Wolff. *Energy Down the Drain: The Hidden Costs of California's Water Supply.* Natural Resources Defense Council and Pacific Institute, August 2004, page 2. http://www.pacinst.org/reports/energy_and_water/energy_down_the_drain.pdf.

18. Pacific Institute for Studies in Development, Environment, and Security, *The World's Water, 2006–2007: The Biennial Report on Freshwater Resources*, 2006.

19. As quoted in the World Economic Forum Water Initiative, *The Bubble Is Close to Bursting*, 2009.

20. Mark Leon Goldberg, "UN Advisory Body Calls for Universal Access to Modern Energy," *UN Dispatch*, April 28, 2010, http://undispatch.com/un-advisory-body-calls-for-universal-access-to-modern-energy.

21. International Energy Association, *World Energy Outlook, 2008*, 2008.

22. Project Catalyst, *Project Catalyst Brief*, 2009.

23. International Energy Agency, *World Energy Outlook, 2009*, 2009.

24. World Economic Forum Water Initiative, *The Bubble Is Close to Bursting*, 2009.

25. Danish Hydraulic Institute, *A Water for Energy Crisis?*, 2007.

26. International Energy Agency, *World Energy Outlook, 2009*, 2009.

27. International Energy Agency, *From 1st- to 2nd-Generation Biofuel Technologies*, 2008.

28. International Water Management Institute, *Water for Food, Water for Life: A Comprehensive Assessment of Water Management in Agriculture*, 2007; and Danish Hydraulic Institute, *A Water for Energy Crisis?*, 2007.

29. Todd Woody, "Alternative Energy Projects Stumble on a Need for Water," *New York Times*, September 29, 2009, http://www.nytimes.com/2009/09/30/business/energy-environment/30water.html.

30. Geoff Schumacher, "Solar, Water Don't Mix," *Las Vegas Review-Journal*, October 2, 2009, http://www.lvrj.com/opinion/solar-water-dont-mix-63234432.html.

31. US Department of Energy, *Concentrating Solar Power Commercial Application Study*, 2009.

32. Andrew Eder, "Heat Wave Ignites Problems in ET: Weather Causing Mayhem with Computer Servers, Water Supplies," KnoxNews.com, August 18, 2007, http://www.knoxnews.com/news/2007/aug/18/heat-wave-ignites-problems-in-et/.

33. Modeling by the Hadley Centre, published in 2004 in *Nature*, suggests that by the 2040s, over half the years in Europe could be warmer than 2003. (Peter A. Stott, D. A. Stone, and M. R. Allen, "Human Contribution to the European Heatwave of 2003," *Nature*, 432, 610–614 [December 2, 2004].)

34. US Department of Energy, *Energy Demands on Water Resources: Report to Congress on the Interdependency of Energy and Water*, 2006.

35. Institute for the Analysis of Global Security, *The Connection: Water and Energy Security*, 2004.

36. "Water Desalination Report," *Global Water Intelligence*, http://www.global waterintel.com/publications-guide/water-desalination-report/.

37. World Economic Forum Water Initiative, *The Bubble Is Close to Bursting*, 2009.

38. This insert is reproduced from the 2009 Forum/IHS CERA report *Thirsty Energy: Water and Energy in the 21st Century*.

39. "World Food Situation: FoodPricesIndex," http://www.fao.org/worldfood situation/FoodPricesIndex/en/.

40. "Ethanol's Grocery Bill: Two Federal Studies Add Up the Corn Fuel's Exorbitant Cost." *Wall Street Journal*, June 3, 2009.

41. In early 2008, Saudi Arabia announced that it would phase out its own cereal production, realizing that the fossil water used for irrigation of farms might quickly run out.

42. That is, 22 pounds corn/gallon ethanol. Gallon ethanol = 19,400 kilocalories (kcal). With 10 liters of ethanol per 100 kilometers (only with a fuel-efficient car): 4 kilometers from 2,100 kcal.

43. Intergovernmental Panel on Climate Change, *Climate Change, 2007: Mitigation of Climate Change*, 2007.

44. It is only now, for example, in a paper prepared for the Bali 2008 conference, that responsible scientists have started to worry that this might have been misleading. See Wetlands International, "Biomass: The Zero-Emission Myth," http://www .wetlands.org/LiznkClick.aspx?fileticket=yIVmODL072c%3d&tabid=56.

45. The amount of sulfate aerosols (particulates) trapped in ice samples had also risen, though it has declined in recent years with better pollution controls. Unlike greenhouse gases, sulfate aerosols are short-lived and can have a cooling effect. There is still debate about some aspects of the causality of CO_2; warming tends to increase the amount of CO_2 in the air (coming mostly from the oceans).

46. Crutzen and colleagues have calculated that growing some of the most commonly used biofuel crops releases around twice the amount of the potent greenhouse gas nitrous oxide (N_2O) than previously thought—wiping out any benefits from not using fossil fuels and, probably worse, contributing to global warming. For rapeseed bio-diesel, which accounts for about 80% of the biofuel production in Europe, the relative warming due to N_2O emissions is estimated at 1 to 1.7 times higher than the quasi-cooling effect due to saved fossil CO_2 emissions. For corn bio-ethanol, dominant in the US, the figure is 0.9 to 1.5. Only cane sugar bio-ethanol—with a relative warming of 0.5 to 0.9—looks like a viable alternative to conventional fuels. See "Biofuels Could Boost Global Warming, Finds Study," *Chemistry World*, September 21, 2007, http://www.rsc.org/chemistryworld/News/2007/September/21090701.asp.

47. Björn Pieprzyk, Norbert Kortlüke, Paula Rojas Hilje (Im Auftrag des Bundesverbands Erneuerbare Energie e.V.), Auswirkungen fossiler Kraftstoffe. Treibhausgasemissionen, Umweltfolgen und sozioökonomische Effekte. Endbericht, 2009, http:// bee-ev.de/_downloads/publikationen/studien/2009/091123_era-Studie_Marginal_ Oil_Endbericht.pdf.

CHAPTER 3

Trade

This chapter explores the water-trade nexus. It benefits greatly from the perspectives of many public, private, academic, and NGO representatives who have taken part in various Forum sessions and workshops on water issues over the last three years, including representatives from the World Economic Forum Agenda Council on Trade.

Background

Approximately 1,300 liters of water are necessary to produce one kilogram of wheat.[1] One kilogram of wheat is much easier to ship than 1,300 liters of water. In the same vein, between about 10,000 and 20,000 liters of water are required to produce one kilogram of beef.[2] One kilogram of beef is much easier to ship than up to 20,000 liters of water.[3]

As the earlier chapter on agriculture set out, the demand for grain and the demand for beef are projected to nearly double in the coming decades, mostly through economic growth across Asia. Within this context, what makes more sense if you are a water-stretched Asian economy? Allocate water away from your fast-growing industrial and energy sectors to produce more grain and meat at home to meet this rising demand? Literally import the agricultural water you need? Or instead import the grain and meat you need from somewhere else, thus by default "virtually" importing the water it took to produce these food products. Many would say the economic argument would hold sway. The country will choose to import more of its food.

Extrapolate this concept across all kinds of other food and nonfood consumer goods that a fast-growing economy demands, from melons to makeup, from potatoes to paint, from tomatoes to toothpaste, and the importance of trade to water begins to take shape. The water and trade nexus will be especially important for those water-constrained but expanding economies across North Africa, the Middle East, and Asia over the next few decades. By importing cereal, meat, and other food and consumer products (imports of "virtual" water), countries without much water can reduce their domestic agricultural and industrial water use. By 2025, some estimate that an increase in cereal imports could save Asia up to 12% of its irrigation water consumption.[4]

Virtual water, conceived over twenty years ago by Professor Tony Allan, of King's College and the School of Oriental and African Studies in London, can be defined as follows:

> Virtual water (also known as embedded water, embodied water, or hidden water) refers, in the context of trade, to the water used in the production of a good or service. For instance, it takes 1,300 cubic meters of water on average to produce one metric tonne of wheat. The precise volume can be more or less depending on climatic conditions and agricultural practice. Hoekstra and Chapagain have defined the virtual-water content of a product (a commodity, good, or service) as "the volume of freshwater used to produce the product, measured at the place where the product was actually produced." It refers to the sum of the water use in the various steps of the production chain.[5]

Professor Allan was awarded the Stockholm Water Prize in 2008 for this concept. In awarding him the prize, the Stockholm International Water Institute stated that "virtual water has had a major impact on global trade policy and research, especially in water-scarce regions, and has redefined discourse in water policy and management. By explaining how and why nations such as the United States, Argentina, and Brazil 'export' billions of litres of water each year, while others like Japan, Egypt, and Italy 'import' billions, the virtual water concept has opened the door to more productive water use."[6]

A further and more recent development relating to the "virtual" import of water embedded in food or consumer goods is the "water footprint" of a product, an industry, or indeed a country. Professor Arjen Hoekstra, who holds the chair in multidisciplinary water management at the University of Twente in the Netherlands, is widely credited as the creator of the water footprint concept. The water footprint is an indicator of freshwater use that looks at both direct and indirect water use of a consumer or producer. The water footprint of an individual, community, or business is defined as the total volume of freshwater that is used to produce the goods and services consumed by the individual or community or produced by the business. Water use is measured in terms of water volumes consumed (evaporated) or polluted per unit of time. A water footprint can be calculated for a particular product, for any well-defined group of consumers (e.g., an individual, family, village, city, province, state, or nation) or producers (e.g., a public organization, private enterprise, or economic sector).[7] The water footprint is a geographically explicit indicator, showing not only the volumes of water use and pollution but also the locations.[8]

As a result of the rise of water footprint thinking over the past several years among academics and NGOs, water-related facts and figures are increasingly being assembled, in a manner analogous to the calculation of carbon footprints. For example, on the webpage of the World Wide Fund for Nature, the following water footprint facts are presented:

- The production of one kilogram of beef requires between ten thousand and twenty thousand liters of water.
- To produce one cup of black coffee without sugar, we need 140 liters of water.
- The average annual water footprint of China is 950 cubic meters per person. Only about 8% of the Chinese water footprint is related to the consumption of imported products.
- In the United Kingdom, the average annual water footprint is 1,695 cubic meters per person. About 62% of the nation's water footprint is related to the consumption of imported products.
- The water footprint for producing the cotton required by the average person in the United Kingdom is 210 liters per day, whereas the average daily direct use of water in the house is only 150 liters per person.
- The average annual water footprint of a person in the US is 2,900 cubic meters.[9]

As an added resource, a Water Footprint Network exists and a Water Footprint Calculator is available on their webpage.[10]

Many leading businesses and business organizations, such as the World Business Council for Sustainable Development, are now engaged in helping to develop methodologies and applications for the water footprint concept. At the 2010 Stockholm Water Week, for example, the beer company SAB-Miller, together with the World Wide Fund for Nature and the German Development Agency GTZ, discussed a report that explains the water footprint of the whole value chain for SABMiller's beers covering South Africa, Peru, Tanzania and Ukraine. In the previous year, 2009, SABMiller published the first ever corporate Water Footprint report, which covered South Africa and the Czech Republic.[11] At the same event, the Coca-Cola Company and the Nature Conservancy discussed a water footprint report that examines three pilot studies that were conducted on Coca-Cola products and ingredients.[12]

For South Africa, the net water footprint for a liter of beer was calculated as 155 liters using the water footprint methodology (excluding gray water), of which crop cultivation and imports made up 95% of the footprint.[13] SAB-Miller Head of Sustainable Development Andy Wales explains, "Water footprinting enables SABMiller to understand which parts of our supply chain might face water scarcity, or poor water quality, in the future, and means that we can plan now to deal with these future challenges."[14]

In partnership with third-party researchers, the Coca-Cola Company and the Nature Conservancy calculated the water footprints of Coca-Cola in a 0.5 liter PET bottle produced by Coca-Cola Enterprises in the Netherlands, beet sugar supplied to Coca-Cola bottling plants in Europe, and Minute Maid orange juice and Simply Orange produced for the North American market. Estimates are that the green water footprint of the 0.5 liter Coca-Cola beverage is fifteen liters, the blue water footprint is one liter, and the gray water footprint is twelve liters. The average green water footprint for sugar from sugar beets across all regions of Europe is estimated to be 375 liters/kg sugar, the average blue water footprint is 54 liters/kg sugar, and the average gray water footprint is 128 liters/kg sugar. The size and color composition of the water footprint varies depending on the region from which the beets are sourced. For Simply Orange sourced from Florida, the green water footprint is 386 liters per liter of product, the blue water footprint is 154 liters per liter of product, and the gray water footprint is 100 liters per liter of product.[15]

"More important than the numbers associated with a water footprint are the impacts of water use," says Brian Richter, Freshwater Program Codirector at the Nature Conservancy. "When properly managed, even large volumes of water use can be sustainable in locations where the resource is sufficient to support the use and sustain ecological health. The number associated with a water footprint is not the end game, but rather a starting point to addressing the sustainability of the water source."[16]

It is often stressed by those working on the issue that water footprinting is not an end in itself, and that water footprints are not yet ready for use on product labels for internationally traded goods, because of the natural variability caused by a wide range of factors. Some argue that the actual water footprint number (and therefore the concept of water footprint labeling) is not the key outcome. Rather, it is the calculation and breakdown of the water footprint number into green, blue, and gray water that provides insight into water use across the value chain.

Despite these promising academic-, NGO-, and business-orientated activities to develop a better account of the link between water use in the value chain of internationally traded products, our current international arrangements lag far behind. The wider international trade regime, for example, does not take account of even the most basic water issues at all. At a fundamental level, as James Bacchus (the former Chair of the Appellate Judges of the World Trade Organization) says in his perspective at the end of this chapter, "It is unclear under the rules and the rulings of the World Trade Organization when, and to what extent, water itself can become a product, a commodity subject to the rules of trade. . . . [If] a price [or a label] must be placed on water to improve global water use . . . what are the implications under WTO rules?" It seems our global trade institutions are out of step with both the fast-looming issue of water security itself, as well as those who are already seeking ways to address it within the international system.

Trends

According to the United Nations Environment Programme (UNEP), total world cereal demand is projected to grow from 585 million tons today to 828 million tons by 2025, a rise of 42%.[17] Due to water scarcity and other challenges, not every country can grow all the food or fiber it will need under these growth scenarios. The world system will need to include more agricultural trade.

But agricultural exports have actually *decreased* in the share of international trade, from 46% in 1950 to 9% in 2001.[18] A report by United Nations Economic and Social Commission for Asia and the Pacific suggests that rice has been the least traded among the major cereals, with global exports as a share of production not exceeding 10% since 1995. Even in the case of wheat, which is traded the most among the major cereals, the share of global exports has not been significantly higher than a quarter of total global production.[19] This point is further corroborated by the fact that global stocks of major cereals have also been declining since the late 1990s. The sharpest decline has been in case of maize, with global stocks declining nearly 54% since 1999/2000.[20]

Further, the volume of agricultural goods that are traded take place mostly within a small club of countries, and a wider range of measures abound to avoid an opening up of these trade flows, in the name mostly of protecting domestic farmers. In 2001, 60% of global agricultural export was from the US, the EU, and Canada, and 60% of agricultural import was from the US, the EU, and Japan, with average tariffs at 30%. This seems to runs counter to the system the world actually needs. In a 2009 report on water for the World Economic Forum, Mohamed Ait-Kadi, President of the General Council of Agricultural Development in Morocco, suggested that such protectionist agricultural policies have proven costly to governments and consumers alike because of the labyrinth of subsidies, price supports, and trade barriers they entail.[21]

Recall from the earlier section on agriculture that increasing water scarcity in the next decades could cause annual grain losses equivalent to 30% of current world yield, at the same time as we want to *increase* food production by 70–100%. Consequently, there is less overall trade in agriculture when more is needed, and too much protectionism when much less is needed. Food prices are becoming much more volatile, as recent price fluctuations in 2008, 2009, and 2010 have shown. It is unlikely that these trends will reverse over the next two decades; in fact, it is more likely that they will escalate. A shortage in food, with the requisite economic, social, and political ramifications, is an increasingly possible outcome before 2030.

On a more fundamental note than even the issue of trade flows, commodity prices, and food shortages, no correlation exists between the places around the world that are hydrologically best suited to grow food and those that actually do. Three of the world's top ten overall food exporters (Australia, Spain, and the US) face serious national or regional water security challenges over the next two decades with regard to their agricultural sectors. Australia, China, India, Turkey, and the US make up half of the world's top-ten wheat exporters, and all face well-documented water challenges within their agricultural sectors, which will increase through 2030.[22] Taking just one example, and as other parts of this book explain, climate change may reduce agricultural yields across many countries as a whole by 10–25%, including up to 40% in India alone.[23]

The United Nations Economic and Social Commission for Asia and the Pacific report referred to above has a rather gloomy assessment on the challenge of trade, agriculture, and declining food stocks in the world system: "Given such a scenario, countries would indeed be risking their futures if they decided to rely on the global market for their food supplies."[24] And many water-insecure countries seem to be taking this advice to heart.

In 2008, Saudi Arabia gave up being self-sufficient in wheat production. It set up an investment fund to acquire land overseas to grow the crops it needs, possibly in Pakistan or the Horn of Africa. Similarly, China is acquiring agricultural land in southern Africa to help grow the food and fiber it needs at home. Daewoo Logistics famously looked in 2008 to lease land from the government of Madagascar to grow food for South Korea, before political problems in Madagascar stopped the deal.[25] Other countries in South Asia and the Gulf have been making similar moves. Between 2006 and 2009, many such land deals have taken place, totaling more than twenty million hectares in developing countries.[26] This is about the size of all the agricultural land in France.[27] Most are government-to-government deals with state-owned enterprises or investment companies acting as agents for the state. Japan now has three times more land abroad than at home. Saudi Arabia, Kuwait, South Korea, and China have secured deals in Sudan, Ethiopia, DRC, and Pakistan.[28] Many NGOs and media commentators have termed this trend as a "land grab."[29]

In effect, one could better view these "land grabs" as "water grabs": these countries have plenty of land at home; what they don't have is water. This is a new and potentially significant trend—the virtual water thesis writ large. Arguably, the trend reflects the failure of national governments and the international trade system to address the structural water-scarcity problem within the world's agricultural system.

Forecast

It is likely that these trends—a dysfunctional trade regime and an increase in direct lease-land deals—will continue. In fact, land deals may accelerate. When blue water availability drops below 1,500 cubic meters per capita per year, countries tend to begin to import food, particularly water-intense crops. Twenty-one countries fell below this threshold in 2000 and another fourteen will join them by 2030.[30] There will be many more countries looking to the world system to help source their food. Without a step change in the improvement of water use efficiency in agriculture and a functional trade regime, bilateral land-for-water deals become a rational approach in order to ensure national food security.

But it is not just an issue of water scarcity that may accelerate the volume of these land-for-water deals. For many of the fast-growing economies in Asia and the Middle East, there is also an increasing set of water trade-offs to navigate. As economies expand, governments have to choose whether to allocate water to agriculture or to expanding cities and industries. This is a particular challenge that China and South Korea face (and that Japan has faced), for example. When a country devotes 40% of its renewable water resources or more to irrigation, it starts to face these water allocation issues.[31]

By 2030, under business as usual, all of South Asia will reach the 40% threshold, and the Middle East and North Africa will have hit 58%.[32] Agriculture almost always loses out to the industrializing economy in such water allocation decisions, especially to the energy and manufacturing sectors. The consequence will be that rapidly industrializing economies across South Asia, the Middle East, and North Africa, which support approximately 2.5 billion people, will also be forced to look elsewhere for water-rich land for their food.

Combined, these trends suggest that by 2030 nearly 55% of the world's population will be increasingly dependent on food imports as a result of insufficient domestic water. If the trade system is not fixed, one could expect acceleration in land-for-water deals. Under these circumstances, we could see multiple countries across Asia and the Middle East competing with one another to secure bilateral land-for-water deals with cash-poor but water-rich nations, such as the Democratic Republic of Congo or other equatorial African nations. We could also witness such water-rich but previously cash-poor nations realizing the spoils of a new market in lucrative land-for-water deals. Depending on the relative strength of governance systems for managing water in these nations, the land-for-water market could be a positive or a negative development.

Implications

"Australia built the pricing mechanism, incorporated the environmental cost, and gave stronger economic signals to farmers," says David Crean of Australia, formally Minister of Trade, now Minister of Regional Government. "However, there is no point of talking about water security et cetera if we are not also talking about openness in trade."[33] If the global trade system for agriculture is not fixed, the geopolitical implications emerging from the various crises of national water security could be profound. More nations will focus on resolving their water "interests" through unilateral rather than multilateral arrangements; the world system will witness a plethora of new alliances between water-poor, cash-rich nations and water-rich (and likely cash-poor) nations. Unlikely bedfellows will emerge.

The Food and Agriculture Organization (FAO) warns that the race to secure farmland overseas risks creating a "neocolonial" system.[34] A rapid retreat from a globalized, 21st-century world back into a 19th-century-style network of bilateral alliances and trade deals is possible, with all of the associated political and economic complications this could bring.

Such a shift in the geopolitical landscape as a result of alliance trends played out through water, agriculture, and trade could also bring the roles of international organizations and NGOs into question. What will be the relevance of the FAO or UNEP in this new geometry? Companies, too, may face a baffling new landscape where the rules seem to have significantly changed—or are not being followed at all. Without a multilateral framework to set broad rules or behavioral norms for water stewardship and trade, what will be the future utility of a company-focused water footprint analysis? The international playing field for securing and managing water resources may become far from level or transparent.

The corollary to this is, of course, that multilateral trade requires peace. When there is peace, observes Professor Tony Allan, the trade in water intensive commodities can address local water scarcity and the local famines caused by occasional droughts and floods. Peaceful trade can avert further conflict.[35] This possibility provides further impetus for completion of the Doha round of trade negotiations and for agreement on further new trade arrangements.

There are also environmental implications to these trends. Although water is usually categorized as a local resource, the response to a local water crisis as set out here (within the context of a failing international trade regime) is to establish political, economic, and agricultural links with places that have more water. These local water crises will necessitate a major reconfiguration of international trade to enable country-to-country trades in "virtual water" to alleviate domestic water constraints. Consequently, there are serious environmental implications if an increase in trade for agriculture due to water scarcity does not take account of water scarcity.[36]

Consider the "virtual water trade" as maps that can be constructed between and within countries and other geographies. Imagine the damaging impact of growing a water-intensive crop in a country that is water-scarce, and then exporting that commodity to a country that is water-abundant. Not only does the "virtual" or "embedded" water leave the watershed where it was grown, but it is no longer available to recharge the aquifers, thereby worsening the long-term scarcity outlook for the exporter.[37]

The Way Forward

Water supply crises have easily been addressed by other highly developed societies and economies. Consider Singapore: it only has 5% of the water it needs, it has no energy resources, yet it has a very advanced economy.[38] If the international arrangements could be adapted to reflect water scarcity issues, trade in virtual water could also hold real promise for triggering a better spatial location of water-intensive production. But fair terms of trade are central to resolving this issue—tariffs and low food prices for key global markets have prevented a sensible transition to improved productivity in poor rural areas of the world, particularly in Africa.

The developments in water footprinting methodologies could also help. Even without labeling as an end point, a deeper understanding of water use within the value chain of globally traded goods and services could be a useful methodological contribution to help officials in due course recalibrate international trade arrangements.

Another dimension that is worthy of deeper investigation is to look again at regional and traditional systems of localized trading in water rights and allocations. At a localized level, these forms of "trading" systems have proved historically resilient to environmental and economic stress. Much could be learned from how they work, the institutional arrangements and cooperative behaviors they instill, and the improvements in water resource management they create.

Casting back into history, consider Aflaj, as was mentioned in chapter 1. Under that 4,500-year-old water rights exchange system, Omani communities secure enough free water to drink or bathe; beyond that, water's value fluctuates by owner, season, or irrigated crop. Oldest of all, perhaps, is the timeless reciprocity network *xaro*, where Bushmen self-regulate their Kalahari economy by informal bartering of water resource goods, services, or information within and between bands.

More recently, across northern Chile, eastern Australia, or the Western US, regional governments endowed farmers, miners, and ranchers with ownership of "usufruct rights" to private shares of what had been public water resources. Today, under conditions of increased water stress, competing interests can and do buy or lease those rights to secure water for cities, other farms, fisheries, or the stream itself. If designed and implemented in a fair and transparent manner, such trading schemes can and do help promote efficiency as water shifts towards holding a greater economic value.

Each of these distinct water-trading regimes arose uniquely and independently, but they all share common characteristics. They entrust people with ownership and reward voluntary exchanges to reduce social friction and sustain the common water resource. With the new focus on behavioral economics, could serious multidisciplinary research be done to explore how to scaling these trading systems up to national and international levels to help us manage the future we have forecast above? This may seem anathema today, but if established democratically and conducted transparently, could these kinds of trading systems hold out the possibility of transforming the current trajectory of widespread global scarcity into a more efficient situation of relative abundance?

Just think. Through the Global Water Court of 2030, the Democratic Republic of Congo bids out rights on a twenty-year basis to parcels of its water endowment, as part of a wider economic development plan. Public and private (and NGO) entities can bid for these rights through a sealed auction. The Court helps DRC to screen the bids and avoid unscrupulous or overoptimistic bidders. The government of DRC, with the help of international finance institutions, securitizes the future revenue flows it will generate from the sale of these water rights, and is able to issue hydro-bonds to the international capital markets as a result. This generates the capital DRC needs to reinvest up front in important infrastructure or other social and economic assets the country needs, which creates jobs and boosts GDP. Is this an unattainable future?

Perspectives

The following personal perspectives amplify the main themes touched on by this chapter. They help to illustrate the range of current viewpoints on the water-trade nexus. The views expressed do not necessarily represent those of the World Economic Forum, nor do they necessarily represent the views of the other individual contributors or the various contributing companies or institutions.

- James Bacchus, currently Chair of the Global Trade and Investment Practice at Greenberg Traurig LLP; former member of US House of

Representatives; and former Chairman of the Appellate Body of the World Trade Organization, provides his overview of the water-trade nexus and ideas on how the WTO could reform to reflect these challenges.

- Stuart Orr, Freshwater Manager, WWF International; and Guy Pegram, WWF Adviser, South Africa, provide their thoughts on the risks and reward of water and trade.
- Herbert Oberhänsli, Head of Economics and International Relations, Nestlé SA, Switzerland, looks at how trade can make a different to the interlocking crises of water scarcity.
- Professor Tony Allan, Head of the King's College London Water Research Group, sets out a wider range of soft, trade-related ways to secure our future water needs, which involve action in the international system rather than necessarily the building of more water supply infrastructure.

The Water-Trade Nexus

JAMES BACCHUS, CHAIR, GLOBAL TRADE AND INVESTMENT PRACTICE, GREENBERG TRAURIG LLP; FORMER MEMBER OF UNITED STATES HOUSE OF REPRESENTATIVES AND FORMER CHAIRMAN OF THE APPELLATE BODY OF THE WORLD TRADE ORGANIZATION

In the intensifying global scramble for all-too-limited natural resources, the issues of water, food, and energy are interlinked. And all in turn are linked with trade. The link with trade is especially strong on the critical issue of water scarcity worldwide. World water demand could exceed world freshwater supply by 40% by 2030. The Organisation for Economic Co-operation and Development forecasts that if current trends in water use continue, nearly four billion people will face water stress.

World trade practices and patterns affect water use in numerous ways. Thousands upon thousands of traded products and services depend on water, and affect the use of water, every day, in endless ways. Yet world trade rules largely take no account of the growing global water crisis. At the most basic level, it is unclear under the rules and the rulings of the World Trade Organization when, and to what extent, water itself can become a product, a commodity subject to the rules of trade.

How does water differ from other natural resources? Is access to water a human right? Should people ever be required to pay for it? Some economists and other experts suggest that a price must be placed on water if we hope to improve global water use. If this is so, what are the implications under WTO rules?

Amid much misinformation about what WTO rules do and do not currently require, this issue is rapidly emerging in highly emotional debates worldwide. The 153 countries and other customs territories that are Members of the WTO should join this debate now. They should clarify the status of water as a product through multilateral negotiations—and not leave it to potential litigation in WTO dispute settlement.

WTO Members should also address the issue of "virtual water"—the volume of water that is used to produce a product and is therefore "virtually" embedded in it. The flow of "virtual water" through international trade has significant effects on patterns of water scarcity. Importing water-intensive products reduces national water demand. This is true of the water-scarce countries of the Middle East and North Africa. Exporting water-intensive products increases national water demand. This is true of the US and Australia. In this way, water can be saved as a result of international trade.

It has been suggested by some that WTO rules should be changed to permit WTO Members to discriminate between and among otherwise "like"-traded products based on how much water is used to produce them. This could undermine the fundamental rules of nondiscrimination that are the heart of the multilateral trading system. A more promising approach would be to seek transparency through product labels that would inform consumers about water use. This could be done consistently with current WTO rules on labeling requirements and other technical regulations.

On average, 70% of freshwater use worldwide is for agriculture. Better water use in agriculture is thus key to resolving the global water crisis, and this cannot be accomplished without better rules on agricultural trade in the WTO. More efficiency in global agricultural production and trade will result in more efficiency in global water use. Additional trade liberalization in agriculture will speed the flow of "virtual water" in ways that will ease water scarcity. The early and successful conclusion of the long-delayed Doha Development Round of global trade negotiations is therefore important to resolving the water crisis.

There is urgent need as well for WTO rules that encourage efficient water use in agricultural production. WTO rules on agriculture already include some limited provisions relating to environmental programmes. More extensive rules should be negotiated that deal specifically with the global water crisis by encouraging sustainable water use in agricultural production.

The International Energy Agency *World Energy Outlook* for 2009 predicts a 40% increase in energy demand by 2030. Without better rules, this increased demand will worsen the water crisis. In the US and the EU, for instance, about 40% of freshwater use is for the energy sector.

Increased water demands inspired by increased energy demands should likewise be taken into account more comprehensively in WTO trade negotiations. So, too, should the myriad ways in which the global challenge of climate change is affecting water availability and water use.

Lastly, there is the pressing issue of global governance. There is no World Water Organization comparable to the World Trade Organization. There are no world water agreements comparable to the world trade agreements that make up the WTO treaty.

New international agreements and new international institutional arrangements are much needed to bring the world together to confront the many complexities of the global water crisis. In seeking such agreements, and in fashioning such arrangements, those who hope to resolve the water crisis could profit from serious consideration of the historical evolution and the structural architecture of the world trading system.

The Risks and Rewards of Water in Trade

STUART ORR, FRESHWATER MANAGER, WWF INTERNATIONAL; AND
GUY PEGRAM, WWF ADVISER, SOUTH AFRICA

Whether absorbed in the field or soaked up in the value chain, every commodity requires water. The amount of water needed is highest for agricultural food and fiber commodities, but a significant amount is embedded[39] in consumer goods and heavy industry materials.

Extractive industries are seldom constrained by water, but the global trade in agricultural commodities and their prices on international markets increasingly depend on seasonal variations in climate and water. The FAO food price index increased by 50% during 2007, due to a combination of growth in biofuels, increasing demand, high oil prices, speculation in food markets, and extreme weather events. After a half century of steadily declining prices—due largely to high productivity yields of the Green Revolution and more reliable water supply—the sudden spike came as a shock.

Food prices dropped back to 2006 levels after the onset of global recession in September 2009 and then rose again in 2010, underscoring the economic and speculation-driven instability of global commodity prices. The problem now is that even when world commodity supplies increase to record levels, the higher prices put food out of reach of the poor, condemning one hundred million people to undernourishment and undermining the global target to eradicate hunger.

This interaction between climate, water, food, and energy is manifest in sugar. Sugar's price broke record levels in August 2009 due to a combination of failing rains in India and Brazil, conversion of cane crops into ethanol fuels, projections of economic recovery, and a greater sweet tooth in Asia. Amplify all this with commodity investors, and the price of sugar doubled in just six months. True, that's how markets work. But speculators pose unforeseen risks to countries, companies, and communities that depend on certain crops in their supply chains for food security. Even without speculation, a rising population, a volatile climate, and finite water resources will guarantee price instability. The political, social, economic, and financial consequences of volatile prices will fall hardest on those countries and companies that most depend on water-embedded commodities.

The coming nature of these risks were foreshadowed in 2008 at the height of the food price spikes, when many countries sought short-term refuge from political instability and food riots by erecting protective trade barriers, only to suffer over the long term. Countries may begin to impose controls or tariffs on the export of commodities with significant embedded water, despite the implications for international trade law. While water itself is not at the forefront of the current ongoing trade negotiations, it has surfaced in agricultural negotiations as either a "good" or "resource."

Even as business interests lobby for pricing of and markets for water, and even as trade may expand between users within a basin, water will remain highly regulated, due to hydrological constraints and political-economic imperatives. As a result, the trade in water-embedded commodities is likely to intensify, further compounded by speculation. Consequently, for the World Wide Fund for Nature, a diverse array of market variables will pose significant risks for freshwater ecosystems and the people who depend on them.

That's why oversight of energy and food markets must account for the water embedded within them. Judicious regulations can and should mitigate political and financial risks associated with the instability of commodity prices. This will help reduce the potential for poor decision-making around water resources development and use by (a) governments forced to seek food security through protectionism, (b) commodity speculators who invest in agricultural enterprises to capture commodity production, and (c) companies expanding production into inappropriate basins to protect their supply chains.

The recent media focus on agricultural acquisitions, or "land grabs," introduces an international investment issue that will become more relevant under a more volatile climate and water-limited world. Foreign investments are protected under international law, as are the "conditions" implied at the time contracts are signed. That builds trust. But potential constraints on management flexibility—and thus on adaptation strategies—may erode trust in those countries receiving this investment, especially where sovereign or multinational companies lease or buy land for dedicated crop exports

The future is by definition uncertain. But the linkages between water, trade, and investment in agricultural commodities all point towards greater instability and risk. Governments and companies most dependent on water-embedded food and energy will need to align their interests with societal expectations to avoid the erosion of crucial natural resources.

Interlocking Crises of Water Scarcity: How Trade Can Make a Difference

HERBERT OBERHÄNSLI, HEAD, ECONOMICS AND INTERNATIONAL RELATIONS,
NESTLÉ SA, SWITZERLAND

In 2008, as the Spanish city of Barcelona ran dry, Marseille, in neighboring France, rushed to import several shiploads of water to carry it through the hot summer months.[40] This was, admittedly, high drama. It made news for weeks. The world became aware of the gravity of the water issue like never before and witnessed the logic and benefits of water trading as the exchange unfolded in real time. But this high-profile story also distracted from the real issue concerning water and trade: how to feed more people with thirstier appetites while using less water. If a liter of water produces a calorie of food, nine billion people require twelve trillion liters each day just to survive. That assumes perfect stability and no waste. Yet aquifers are falling, rivers are running dry, canals are leaking, dams are silting up. At the same time, demand for food is growing further, with an increasing global population and more prosperity. To put it mildly, all this puts the global food supply at risk.

Within fifteen years, water scarcity "will affect the livelihoods of one-third of the world's population," wrote Frank Rijsberman in 2003, at that time head of the International Water Management Institute. "We could be facing annual losses equivalent to one-third of global grain crops today."[41] A recent UN map[42] highlights problem hot spots: the US Great Plains, the Middle East and North Africa, and parts of Spain, Pakistan, northwestern India, and northeastern China. All are vital agricultural regions. To illustrate orders of magnitude, once the water crisis does erupt, it would require more than thirty-five million "Barcelona-size" shiploads of water each year to be transferred to the water-stressed areas still growing food today in order to avoid the worst.

In early 2008, Saudi Arabia realized that, for them, water was more valuable than oil, and decided to stop exploiting its more precious liquid asset.[43] Instead, similarly dry countries like that can buy crops, or the property itself, from a wide range of rainy but massively underused landscapes from sub-Saharan Africa (about six hundred million hectares) and Latin America (about three hundred million hectares).[44] Agricultural yields are relatively low in these regions, but that could change if farmers were given a strong signal that productivity would be rewarded.

Those signals are long overdue. Liberal trade efficiencies would boost GDP and incomes in developing countries in the short term. Better still, the OECD estimates that full liberalization could reduce overall agricultural freshwater withdrawals by 10%. Still, trade in "virtual water" works only if done hand in hand with necessary internal reforms that reveal the true value of scarce water.

These measures include liberalization, modernization of regulations, and, in certain instances, pricing.

The term "pricing of water" is highly contentious and deserves explanation. Water for fundamental human needs—drinking, cooking, and basic hygiene—is a human right. Governments must secure adequate and affordable access to that minimum amount for all people, if necessary, free of cost. Any use beyond basic needs, like watering the lawn or filling a swimming pool, should carry with it at least the full cost of the infrastructure.

Beyond this, freshwater use for industrial or agricultural production is most efficient and sustainable when water use decisions depend on opportunity costs. And costs are largely a function of private ownership shares that can be traded. "There is only one way of getting users to consider opportunity costs," argues Harvard's John Briscoe, formerly of the World Bank, "and that is to give users well-specified, transferable water rights." He notes how such rights have long existed in the arid western US, for decades in Chile, Australia, and Mexico, and more recently in parts of India and Pakistan. Once users have these rights, they automatically decide whether to forgo use of water in exchange for compensation from another user who may place a higher value on the water. His conclusion: "Reallocating water then becomes a matter of voluntary and mutually-beneficial agreements between willing buyers and willing sellers and not a matter of confiscation via pricing at the scarcity value of the resource, or the endless search for new sources of supply."[45]

When farmers can't trade private rights, the result is waste. In Valais, Switzerland, private water rights have been in existence for eight hundred years, but shares can't be rented. So farmers may flood their fields, as they do in the western US, under the mantra "use it or lose it." To avoid being wasted, water requires a price. But before nations try to overhaul and liberalize the entire complex global trading system, they might first work at home. Local water markets could form a cornerstone of badly needed reforms.

The alternative of free trade is the new trend of restrictive bilateral contracts, where dry countries buy parts of wet ones. The media has reported this phenomenon without grasping what's at stake. Most articles describe the value of all trades in terms of land size, such as something the size of "the potential cropland of Germany." That grossly misses the point. Money is not changing hands to buy land, but rather the water use rights embedded therein. By that accounting, the buyers are getting a bargain. On the basis of one crop per year, the acreage transferred represents between fifty-five and sixty-five cubic kilometers of freshwater entitlements—that is, three million "Barcelona-size" shiploads per year.[46] Since this water has no price, the investors essentially take it over for free.

Soft Approaches to Sustainable Intensification for Water Security

TONY ALLAN, HEAD, KING'S COLLEGE LONDON WATER RESEARCH GROUP

While a political decision to cut subsidies for dryland crops and reinvest in cultivating wetlands may at the macro-level be economically rational to the water professional or micro-economist suggesting water reform recommendations, it would hardly seem efficient or equitable to the newly unemployed rural irrigator—to say nothing of the local economies that depend on them. In this regard, a soft, trade-related approach to water security is vital because most nations are net food importers. Only one in ten of the world's two hundred economies are net exporters of food. So for individual economies, imported food brings water security as embedded or virtual water is "traded" from water-surplus to water-deficit economies. A water-deficit economy that imports a ton of wheat avoids the economic and political stress of competing to produce the commodity. This "trade," however, is economically invisible and politically silent.

The important outcomes largely depend on incentivized decisions by farmers and consumers. Food water is the big water user, and consumers purchase and consume the food that is associated with this 80% of water use. Consumers drive the demand for food. What they choose to consume is pivotal. That is why water security needs to be considered through four lenses above and beyond straightforward micro-economic analysis.

First, farmers manage all the "green water" used to produce 70% of total crop and livestock production. Engineers provide the remaining 30% of "blue water" from surface and groundwater sources. With these blue and green waters, farmers combine other inputs. Subsistence farmers combine water, land, labor, and seeds. Farmers in OECD economies combine water, land and scores of agri-technology inputs with huge inputs of energy. The skills they deploy determine the level of returns to water, and on these skills rests global water security (again, because they manage 80% of our water). But farmers face many uncertainties. Climate and water are unreliable. The market can be cruel. Markets could make their returns safer and higher; transportation and storage could improve efficiency and access to markets; communication could help them to adapt to fast-changing weather.

Second, farmers need a level global playing field. The continent where farmers need most to increase returns on water—Africa—is held back by the unfair global trading system. US and EU subsidies determine global wheat prices. Poor farmers in Africa are repeatedly knocked back by low-priced food imports and can never gain surpluses to make essential investments. Instead, their capital base has been progressively eroded as yields decline, rather than trebling to meet demands locally.

Third, eliminating food waste would eliminate water waste. In advanced countries, nearly a third of all purchased food ends up as household trash. Conversely, developing economies sacrifice another 30% of all food to rot en route from farm gate to marketplace. Secure storage and refrigeration are known, proven, and affordable technologies. Why mobilize 40% more new water when we can save 60% of all food that water would grow?

Finally, and perhaps most importantly, the water resource issue depends on consumer choice. The food consumption that determines water consumption is driven by demography and choice of diet. One can slash population growth, as China has, or shrink, as some European countries have. But if even a static population goes from a vegetarian diet to eating beef, they double the per capita daily pressure, from 2.5 to 5.0 cubic meters per day, for food.

By all means, close the demand/supply gap in global water needs, by 2030 estimated to be 40%. Enable access to 40% more water by mobilizing new water and intensifying water use in all sectors. But don't forget the bigger savings in water gained by securing farmers' livelihoods and options while persuading consumers to behave rationally.

Notes

1. See "The Concepts of Water Footprint and Virtual Water," http://www.gdrc.org/uem/footprints/water-footprint.html.

2. World Wide Fund for Nature, "Reducing the Impact of Humanity's Water Footprint," http://wwf.panda.org/what_we_do/footprint/water/.

3. World Wide Fund for Nature, "Water Footprint," http://www.wwf.org.uk/what_we_do/safeguarding_the_natural_world/rivers_and_lakes/water_footprint/.

4. Tony Allan, King's College, personal communication.

5. Definition taken from Hoekstra, A. Y., and Chapagain, A. K. (2008), *Globalization of Water: Sharing the Planet's Freshwater Resources* (Blackwell Publishing, Oxford, U.K.). See also http://virtual-water.org and http://www.waterfootprint.org/ for further definitions and various examples of "virtual water."

6. Stockholm International Water Institute, "'Virtual Water' Innovator Awarded 2008 Stockholm Water Prize," http://www.siwi.org/sa/node.asp?node=25.

7. Within the water footprint, three types of water are assessed: green water, blue water, and gray water. Blue water is defined as water withdrawn from groundwater and surface water, and it does not return to the system from which it came. Green water is evaporated through crop growth that originates from soil moisture (which comes from rainfall). This is relevant to agricultural products. It is assumed that such a loss is not available to the area immediately downstream of where the crops are grown, and therefore it is considered a water use. Gray water refers to the volume of polluted water associated with the production of goods and services, quantified as the volume of water that is required to dilute pollutants to such an extent that the quality

of the ambient water remains above agreed water quality standards. For crop production this would be the volume of dilution to reduce to agreed standards nitrate and phosphate (fertilizer) levels and pesticide levels leaching from soils.

8. Water Footprint Network, "Glossary," http://www.waterfootprint.org/?page=files/Glossary.

9. World Wide Fund for Nature, "Water Footprint," http://www.wwf.org.uk/what_we_do/safeguarding_the_natural_world/rivers_and_lakes/water_footprint/.

10. Water Footprint Network, "Your Water Footprint: Extended Calculator," http://www.waterfootprint.org/?page=cal/WaterFootprintCalculator.

11. SAB Miller and the World Wide Fund for Nature, *Water Futures: Working Together for a Secure Water Future*, 2010. http://www.sabmiller.com/files/reports/water_future_report.pdf

12. The Coca-Cola Company and the Nature Conversancy, *Product Footprint Water Assessments: Practical Applications in Corporate Water Stewardship*, 2010.

13. SAB Miller and the World Wide Fund for Nature, *Water Futures: Working Together for a Secure Water Future*, 2009.

14. SABMiller, "WWF and SABMiller Unveil Water Footprint of Beer," August 18, 2009, http://www.sabmiller.com/index.asp?pageid=149&newsid=1034.

15. The Coca-Cola Company, "The Coca-Cola Company and the Nature Conservancy Release Water Footprint Report," September 8, 2010, http://www.thecoca-colacompany.com/presscenter/nr_20100908_water_footprint_report.html.

16. Ibid.

17. United Nations Environment Programme, *The Environmental Food Crisis*, 2009.

18. Food and Agriculture Organization of the United Nations, *The State of Food and Agriculture*, 2008.

19. Biswajit Dhar, "Agricultural Trade and Government Intervention: A Perspective from a Developing Country." In *Agricultural Trade: Planting the Seeds of Regional Liberalization in Asia: A Study by the Asia-Pacific Research and Training Network on Trade*. UN Economic and Social Commission for Asia and the Pacific, 2007, pp. 211–223. http://www.unescap.org/tid/publication/tipub2451.pdf.

20. Ibid.

21. World Economic Forum Water Initiative, *The Bubble Is Close to Bursting*, 2009.

22. "The World Top Ten Wheat Importers and Exporters," *Reuters*, July 13, 2009, http://in.reuters.com/article/idINSP49082020090713.

23. Cline William, *Global Warming and Agriculture: Impact Estimates by Country*, 2009.

24. Biswajit Dhar, "Agricultural Trade and Government Intervention: A Perspective from a Developing Country." In *Agricultural Trade: Planting the Seeds of Regional Liberalization in Asia: A Study by the Asia-Pacific Research and Training Network on Trade*. UN Economic and Social Commission for Asia and the Pacific, 2007, pp. 211–223. http://www.unescap.org/tid/publication/tipub2451.pdf.

25. See "Madagascar Scraps Daewoo Farm Deal," *Commercial Pressures on Land*, March 18, 2009, http://www.landcoalition.org/cpl-blog/?p=1235.

26. International Food and Policy Research Institute, *"Land Grabbing" by Foreign Investors in Developing Countries*, 2009.

27. See http://www.nationmaster.com/country/fr-france/agr-agriculture.

28. International Food and Policy Research Institute, *"Land Grabbing" by Foreign Investors in Developing Countries*, 2009.

29. See, for example, GRAIN, "Landgrab Resource Page," http://www.grain.org/ landgrab/.

30. World Economic Forum Water Initiative, *The Bubble Is Close to Bursting*, 2009.

31. Ibid.

32. Ibid.

33. David Crean, personal communication.

34. See, for example, Julian Borger, "Rich Countries Launch Great Land Grab to Safeguard Food Supply," *Guardian*, November 22, 2008, http://www.guardian .co.uk/environment/2008/nov/22/food-biofuels-land-grab.

35. Tony Allan, personal communication.

36. See World Wide Fund for Nature, *Water at Risk*, 2009. http://assets.wwf.org .uk/downloads/understanding_water_risk.pdf.

37. Ibid.

38. See Cecilia Tortajada, "Water Management in Singapore," *Water Resources Development*, June 2006, http://www.adb.org/water/knowledge-center/awdo/br01 .pdf.

39. The term "embedded water," also known as "virtual water," is often used, too, but in some discussions this term is also used normatively to refer to the comparative advantage in production in different places.

40. Cited in: http://economist.com/node/12494630?story_id=12494630, November 19, 2008.

41. UNEP/GRID-Arendal. Water Scarcity Index. UNEP/GRID-Arendal Maps and Graphics Library. 2009, http://maps.grida.no/go/graphic/water-scarcity-index.

42. In all, Barcelona received nineteen thousand tons of water per each of the ten boatloads from Marseille, as well as water from Tarragona and a desalination plant in southern Spain.

43. Andrew England, "Saudis to Phase Out Cereals," *Financial Times* April 11, 2008, http://us.ft.com/ftgateway/superpage.ft?news_id=fto041020082230338263&page=2.

44. A comprehensive database on soils and land types can be found in FAO/ IIASA/ISRIC/ISSCAS/JRC, 2008. Harmonized World Soil Database (version 1.0). FAO, Rome, Italy and IIASA, Laxenburg, Austria. Go to http://www.iiasa.ac.at/ Research/LUC/External-World-soil-database/HTML/.

45. John Briscoe, "Valuing Water Properly Is a Key to Wise Development," *Wall Street Journal*, June 23 , 2008, http://online.wsj.com/article/SB121417640 158095337.html?mod=googlenews_wsj.

46. Despite these high numbers, it is still a perception underpinned by the Barcelona water story that made the headlines. It even triggered the interest of Hollywood, with a James Bond movie and several "documentaries" constructing a story of tap-water barons withholding water resources from the population in order to increase personal profits.

CHAPTER 4

National Security

This chapter explores the water–national security nexus. It benefits greatly from the perspectives of many public, private, academic, and NGO representatives who have taken part in various Forum sessions and workshops on water issues over the last three years.

Background

Historically, the availability of easily accessible freshwater has proven to be a key determinant in development. A study showed that those countries which twenty-five years ago had low incomes (below US$ 750 per year per person), yet had access to adequate safe water and sanitation, grew on average 3.7% per year; on the other hand, countries with the same per capita income and limited water access grew at only 0.1% per year during the same period. Research such as this illustrates that access to freshwater cannot be discounted as an important variable in economic growth.[1]

Other work supports these findings. Researchers have found that societies and nations that inherited a legacy of difficult hydrology have remained poor—their findings confirm that greater rainfall variability is statistically associated with lower per capita incomes.[2] The work also found a direct correlation between investments in irrigation and significant declines in poverty (in this case, in India)—irrigated districts averaged 25% poverty rates against 70% poverty rates in unirrigated districts.[3] Similar trends can be found elsewhere. Sub-Saharan Africa, for example, loses 5% of GDP annually due to poor water services provision, which is far more than the region receives in aid.[4]

The converse is also true. Water insecurity, whether caused by environmental trends, economic growth, or a combination of both, can have a material impact on the economy. The "big dry" drought in Australia shaved at least 1% off the country's GDP in 2006/2007.[5] In the US, water shortages are reported to have cost the agricultural sector US$ 4 billion a year over the past two years. And California's current water crisis management will cost taxpayers an estimated US$ 1.6 billion per year by 2020.[6]

Yet could the economic impact of water security really stretch to challenge the very viability of a state in today's economy?

Trends

As six billion people become eight billion over the next two decades, as aggregate wealth increases, and as urbanization continues apace, human consumption of water will rise at an accelerating rate. We will need more food and we will demand more high-protein food. We will demand and use more energy. We will use more petroleum, buy more consumer goods, flush more toilets, use more showers, and water more lawns and golf courses than ever before in history.

It is important to note that as we grow wealthier, we demand more water. Population growth and water consumption follow a nonlinear relationship. From 1900 to 2000, for example, blue water use grew ninefold against population growth of factor of four. In 1950, with a global population of around 2.5 billion people, about 1,400 cubic kilometers of freshwater was withdrawn. In 2000, with a global population of around 5.2 billion, about 5,200 cubic kilometers of freshwater was withdrawn. This represents an increase of about a factor of four, compared with a population increase of just over a factor of two in the same period.[7]

But regional and temporal differences in the relationship between population growth, economic growth and water consumption abound. In the US, total water use peaked around 1980 and declined by one-tenth by 1995, despite the simultaneous addition of some forty million people to the American population.[8] In China, however (which holds the fourth largest freshwater resources in the world), economic growth has meant skyrocketing demand for water, creating overuse, inefficiencies, pollution, and unequal distribution. This creates paradoxical situations in which, for example, two-thirds of China's approximately 660 cities have less water than they need, while at the same time Chinese industries, which are generally water inefficient, use 10–20 percent more water than their counterparts in developed countries. Despite these various complexities, it is a reasonable assumption to make that human demand on the world's freshwater resources at least through 2030 will grow in aggregate much more quickly than the large population growth we expect, in particular to meet demands related to fast economic growth.

Recall from the opening chapters of this book that more than 1.4 billion people currently live in river basins where the use of water exceeds minimum recharge levels. Consequently, and more worryingly still, these water demands will occur just as our historic freshwater supplies are growing dangerously unstable. Recall also the analysis that suggests we will face a 40% gap between global water demand and available freshwater supply by 2030. This gap between water demand and supply will not open up in the same way all around the world. Very local differences (and dramas) may start to emerge.

The challenge is exacerbated by the fact that these multiple pockets of looming water scarcity to 2030 will often occur exactly within those economic regions that at the same time are becoming more populous and urbanizing and industrializing the fastest. Aside from water-blessed Brazil and Russia, a core group of countries elsewhere within Latin America, West Asia, the Middle East, and South Asia (such as Bangladesh, Egypt, Indonesia, Iran, Korea, Mexico, Nigeria, Pakistan, Philippines, Turkey, and Vietnam) are expected to be some of the fastest growing economies through 2030. Alongside China and India, many of these "N-11" countries (according to Goldman Sachs)[10] contain some of the most water-stressed areas of the world.[11] An important nexus between water, population growth, and national security starts to emerge.

There are, however, further layers of complexity. The World Bank estimates a 6% average growth rate across these fastest growing developing countries in the medium term. When population growth and economic growth forecasts are combined, however, something extraordinary happens. The World Bank predicts that by 2030 the number of *middle-class* people in the developing world will be 1.2 billion—a rise of 200% since 2005. This means that the developing world's middle class alone by 2030 will be larger than the total populations of Europe, Japan, and the US combined. Professor Jack Goldstone of the George Mason School of Public Policy builds on this forecast to suggest that by the middle of this century, the global middle class—those capable of purchasing durable consumer products, such as cars, appliances, and electronics (many, of course, with large water footprints)—will basically be found in what is now considered the developing world. He also inserts an interesting geopolitical twist to this growth trajectory—worldwide, of the forty-eight fastest growing countries today (those with an annual population growth of 2% or more), twenty-eight are majority Muslim or have Muslim minorities of 33% or more.[12]

In the next two decades, therefore, we face the scenario of a fast-growing, significantly Muslim middle class emerging across what is now termed the developing world. A new geopolitical geometry for international business and economic affairs will evolve as a result. But this growth will rest uneasily on a fast-approaching water security challenge facing nations in many of these areas.

From the previous chapter, we know that in principle trade should offer an opportunity to sustain economic growth in these countries despite their water shortages, if they can use international systems to leverage the comparative hydrological advantages of others. But the agricultural trade system is not working. The previous chapter also explored the first signs of a geopolitical pattern that is emerging as a result of this trade failure: if a growing, relatively wealthy nation can't acquire the "virtual" water resources it needs to feed its population through trade, then it will take the rational response of engaging in bilateral land-for-water deals with hydro-rich (but usually cash-poor) governments— South Korea into Madagascar, or Libya into Ukraine, for example.

In this fast changing world, where might the first tipping points occur when water and national and international security issues start to bump into one another? Let us turn to the Horn of Africa.

Yemen is now increasingly in the news in the US and western Europe as a nation of dwindling economic fortunes offering fertile ground for terror groups.[13] Diplomatic discussions are increasing as to how best to engage with Yemen to curb this perceived threat. Yet could there be a deeper reason for Yemen's national security misfortunes that Western security analysts are overlooking?

Half the population in Yemen is under eighteen years of age. Officials are paid with revenues from dwindling oil reserves. But, much more profoundly, the country is expected to quite soon literally run out of water.[14] Like many arid countries with expanding populations, Yemeni fossil water tables have been historically overabstracted; they are currently falling up to seven feet a year. The country has twenty-one diminishing aquifers. Subsidized fuel for well pumps encourages farmers to chase the diminishing water still further. Where is the water going? Reports suggest that about 30% of Yemen's available freshwater is used to flood fields twice a year to grow khat, a chewing leaf that provides a stimulant, something socially similar to having a cup of coffee or a cigarette in the West (and also permissible under Islam). Some hydrologists estimate that, due to the mining of fossil water mainly for khat agriculture, within five years Sana'a, Yemen's capital of two million people, will run out of water.[15]

The drying up of Yemen may not result in war. The decades of rhetoric about impending international "water wars" have now largely subsided, after scholars such as Aaron Wolf documented how, over thousands of years, no classic conflagration between sovereign states has ever broken out over water.[16] But the Yemen example could become the first case study of a nation-state in modern times gradually collapsing due to extreme water scarcity. As this slow decline happens, subtler and more troubling realities about the water–national security nexus may be realized, with ethnic divisions, local level conflicts and political opportunities for militants surfacing, especially at the sub-national level, while the nation slowly fails.[17]

What might be the lessons for the security analysts from all this? If the West would rather not have Yemen slowly disintegrate, which water-rich nation can be primed to export khat to Yemen, such that this trade in "virtual" water for khat will save the nation from disappearing due to its own addiction?

Elsewhere, other bumps within the water–national security nexus could create tipping points for much more serious national crises that would get the world's attention, again due to the fundamental problem of environmental degradation of the watercourse. In China, some estimates conclude that environmental degradation and pollution, much of it water-related, costs the national economy between 8% and 12% of GDP annually.[18] If the political and social contract between the polity and the populous in China is to come under stress in the next few decades, thereby causing an existential crisis for the government of PRC, then the issue of environmental degradation, particularly surrounding water services and resources, is as likely a trigger point as any. Note, for example, that out of China's 669 cities, 60% suffer water shortages and nearly half lacked wastewater treatment facilities when inspected in 2005.[19] Consequently, water will likely be a key domestic environmental (and political) issue for China to focus on over the next decade or so as it seeks to rebalance the environmental impacts of its economic growth, similar to Japan and South Korea before it. One should note, of course, that China has also taken steps over the past decades to address the demographic challenge it faced.

The 2005 Millennium Ecosystem Assessment also warns that it is not possible for a nation to sustain food production or economic growth when the environment is being compromised too severely.[20] Other experts have built on this observation and wonder if over the next two decades and in some national contexts—poorer developing countries, for example—large multinational companies might start to actually relocate *away* from those nations with poorly managed water resources. This could be broadly analogous to the situation in the last twenty years where lower wages in emerging countries such as China and India became much more attractive locations for manufacturing.[21] Will water security concerns start driving major economic decisions, which will in turn affect the national economy and national security as a result, especially in some developing countries?

Forecast

"The potential for conflict over water will only increase with current global economic tensions," says Patricia Wouters, Director of the UNESCO Centre for Water Law, Policy, and Science, University of Dundee. "The current reaction to economic failure has seen nation states adopt a go-it-alone strategy. There is fragmentation of global governance structures, a blurring of the public-private boundary lines (look at the nationalization of banks across the world), and a functional breakdown of regional architecture. The same reactions are foreseeable when water scarcity (considered in the broadest sense) starts to affect economic development."[22]

The number of people living in water-stressed countries will increase from about seven hundred million today to more than three billion by 2025 (about 35% of the predicted global population).[23] Compounding the water security problem for many nations is the fact that fast-growing economies, especially in the Middle East and Asia, will likely allocate much more to the growing demands of their urban, energy, and industrial sectors over the next two decades. As discussed in previous sections, when 40% of renewable water resources are devoted to irrigation, fast-growing economies are often forced to decide between allocating water to the agricultural sector or to the urban municipal and industrial sector. By 2030 under business as usual, all of South Asia will reach the 40% threshold, and the Middle East and North Africa region will have hit 58%. In Asia, the forecast by 2030 is for a 65% increase in water for industrial use and a 30% increase in water for domestic use, against a 5% increase in water for agriculture. Similar ratios apply across the EU, Latin America, the US, and West Asia.

Environmental trends related to economic growth will compound the security challenge for water-insecure nations. The Millennium Ecosystem Assessment found that water-based ecosystems are now the world's most degraded natural resources. Seventy major rivers around the world are close to being totally drained in order to supply water for irrigation systems and for reservoirs, including the Colorado, Ganges, Jordan, Nile, and Tigris-Euphrates. In China, the Yangtze and Yellow Rivers are dry in their lower reaches for much of the year. An estimated one-quarter of the flow of the Yellow River is needed to maintain the environment. Human withdrawal currently leaves less than 10%. In 1997, it was dry six hundred kilometers inland for 226 days, causing agricultural losses of US$ 1.6 billion.[24]

In Australia's Murray Darling basin, irrigated agriculture uses almost 80% of available water flows. The environment needs about 30% of the flow. Extensive environmental damage is occurring as a result, including salinity, nutrient pollution, and the loss of floodplains and wetlands. In recent years, virtually no Murray River water has made it to the sea.

The upper reaches of the Orange River in southern Africa have been so modified that the combined reservoir storage in the basin exceeds annual flows. In 1960, the Aral Sea was the size of Belgium. After fifty years of water engineering projects, it has shrunk to 20% of its former size, with severe ecological consequences. Lake Chad has shrunk to 10% of its former volume. In China, 543 medium- and large-sized lakes disappeared between 1850 and 1980 due to irrigation projects.[25]

In many parts of the world, glaciers act as water banks. Across much of Central Asia, Latin America, and South Asia, rural livelihoods depend on glaciers. The glaciers of the Himalayas and Tibet alone feed seven of the world's greatest rivers—the Brahmaputra, Ganges, Indus, Irrawaddy, Mekong, Salween, and Yangtze—that provide water supplies for more than two billion people. Today, these glacial banks are melting at an accelerating rate. In the 1990s, glacial mass fell at three times the rate of the previous decade. Despite the flash flooding this melt causes (river flow increasing by 30%), the most profound consequences of this will be experienced in the decades ahead when the banks are gone.

Most analysis, despite the well-publicized errors in the recent Intergovernmental Panel on Climate Change (IPCC) reports, suggests that the majority of these glaciers will disappear by 2100 under current trends.[26]

- The Andes: In Peru, glacial coverage has shrunk by 25% over the past thirty years. Small- and medium-sized glaciers in the Andes are predicted to disappear by 2100.
- Central Asia: Almost all freshwater in Kazakhstan, Kyrgyzstan, Tajikistan, Turkmenistan, and Uzbekistan originates from permanent snowfields and glaciers in the mountains of Kyrgyzstan and Tajikistan. Satellite images show that glaciers in this area have shrunk by 33% since 1949. Under current trends, Tajikistan's glaciers will disappear within a century.
- China and Tibet: Glacial retreat in Tibet has been described as an ecological catastrophe. Most glaciers could disappear by 2100.
- Nepal: Glaciers are shrinking up to seventy meters per decade.

So what will likely happen? Symptoms of water stress are generally felt first in those sectors where the economic return of water is the lowest. This means that the first signs of water stress are experienced through the environmental degradation of natural ecosystems that depend substantially on the availability of freshwater. The second sector that will feel the effects of water stress is the agricultural sector. The industrial sector follows agriculture, and the domestic sector is the one that generally suffers in the last instance of water scarcity.[27] But this distinction between sectors is somewhat simplistic given that they are all interconnected, and a crisis in, for example, the agricultural sector may propagate further crises in the agro-industry (or the energy production industry) and, in turn, trigger problems for the food security of the population. The above-mentioned symptoms may also lead to conflicts and increased competition between and within the different economic sectors and between and within states.

As a response to a perceived threat of water and national security challenges, there may be a temptation to invest in more large, hydraulic, supply-side projects for the nation. A default reaction may well be for governments to devote more time, energy, and resources to think about large-scale ways to move water from where there is a lot of it to where there is not enough (such as the various large canal projects on the drawing boards in China, India, and Jordan). But government decisions on how to create new water supplies from large investments in infrastructure or new technologies are not always based on good micro-economics or cost-benefit analysis. Too often, a decision is made based for short-term political gain, not for the longer-term value accruing to society. Notwithstanding the environmental, social, or political effects arising from such mega-projects, on a much more practical level the energy costs associated with transporting water such long distances may also be huge. Will more energy production capacity be required, ironically requiring even more water supplies? As the earlier energy-water nexus chapter concluded, a better strategy in the face of water and national security challenges may be to focus in an integrated manner on the dual challenge of improving both water-use and energy efficiency.

Trans-boundary tensions are also likely to escalate as water security issues deepen within and between nations. The scale of national interdependence on international water basins is huge. One hundred and forty-five countries in the world, accounting for more than 90% of the world's population, are in shared basins: more than thirty countries are located entirely within trans-boundary basins.[28] As government responses to water security issues increase, so, too, will tensions between those nations sharing the same water basin. The Balkans region of southeastern Europe is a good case in point. Here, 90% of the territory that the nations each own a part of lies in international river basins. Most of these fledgling nation-states rely on their own hydropower, yet future climate trends suggest that evaporation levels will increase dramatically, forcing the region to try and work together to create an integrated energy market. Could the Balkan states, mostly less than two decades old, use the challenge of water security as a springboard for enhanced regional cooperation on such historically sensitive issues as water and energy?

Finally, it is also foreseeable that humanitarian assistance may have to increase dramatically if, as some commentators foresee, large-scale migration results from the twin forces of climate change and water scarcity. The International Committee of the Red Cross estimates that there are already twenty-five to fifty million climate change/water security refugees, compared to the official international refugee population of twenty-eight million. The IPCC suggests that 150 million environmental refugees could exist by 2020.[29] Currently in international law there is no such thing as an environmental refugee. The human and political security implications of a mass movement of this nature could be profound.

Implications

"Among the many things I learnt as a president," said Nelson Mandela at the 2002 World Summit on Sustainable Development, "was the centrality of water in the social, political, and economic affairs of the country, the continent, and the world."[30] Could the mid decades of the 21st century world system see an emergence of water "haves" and "have-nots" nation-states, similar to the 20th century geopolitics of oil? By 2030, it may be that those countries that have not achieved water security will find it increasingly difficult to do so. All countries will need to attain a reasonable measure of water security to attract investment and compete effectively in global markets. Unlike money, water cannot be physically accessed from the world markets through a rescue package to pay off a historically accumulated hydro-debt. Actual hydrological water bankruptcy is a real threat for some of these economies, with the danger of political collapse following soon thereafter, as the early case of Yemen is beginning to illustrate. As economies grow and diversify, countries with more natural water resources will become more attractive locations for investments. At some point, will water scarcity limit the competitive advantage of a state? By 2015, could the World Economic Forum have begun an annual Water Competitiveness Report to help rank the fluctuating water security of nations and their policies as a guide to investors?

If the idea of nations failing in the near future due to a lack of water sounds far-fetched, consider civilization's past. Records are clear that entire states have disappeared as a consequence of the failure of water systems.[31] Cambodia's medieval Khmer empire of Angkor, often cited as the most extensive pre-industrial, low-density urban complex, with a single hydraulic system, was destroyed when the system failed due to protracted water stress. A similar fate is believed to have caused the decline of the Mapungubwe and Zimbabwe in southern Africa, and also the Mayan, Anasazi, and Hohokam city-states of North America during a prolonged period of drought.[32]

The difference between ancient history and now, however, is that these early polities were mostly autonomous entities prior to their collapse. They were largely insulated from extensive trade and economic linkages outside their culture. Given the interconnected ways that water weaves itself through today's global economic web, if one or two river basins, cities, or even nations collapse through water shortages in the coming decades, then the integrity of the wider system should remain intact. But if multiple water "hot spots" run dry, one after the other, the multitude of small tears in our water-food-energy-climate nexus could reach a point where the overall integrity of the system is challenged and collapse occurs. How many crop-producing regions of the world need to face severe water challenges before a significant food or fiber crisis occurs? How would the markets react? How severe would national protectionist measures become among the "haves"? What would happen to the "have-nots"?

As a preemptive response to such endemic security challenges, could the 21st century see an emergence of economic and political power among water-endowed countries, akin to the 20th-century geopolitics dominated by the rise of oil-rich states? Brazil, Canada, Iceland, northern Europe, and Russia are hydro-blessed in ways that India, Mexico, China, and the Middle East are not. By 2030, might they form an Organization of Water-Endowed Countries, emerging as a powerful new economic cartel that, by allowing access to and encouraging collaboration across their water-endowed nations, helps to maintain balance in key geopolitical matters, such as food security and agricultural trade?

The Way Forward

According to Peter Rogers of Harvard University, "Water scarcity is a governance crisis and not a [water] resource crisis per se."[33] Geography need not be destiny. In the water–national security nexus sketched out above, it appears that water scarcity is largely a challenge that good national and international governance can address. Indeed, technological innovation, sound policy, political responsiveness, diverse markets, and economic interdependence can more than make up for a poor initial natural endowment.

The first, cheapest, and most effective option to address any stress in the water-national security nexus is the one alternative most likely to reduce friction and conflict within and between nation-states: forward-thinking domestic governance that invests in institutions for enhanced water use efficiency. As the US has shown, population and economic growth need not drive up demand for water: water use per capita or per unit of GDP *can* be reduced. Further evidence suggests a double win to be gained by focusing on water and energy efficiency programmes in an integrated manner.

Water scarcity brings stress, and stress can lead to conflict, segregation, or mass migration. But conflict is hardly inevitable. Faced with a security threat, governments can choose to establish legally protected and clearly defined and economically transferable water rights. Such voluntary, hereditary property rights evolved over the last two centuries in parts of Spain and in the arid western US. In recent decades, Chile, Australia, and Mexico have established water rights–based institutions, followed, more recently, by Pakistan and India.

Water rights work because they allow individuals, communities, and nations to weigh up what economists call "opportunity costs." That is, they enable people to appreciate how water not used for one activity can be invested in another. This reveals the cost that others might pay to use that water.

People will tend to allocate water to its most valuable uses (as revealed by those who are willing to pay the most for it). With leadership from government establishing the necessary checks and balances, such as safety nets for the poor (a free basic level of provision, as in South Africa) and assured flows to environmental goods and services (as the government of the Australian state of Victoria did during the drought, by buying back water rights from farmers to ensure the integrity of the river ecosystem), then an optimal allocation of water can occur, benefiting society the most. It is clear within this system that the important role of government is as a regulator and rule- and price-setter where relevant—this is not an unfettered market for water.

Such systems are far away from many present circumstances. Presently, in most cases, water is allocated free to all or rented by large entities operating within a small cartel, which worsens national security to the extent that it limits choice, competition, and reasons to conserve. Rents paid are rarely as much as it cost to provide the water. A cartel can charge more to make people use less, but it can never account for all the lost opportunities that would have been revealed through competition.

Among the technological options on offer, countries can "create water" through desalination in coastal cities. Australia, several Gulf States, and others have embarked on this route, although the increased energy demands of this strategy are rarely properly integrated into a combined water and energy policy. In other cases, domestic governance reforms and promotion of key technologies can focus on improving water use efficiency. Crop technologies are also a core strategy, which can work in tandem with water use efficiency approaches. Israel and California have both taken this route, squeezing more crops per drop through the promotion of extensive drip-irrigation schemes in their agricultural sectors, for example, but also by enabling the market to drive more water allocations to cities, encouraging innovation in water use efficiency in agriculture. Cities can also take the choice to literally "import water," as Barcelona did in 2008 (when it temporarily shipped in water across the Mediterranean from Marseilles). But such dramatic supply-oriented solutions are clearly not sustainable, and they do not fully address the structural water security challenge that exists. More usefully, nations like Egypt and China can opt to import more virtual water embedded in water-intense grains and soybeans rather than try to grow them domestically, if the international markets allow. Still other countries like Saudi Arabia and Japan have "outsourced" water by investing in water-rich lands in Sudan or Madagascar to grow crops. If managed transparently, as suggested at the end of the trade chapter, this approach, too, could yield value to all parties in an economically efficient manner.

In short, governments and regions in water-scarce areas that proactively address the water–national security nexus, and which take a lead in progressive water policy reform, will likely enjoy an economic triple win over the coming decades: they will retain and attract companies, they will attract more inward investment into their water infrastructure, and their economy will be strengthened as a result of improved water management. Those that do not will face a very different future. It is up the international community to create an international framework conducive to trade and development, such that governments in water-scarce areas are enabled and emboldened to take these important and necessary steps.

Perspectives

The following personal perspectives amplify the main themes touched on by this chapter. They help to illustrate the range of current viewpoints on the water–national security nexus. The views expressed do not necessarily represent those of the World Economic Forum, nor do they necessarily represent the views of the other individual contributors or the various contributing companies or institutions.

- Claudia Sadoff, Lead Economist and Team Leader, South Asia Water Initiative, World Bank; Member, Global Agenda Council on Water Security, 2007–2009, explores some of the geopolitical challenges we might expect in relation to trans-boundary water issues by 2025.
- Patricia Wouters, Director, UNESCO Centre for Water Law, Policy, and Science, University of Dundee, offers the concept of hydro-solidarity as a potential foundation for national security in the future.
- Francis Matthew, Editor at Large, Gulf News, Dubai; Member, Water Global Agenda Council on Water Security, 2008/2009, explores how one can tell the story of the water security crisis in the Arabian Gulf.
- Ralph Ashton, Convenor and Chair, Terrestrial Carbon Group, September 2010, sets out the competing challenges facing our land and resource assets in the coming decades, and the threat to national sovereignty this may pose unless new initiatives are taken.
- John Briscoe, Gordon McKay Professor of the Practice of Environmental Engineering, Harvard University Schools of: Engineering and Applied Sciences; Public Health; and Kennedy School of Government, explores the case of Pakistan where, against a critical backdrop of water insecurity in the Punjab, innovative water trading policies have been developed.

Trans-boundary Waters and Geopolitics by 2025

CLAUDIA SADOFF, LEAD ECONOMIST AND TEAM LEADER, SOUTH ASIA WATER INITIATIVE, WORLD BANK; MEMBER, GLOBAL AGENDA COUNCIL ON WATER SECURITY, 2007–2009

More than two hundred and sixty rivers, covering half the earth's surface, traverse at least one border. As they cross that political divide, the two or more countries sharing one current are forced to confront a geopolitical issue: do they fight over the management and use of their trans-boundary waters, or find collaborative ways to share?

As water resources become scarcer relative to demand, countries will—by necessity—increasingly turn to these shared resources with expectations to develop and utilize them. By 2025, three quarters of the world's countries will sharpen their focus on these rivers, confronting the risks of action and inaction.

Shared river basins tend to be large, perennial watercourses whose quantity and reliability make them particularly valuable. Trans-boundary currents also often hold significant untapped potential that can only be captured through cooperative basin-wide management.

To complicate matters, climate change is likely to make river flows less predictable and more extreme, and thus more difficult to manage. As demands escalate on volatile river flows, our shared challenge lies in how nations can do more with less—and less reliable and potentially more harmful—water resources.

Two opposing pressures will raise the geopolitical stakes. Inevitably, a growing demand for water will raise tensions between "co-riparian" countries, pushing leaders to compete for shared trans-boundary rivers. Yet those same countries will have to cooperate as they become increasingly unable to manage water scarcity and unpredictability on their own.

Cooperation will be needed to enhance the productivity of their shared water resources to meet growing demands for food, energy, water supplies, and ecosystem services. Under collaborative river management, co-riparian nations have three areas of overlapping interest. They can coordinate consumptive and nonconsumptive use patterns to allow each unit of water to be used multiple times. They can curtail the river basin's evaporative losses. And they can store floodwaters for use during low-flow periods to deliver water where and when it is needed, while also ensuring environmental flows.

Failure to cooperate brings inefficiency. And while today there are still thin margins for error in water, by 2025 the world will not be able to afford to waste a single drop. Cooperation will also be needed to manage the shared risks arising from trans-boundary rivers, and thus strengthen the resilience of vulnerable people and the ecosystems on which they depend. As populations grow, economies develop, and climate change brings more frequent

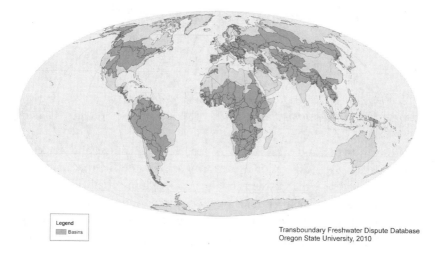

Legend
Basins

Transboundary Freshwater Dispute Database
Oregon State University, 2010

Figure 4.1 International River Basins.

and intense floods and droughts, the risks from volatile water flows will only continue to escalate.

Beyond the obvious direct effects of sudden catastrophic weather events, floods spread sewage, waste, and contamination while droughts deprive rivers of enough water to dilute pollutants. Both extremes undermine the delivery of water services that are essential to health and productivity. Countries sharing trans-boundary rivers will need to collaborate closely in order to understand, predict, and manage the changing hydrology.

Riparian nations have long appreciated the need for trans-boundary water management, but the perceived benefits of cooperation were often outweighed by the costs. In truth, those political and financial costs are real. They remain substantial. But the rapidly escalating risks of inaction are reversing this calculus. Where hypothetical productivity gains can often be obscured or discounted, the devastating impacts of unmitigated floods and droughts are impossible to ignore.

Risks are fast becoming a compelling driver towards cooperation. Countries can better manage water-related risks by working together on basin-wide information networks, river regulation, and early warning systems. As historical experience of the climate becomes less relevant for the future, riparian nations need concerted efforts to forecast and respond to their shared basins' changing hydrologies. Cooperation will be an essential tool to manage risks on shared rivers. Trans-boundary waters can push riparian nations apart or pull them together. Looking forward to the geopolitics of trans-boundary waters in 2025, we may see a choice between conflict and cooperation—but we are certain to see just one wise option.

Hydro-solidarity as a National Security Foundation

PATRICIA WOUTERS, DIRECTOR, UNESCO CENTRE FOR WATER LAW, POLICY AND SCIENCE, UNIVERSITY OF DUNDEE, SCOTLAND

" . . . *the cause of larger freedom can only be advanced by broad, deep and sustained global cooperation among States.*" (Report of The Secretary-General, 2005)

Following two world wars, the UN Charter was crafted and agreed by sovereign states as an operational platform to promote international peace and security and to enhance the fundamental freedoms of all (UN Charter, Article 1). These higher-level objectives, which continue their legacy today, serve as guidelines for nation states as they manage their freshwaters, within and beyond national borders, and comprise the foundation for the notion of hydro-solidarity.

"Hydro-solidarity" is founded upon the notions of collective action, interdependence, and a community-of-interests approach, and provides a platform for reconciling competing demands for shared transboundary freshwaters. The concept offers a fresh perspective and innovative mechanism for implementing the emerging legal notion of water security, described at the Hague World Water Forum as comprised of seven key components: (i) meeting basic needs; (ii) securing food supply; (iii) protecting ecosystems; (iv) sharing water resources; (v) managing risks; (vi) valuing water; and, (vii) governing water wisely.

Addressing this vast range of duties and obligations, especially across national borders, requires considerable effort and must align with domestic political agendas. While transboundary waters may link two or more countries through the same shared water resources, geo-politics tends to separate and push them apart—locating some nation states upstream or downstream; giving some mountains and others valleys; endowing one with fertile soil or ample oil reserves, while leaving others with barren deserts; providing one with a certain political legacy, and the other with another. Thus, while transboundary waters provide an opportunity to draw nation states toward peaceful cooperation, in some cases, the geo-political misalignment results in conflict.

Within such a context, where the globe is actually connected up by a series of criss-crossing transboundary water systems, hydro-solidarity recognizes global interdependencies in the use of the world's water resources and leads to collective action through cooperative mechanisms. This approach increases the opportunities for regional peace and security and is premised on legal and institutional mechanisms (including a range of substantive and procedural rules, such as requirements for data sharing and stakeholder engagement). The hydro-solidarity paradigm spans the spectrum of actors at all scales (individual, local, regional, international and global) and calls for a new understanding of both the risks and benefits of enhanced cooperative water governance across borders of constraint (i.e., national boundaries and disciplinary and sectoral siloes).

How does hydro-solidarity work in practice? Building upon the UN Charter ideals, the rule of law is a fundamental tenet of international relations and is at the heart of national security—each sovereign state is bound to "practice tolerance and live together in peace with one another as good neighbours" (UN Charter). International water law, through treaties and normative customary law, provides a construct for peaceful co-existence, and offers a framework entirely suited to address the world's pressing water security problems. Since the great majority of the world's population depends upon transboundary water resources, solutions must be based upon compromise, through the principles of fairness and rationality epitomized in the governing rule of international water law—that each sovereign state is entitled/obliged to use transboundary waters in an equitable and reasonable manner. A transboundary watercourse state's ability to ensure the water security of its population is improved through an agreed legal framework. The integral constituent elements of water security—availability, access, and addressing conflicts-of-use (the 3-A legal analytical framework)—find expression and meaning in international water law as applied in a domestic setting to address national and regional security issues.

The current world stage is characterized by rapid change and rampant uncertainty. In such a complex reality, water law offers some comfort and conviction by fixing the "rules of the game"; it (1) defines and identifies the legal rights and obligations tied to water use and provides the prescriptive parameters for resource development and management; (2) provides tools for ensuring the continuous integrity of the regime—that is, through monitoring and assessment of compliance and implementation, dispute prevention, and settlement; and (3) allows for modifications of the existing regime, in order to be able to adapt to changing needs and circumstances, within and outside the water box. The existence of an agreed legal regime, especially at a global or regional level, such as the 1997 UN Watercourses Convention, contributes to local and global water security by providing an operational system for addressing specific issues of shared water development and management. The continued promotion of regional peace and security and the fundamental freedoms of all, in line with the UN Charter, are linked directly with the peaceful management of the world's shared water resources.

While water law on its own cannot be considered to be a panacea to the world's water problems, it must be part of the mix. A transparent, credible, and responsive legal framework is essential to addressing water security issues, and is a vital link in the hydro-solidarity chain.

Water in the Arabian Gulf: How to Tell the Story?

FRANCIS MATTHEW, EDITOR AT LARGE, GULF NEWS, DUBAI; MEMBER, WATER GLOBAL AGENDA COUNCIL ON WATER SECURITY, 2008/2009

The water story is hard to tell in its totality. The vast majority of stories to do with water are about natural disasters like floods or droughts, with a typical example being the terrible suffering in Pakistan in the summer of 2010, which grew worse and worse over the weeks and months as the floods moved down from the hills to the plains. The tragedy led to an outpouring of international sympathy and aid, but much of the news coverage then moved off the water story and on to whether the promised aid had actually materialized, and if the Pakistani government was using the aid to the best effect.

This kind of story has been told many times over the years, watching floods in China or Bangladesh, or droughts in Africa. Their common thread is that they are immediate disasters, always massive, and sometimes overwhelming, and the coverage focuses on the human reaction to the event. If these disaster stories do move into the bigger picture, they are now strongly influenced by the worldwide awareness of global warming. So when analysts look at such extreme natural events, they do so through the prism of climate change, relating the event back to the global urgency of dealing with climate change. But by focusing on "saving the world" they miss the water-focused background to the events.

Most stories about water concentrate on the urgent, and in so doing they miss the slow transition in the perception of water from being a free gift to an increasingly valuable commodity. This shift has not become part of the mainstream media agenda, and therefore it has not yet caught the public imagination. This is in part because the story is hidden in so many other, more dominant tales: famine and food shortages, disease and epidemics, global warming, even the Millennium Development Goals.

But the water story is starting to get traction as it become clear that one of the very few genuinely limiting factors to human development is access to clean water. The parched lands of the Arabian Gulf are a case in point, where rich governments can spend money to buy all sorts of development but they cannot invent or buy water. It has to be produced locally. The problem in the Gulf Cooperation Council (GCC) countries is that they seek substantial economic growth and expect a doubling of their presently small populations (from both nationals and expatriates settling in the region).

This means they will need a lot more water and energy, and their neighbors like Iran or Iraq are also short on power and water and therefore offer no op- portunity to import anything. Since the GCC states have no rivers, no rain, and their aquifers are drying up rapidly due to overuse, desalination has to be the answer, but even in the oil-rich Gulf with its vast reserves, gas is a finite asset, and in some areas it is already running out. This is why the Gulf States are switching to nuclear power to fuel their desalination plants and power stations. This is part of the reason why they are so nervous of the present standoff with Iran. They cannot afford to let their own plans get caught up in that US-Iran crisis.

This Gulf example is one example of where water and power have become a national priority, but even in the Gulf most of the public attention has focused on the need for more energy rather than the need for more water. What will turn the water story into a wider tale is the realization of how much water is an integral part of our lives.

The links between water, energy, and food are becoming a very important part of the wider story. For example, it is becoming a bigger story that that most countries could save a vast proportion of their water needs by working on eliminating food waste. The link starting to be being publicized is that a majority of water is used in most countries on agriculture to produce food, and that water is wasted through inefficient use of the water in the fields but also in flinging away large amounts of food, which have consumed substantial amounts of water in their growing and manufacture.

Another part of the water story beginning to gain traction is the concept of virtual water, which assigns a water value to any product based on the volume of water used in its production. This measure will be a useful part of developing a water-aware trade regime, as the indicator allows a consumer to see how many liters of water are needed to produce a cotton shirt, or a can of sweet corn, or even a car. This kind of easy-to-understand measure can take the water story much further into popular folklore than the most detailed of studies.

This is where editors can work to build a popular awareness that water cannot be wasted and should be conserved. In the future, just as people today talk about their carbon footprint, they should also be able to refer to their water use. And once they can measure it, they can seek to reduce it. Such devices will take the water story into people's homes, and that is how it can become a genuinely worldwide cause, attracting the popular imagination enough to force the politicians to first take notice and then to realize that they gain stature (and votes) by backing water conservation.

Land: A Question of Increasing Strategic Importance in Search of Better-Informed Answers

RALPH ASHTON, CONVENOR AND CHAIR, TERRESTRIAL CARBON GROUP

In how many ways did you rely on land yesterday? You quickly list the more obvious: your home, the road to work, your lunch, the park. The bus with its metal from a foreign mine. The coal-fired electricity for your breakfast (or was it biofuel, nuclear, or wind?). Your medicine developed through tropical forest bio-prospecting. You might not have realized it, but soil and vegetation on land across the planet quietly sucked carbon dioxide out of the atmosphere yesterday, reducing greenhouse gas concentrations, thereby reducing climate change.

It probably strikes you that the world has rather a lot of land. But you were quite picky: you needed land with certain qualities. Relatively flat land. Land with adequate water and phosphate. With trees. With metals. With carbon-sequestration capacity. Moreover, availability of suitable land is already being tested by land degradation and desertification, by water and nutrient depletion. And you're not the only person on the planet. Every day, 230,000 people join you, adding their own demands on land. Food and climate change mitigation are among the most pressing.

The Food and Agriculture Organization expects an 11% increase in average per capita calorie consumption between 2003 and 2050. An estimated additional 120 million hectares will be needed to support the traditional growth in food production by 2030. That's a brand-new farm the size of South Africa. How will it get watered? Unless degraded land is rehabilitated, forests and other natural lands will be converted to make way for agricultural production; greenhouse gas emissions will be one side effect, and accelerated demands on water resources will be another.

Improved management of the world's land represents one-third of the climate solution in 2030. This includes both maintaining the carbon in forests, grasslands, and peatlands, and restoring natural systems. Much attention is rightly focused on avoiding emissions from deforestation in developing countries (REDD+). But carbon in other natural systems is critical. The Terrestrial Carbon Group estimates that if land expansion for food and other products continues on current trends (twelve million hectares annually), even if all forests in developing countries were protected, mitigation from forest protection would be reduced by up to 70% because of emissions from "deflected" expansion into non-forested land. On the restoration side, sequestering half a billion tons of carbon in the tropics per year (equivalent to 1.8 billion tons of carbon dioxide, or 10% of the solution in 2020) would require between fifty million hectares (slightly less than the area of Thailand) and 150 million hectares (slightly less than that of Mongolia).

Land for food caters to immediate, individual needs. Land to mitigate climate change responds to longer-term, collective needs. While narrow self-interest might tempt you to prefer food, think again. The United Nations Environment Programme highlights in the 2009 report *The Environmental Food Crisis* that a projected 50% increase in food production by 2050 has not taken into account environmental and water degradation, which together with a changing climate could reduce agricultural yields by 13% to 45%.

So, do we have enough land of the right type in the right place?

While the question arouses controversy and uncertainty in academic and policy circles, countries and private investors are voting with their feet. Investment in foreign land for food and biofuel production (in other words, investment in foreign water) continues apace: western Europeans in eastern Europe and Africa; Gulf States in Asia and Africa; Japanese in Brazil; South Koreans in Russia and Africa. Asian countries will comprise 60% of the world's population by 2050. It is no surprise then that Indians and Chinese are investing in Africa's land. As the global population hurtles towards 9.2 billion in 2050, difficult land use decisions will have to be made. Many will entail trade-offs.

The cumulative effect of these decisions could challenge long-held notions of national sovereignty and private land rights through the forging of new "über"-rights: the right to calories and nutrition, to a certain atmospheric concentration of greenhouse gases, and, crucially, to water. As the World Bank points out in its 2010 report *Rising Global Interest in Farmland,* the "rediscovery" of investment in the agriculture sector could be an opportunity for land-abundant countries to gain better technology and create rural jobs. But if improperly managed, it could result in "conflict, environmental damage, and a resource curse."

Can the "competing" demands for land co-exist in the mid to long term, or will they cancel one another out? If they can, how? If they cannot, what data, policies, and actions can be used to make deliberate land use choices with a more complete and transparent understanding of their implications? To better answer these questions, we need an integrated understanding of land and our land use trajectory towards 2050 at the global and national levels. We need a concerted global effort to bring together experts, agenda-setters, and decision-makers in a safe and informed venue to understand and resolve perceived competing interests, and to build a two-way reinforcing flow between knowledge and policy. Without such efforts, it is difficult to expect wise land management decisions for multiple outcomes. A mid-century train wreck of competing visions is more likely.

The Water–National Security Nexus: The Case of Pakistan

John Briscoe, Gordon McKay Professor of the Practice of Environmental Engineering, Harvard University Schools of: Engineering and Applied Sciences; Public Health; and Kennedy School of Government

Pakistan is a hydraulic civilization, built from the waters and tributaries of the Indus River. Over its recent history, Pakistan has harnessed the Indus to overcome series of daunting water challenges. It made the desert bloom through construction of the world's largest contiguous irrigation system. It devised a hydraulic solution after the line of partition amputated five rivers of the Punjab. It addressed the devastating effects of waterlogging and salinity. As of autumn 2010, it is currently dealing with the aftermath of terrible national floods. These challenges have each threatened the country's existence, and they have always been met in what is a tribute to the great ingenuity of the people who inhabit the basin.

But water management is a dialectic and not a mechanical task; each success gives rise to a new problem. Today's Pakistan faces water problems that arise both from beyond and within its borders. Exogenous threats include climate change, as snowmelt accounts for almost half of the water of the Indus, and the glaciers in the western Himalayas are retreating rapidly. Governing that runoff, the Indus Waters Treaty must evolve to absorb the tensions from Indian Kashmir constructing many hydropower plants. But even without external pressures, Pakistan must reconcile growing and dynamic urban, irrigation, and environmental demands for the Indus River, even as water availability per capita continues to dwindle.

In Pakistan there is one resource even scarcer than water: trust. Water management has long followed the logic of location. If there is any rule of water management, it is that "upstream and up-canal users take what they want, and the downstream tailenders pay the price." The resulting mistrust is both endemic and corrosive.

But geography is not always destiny. In recent years, Pakistani officials have started to address this "trust deficit" through an excellent basic system of allocated water rights. The Indus Treaty allocated specific amounts of water to twenty-six major canal commands; the 1991 Water Accord sanctified the shares going to different provinces. Within the canal commands, a system of rights goes all the way down to the individual turns of farmers, through a system known as the *warabandi*. Led by enlightened political and agricultural leaders, in 2005 the government of Pakistan's biggest and most prosperous province, the Punjab, took entitlements out of the opaque cupboard of the irrigation department and made them public and transparent. For the last three years, the Punjab Irrigation Department website lists the entitlements of each of the canals, and, on a weekly basis, updates deliveries and banked surpluses or deficits. Over time this will be extended all the way down to rights of distributaries.

The consequences of establishing transparent, rights-based systems can be dramatic. They helped Western economies like California or Australia absorb the reductions of up to 70% less available water with very little impact on economic output or jobs. Pakistan has started down this road towards security, efficiency, and growth.

But institutional reforms have also been accompanied by a package of technologies that lets farmers translate their secure water entitlements into maximum agricultural productivity. This modernization process has begun, starting with private-sector one-stop-shops for credit, equipment, seeds, and fertilizers springing up in the Punjab.

Much more needs to be done. The state must reinvigorate its essential planning and regulatory tasks, improve the quality of decision support systems, integrate surface and groundwater, deal with salinity and pollution, and improve the transparency and administration of water entitlements at all levels. But Pakistan, and the Punjab in particular, has clearly begun to address the central water challenges of this generation, and the greatest dividend from these political and economic reforms in water is trust.

Notes

1. Jeffrey Sachs in United Nations Development Programme, *Human Development Report, 2006: Beyond Scarcity*, 2006.

2. David Grey and Claudia W. Sadoff, "Sink or Swim? Water Security for Growth and Development," *Water Policy* 9, no. 6 (2007): 545–571.

3. Ibid.

4. United Nations Development Programme, *Human Development Report, 2006: Beyond Scarcity*, 2006.

5. World Wide Fund for Nature, *Water at Risk*, 2009.

6. See "Why California Is Running Dry," *60 Minutes*, December 27, 2009, http://www.cbsnews.com/stories/2009/12/23/60minutes/main6014897.shtml?tag=contentMain;cbsCarousel.

7. J. R. McNeill, *Something New under the Sun: An Environmental History of the Twentieth-Century World*, 2000.

8. Ibid.

9. Elizabeth Economy, "The Great Leap Backward?" *Foreign Affairs*, September/October 2007, http://www.foreignaffairs.com/articles/62827/elizabeth-c-economy/the-great-leap-backward.

10. See Goldman Sachs, *The N-11: More Than an Acronym*, 2007.

11. United Nations Development Programme, *Human Development Report, 2006: Beyond Scarcity*, 2006.

12. Jack Goldstone, "The New Population Bomb: Four Megatrends That Will Change the World," *Foreign Affairs*, January/February 2010, http://www.foreignaffairs.com/articles/65735/jack-a-goldstone/the-new-population-bomb.

13. Brad Lendon, "Yemen Fertile Ground for Terror Groups," *CNN World*, January 4, 2010, http://articles.cnn.com/2010-01-04/world/yemen.profile_1_yemen-president-ali-abdullah-saleh-qaeda?_s=PM:WORLD.

14. Judith Evans, "Yemen Could Become First Nation to Run out of Water," *London Times*, October 21, 2009, http://www.timesonline.co.uk/tol/news/environment/article6883051.ece.

15. Andrew Lee Butters, "Is Yemen Chewing Itself to Death?," *Time*, August 25, 2009, http://www.time.com/time/world/article/0,8599,1917685,00.html.

16. See, for example, Aaron Wolf, "'Water Wars' and Other Tales of Hydromythology," in Bernadette McDonald and Douglas Jehl, eds., *Whose Water Is It? The Unquenchable Thirst of a Water-Hungry World*, 2003.

17. A recent study estimates that there are four thousand deaths a year in Yemen as a consequence of land and water disputes. This is over ten times the murder rate in an industrialized country. See http://www.yemen-ava.org/pdfs/Yemen-Armed-Violence-IB2-Social-violence-over-land-and-water-in-Yemen.pdf.

18. Elizabeth Economy, "The Great Leap Backward?" *Foreign Affairs*, September/October 2007, http://www.foreignaffairs.com/articles/62827/elizabeth-c-economy/the-great-leap-backward.

19. United Nations Development Programme, *Human Development Report, 2006: Beyond Scarcity*, 2006.

20. Millennium Ecosystem Assessment, *Ecosystems and Human Well-Being: General Synthesis*, 2005.

21. David Grey and Claudia W. Sadoff, "Sink or Swim? Water Security for Growth and Development," *Water Policy* 9, no. 6 (2007): 545–571.

22. World Economic Forum Water Initiative, *The Bubble Is Close to Bursting*, 2009.

23. United Nations Development Programme, *Human Development Report, 2006: Beyond Scarcity*, 2006.

24. Millennium Ecosystem Assessment, *Ecosystems and Human Well-Being: General Synthesis*, 2005.

25. United Nations Development Programme, *Human Development Report, 2006: Beyond Scarcity*, 2006.

26. Ibid.

27. Pasquale Studeto, Chief, Water Development and Management Unit, Food and Agricultural Organization, United Nations, personal communication.

28. United Nations Development Programme, *Human Development Report, 2006: Beyond Scarcity*, 2006.

29. See IPCC (Intergovernmental Panel on Climate Change) (2007), *Climate Change 2007: Impacts, Adaptation and Vulnerability*. Contribution of Working Group II to the Fourth Assessment Report of the Intergovernmental Panel on Climate Change, M. L. Parry et al. (Eds.), Cambridge: Cambridge University Press. It cites coastal flooding, shoreline erosion and agricultural degradation as major factors.

30. United Nations Development Programme, *Human Development Report, 2006: Beyond Scarcity*, 2006, p. 172.

31. See Jared Diamond, *Collapse: How Societies Choose to Fail or Succeed*, 2006.

32. Ibid.

33. World Economic Forum Water Initiative, *The Bubble Is Close to Bursting*, 2009.

CHAPTER 5

Cities

This chapter explores the water-urbanization nexus. It benefits greatly from the perspectives of many public, private, academic, and NGO representatives who have taken part in various Forum sessions and workshops on water issues over the last three years.

Background

Over half the world's population now lives in an urban environment. There are twenty-four megacities in the world with more than ten million people, seventeen of which are in developing countries. China already has more than one hundred cities with more than a million inhabitants; India has thirty-five (the US has nine). By 2050, China's cities will house 73% of its population (up from 46% today), and Indian cities will host 55% of its people (up from 30% today). The UN projects that the urbanized proportion of sub-Saharan Africa will nearly double between 2005 and 2050, from 35% (three hundred million people) to more than 67% (one billion people).[1]

Whereas less than 30% of the world's population was urban in 1950, according to UN projections more than 70% will be by 2050. Note that these are also percentages: the world population was 2.5 billion in 1950; it is forecast to be 9.3 billion by 2050.[2] In real terms, this means that the world will have experienced a huge jump in urbanization between 1950 and 2050, from about 750 million people to 6.5 billion people, or nearly a ninefold increase. We are now in the middle of this century of unprecedented change. Over the lifetime of three generations—our predecessors, ourselves, and our children—urbanization will be one of the most important demographic and sociological world mega-trends that we will experience.

It will be cities and their associated industrial and business activities that will demand the majority of the 40% increase in world energy demand forecast by 2030. It will be cities and their inhabitants that will demand the majority of the 70% increase in food and fiber forecast by 2025. It will be in cities across the developing world of today where the world's new middle class will mostly emerge, predicted to be larger in number than the total populations of Europe, Japan, and the US combined. They will be the main consumers of electricity, oil, food, beverages, household appliances, cars, and the huge variety of other goods and services, all of which, unfettered, will drive the carbon and water footprint of cities across the world higher and higher. It will also be in cities across the developing world where innovation in tomorrow's fashion, music, food, and sustainability trends will be defined.

History also suggests that if this process of rapid urbanization is not also coupled with improvements in quality of life (jobs, income, social inclusion), it will be in cities where the forces of political disillusionment could fester. As well as fueling the growth of the middle class, cities can also become focal points for widespread and concentrated poverty. Large-scale conurbations of the poor can easily breed the conditions for antiestablishment political forces, sometimes in the extreme. This will be particularly the case if the children of the rural migrants who were attracted to the city since the 1950s—that is, today's *new* generation of city inhabitants—fail to experience an improvement in quality of life for them or for their children, compared to their parents. One should not forget the Dickensian urban conditions of 19th-century city life, which affected the attitude of many manual laborers in the Old World, and the profound social, political, and cultural revolutions that were catalyzed as a result, which affected much of the West's political history of the 20th century.

As in the 19th century, when industrialization and urbanization began, the story of a successful city rests to a large extent on how it manages its water. Victor Hugo back in 1862 wrote, "The history of men is reflected in the history of sewers. . . . The sewer is the conscience of the city."[3] His message is as true today as it was then. Urban inhabitants introduce unprecedented strains on water systems and compound the pressure on those managers struggling to balance competing forces. The stresses on water supply and water quality systems in China as a result of rapid transition to an urban economy are an excellent case in point.[4]

For two centuries, Western governments have derived enormous health gains through improved water and sanitation infrastructure. The provision of clean water remains the single most effective means of alleviating human suffering and improving the quality of urban life.[5] Fast-growing cities in developing countries now have to embrace that same priority. At issue for this generation is how, and whether, they can succeed.

In the developing world today, billions of poor residents have no connection to a municipal water supply and instead rely on water vendors. In Dar es Salaam, for example, fewer than 30% of households are connected to a water delivery system. The poorest may pay ten times more for water than the richest households do; adding insult to injury, they often receive poorer quality water as well.[6] Hardly any of the poorest city inhabitants around the world have access to a reasonable toilet. Wastewater treatment facilities are scant.

Many cities also lose vast quantities of water through leaks in their water transport systems. It is common for 30–40% of urban water supply to be lost due to leakage, often euphemistically termed by authorities as non-revenue losses, as many of the poorest may tap into these leaks for their main source of water. In Delhi, Dhaka, and Mexico City, two out of every five gallons of water pumped into the system bleed out through corroded pipes or are sold illegally.[7]

Of China's 669 cities, 60% suffer water shortages; in 2005, nearly half of China's cities lacked wastewater treatment facilities. Water quality as well as quantity issues can also be a major challenge, as cities and their hinterlands are often the focal point for the rapid industrialization process of developing countries. In China, Shanghai is a good example of a city with water quality challenges. Lake Tai, which borders the city of Wuxi near Shanghai, was covered in bright green algae sludge that thrived on the pollutants being dumped into the water by chemicals factories. The situation became acute when the city had to cut off water supplies for days.[8]

In fact, many cities around the world are facing increasingly chronic water quantity or water quality issues. A simple Web search of the world's largest twenty cities in 2010 finds media stories on water shortages within the past three years for all but six of them (see table 5.1).

Some recent examples from smaller cities in developed countries illustrate that the extent of the urban (and increasingly suburban) water management challenge is widespread. In October 2007, for example, Atlanta had eighty-seven days of drinking water left; Raleigh, North Carolina, had ninety-seven days. The culprits were a combination of historically low rainfall and un-bridled urban growth in the southeastern region of the US over the past fifty years. While population growth increased by 20%, increasing demand for tap and lawn water from these new suburbanites significantly overshadowed the decline in water demand from traditionally large water customers, such as ranches, mines, and factories. In the summer of 2008, Barcelona famously had to start importing drinking water shipped in tankers from Marseille, paying US$ 3 per cubic meter, which was triple the "average" cost.

In addition to water shortages and water quality issues, cities are also subject to challenges arising from too much water all at once. Urban systems (especially in smaller towns) in developing countries in particular can quickly find themselves unable to cope with such inundations, resulting in system breakdown, economic losses, and ill health. The recent floods in Pakistan are a good example of this. We should expect all these kinds of stresses to grow through 2030 and beyond.

City	Population	News story on recent water shortage
Mumbai (Bombay), India	12.6 million	Mumbai faces acute water shortage July 2009 http://news.bbc.co.uk/2/hi/8138273.stm
Karachi, Pakistan	10.9 million	Karachi facing shortage of 70 million gallons of water, Sept 2010 http://www.dailytimes.com.pk/default.asp?page=2010%5C09%5C26%5Cstory_26-9-2010_pg7_23
Delhi, India	10.4 million	Water Shortage in South Delhi, May 2010 http://www.hindustantimes.com/Water-shortage-in-South-Delhi/Article1-545037.aspx
Manila, Philippines	10.3 million	Water shortage hits 50% of Metro Manila, July 2010 http://newsinfo.inquirer.net/topstories/topstories/view/20100720-282193/Water-shortage-hits-50-of-Metro-ManilaDPWH-Chief
Seoul, South Korea	10.2 million	South Korea Lacks Clean Water, March 2009 http://asiancorrespondent.com/korea-beat/-p-4139
Istanbul, Turkey	9.6 million	Istanbul Braces for Water Shortage, July 2008 http://www.thenational.ae/article/20080603/FOREIGN/304413336/1013/&Profile=1013
Jakarta, Indonesia	9.0 million	Jakarta's Clean Water Shortage Gets Worse, September 2010 http://www.thejakartapost.com/news/2010/05/06/jakarta%E2%80%99s-clean-water-shortage-gets-worse.html
Mexico City, Mexico	8.7 million	Dry Taps in Mexico City: A Water Crisis Gets Worse, April 2009 http://www.time.com/time/world/article/0,8599,1890623,00.html
Lagos, Nigeria	8.68 million	Tackling Water Shortage, January 2010 http://www.bsjournal.com/articlepage.php?id=3dbf664cd308776
Lima, Peru	8.38 million	Water Isn't for Everyone http://ipsnews.net/news.asp?idnews=46549
Cairo, Egypt	7.6 million	Growing protests over water shortages, Cairo July 2010 http://www.alertnet.org/thenews/newsdesk/IRIN/4912710a260e979c9354033039a7ede5.htm
London, UK	7.59 million	Leaks May Cause Water Shortages, March 2005 http://news.bbc.co.uk/2/hi/uk_news/england/london/4330721.stm
Teheran, Iran	7.3 million	Iran to face severe water shortage in 50 years, September 2010 http://www.tehrantimes.com/index_View.asp?code=208783
Beijing, China	7.2 million	Beijing Water Supplier Faces Severe Water Shortage, March 2009 http://www.chinadaily.com.cn/china/2009-03/21/content_7603383.htm

Table 5.1 World's Largest Cities Facing Water Shortages in the Past Three Years.

Trends

"The seriousness of the water crisis will impinge on our lives much earlier than climate change," says Ajit Gulabchand, Chairman and Managing Director, Hindustan Construction Company, India. "Under-pricing of water encourages waste and blocks the avenues for essential investments in conservation and efficient use."[9] In a decade, three-fifth of all humans will live in cities, and by 2050 seven out of ten humans will do so.[10] This will add three billion new citizens to cities around the world, placing further stress on existing urban water supply and sanitation systems.

In developing countries, US$ 15 billion each year is already spent just on basic water and sanitation services, excluding wastewater treatment. Traditional centralized wastewater treatment services are often too expensive for many city governments in the developing world to provide on top of the basic water and sanitation services they all ready struggle to deliver. Unable to afford the costs, authorities have no choice but to allow wastewater to be discharged straight into water bodies, polluting the ecosystem and causing many problems for downstream populations.[11] These trends will likely continue and worsen.

Yet the very scale of urbanization means the potential market for urban water and wastewater services is also large and growing. Goldman Sachs estimates the global market for water and sanitation infrastructure at US$ 400 billion a year and expanding.[12] By 2015, the OECD estimates that an average annual investment of US$ 772 billion will be required for water and wastewater services around the world.[13] The US EPA estimates that US$ 68 billion will be needed over the next two decades just to restore and maintain existing utility assets in major cities in the US alone. New investment costs would be much higher.[14] The OECD calculates that a further investment of US$ 10 billion annually will be necessary just to meet the water and sanitation Millennium Development Goals (MDGs) by 2015. To collect and treat household wastewater in cities would require investing an extra US$ 180 billion a year in developing countries.[15]

These are extremely large numbers. To put this into context, the total amount of official international overseas development assistance in 2009 was around US$ 120 billion.[16] And there are many competing demands on this development assistance; it cannot all be spent on urban water and wastewater services. In addition, the Copenhagen Climate Accord calls for developed countries to find an additional US$ 100 billion a year by 2020 to help developing countries meet the challenge of climate change.[17] The World Bank and Project Catalyst estimate that meeting the wider clean energy investment needs in developing countries will cost close to US$ 320 billion a year for a decade or more.[18] Worse still, the economies of key traditional donor governments are currently constrained: the US budget deficit is currently around US$ 1.42 trillion, and that of the United Kingdom is about US$ 307 billion. Even China's current account surplus after the financial crisis stands at about US$ 284 billion. This cold economic logic inexorably means that, as in the 19th century in Europe and the US, the trend must become for private-sector capital to somehow be drawn into the developing world's urban water infrastructure market, if the required scale of investment is to be met.

Forecast

Domestic demands on water will rise quickly. Under a business-as-usual scenario, total domestic water consumption will increase 75% from 1995 to 2025, of which 90% will be in developing countries, especially in cities.[19] Poor quality and inefficient water supply services in urban areas will be seen as a brake on economic growth.

A step change in private finance will be required for investment in urban water management, as public funds will not be able to fill the gap. Governments that introduce reforms in water supply management will attract private finance. This does not necessarily mean taking water supply out of public ownership, but it does mean undertaking reforms to ensure that private investor risks are reduced and rates of return become more desirable. International aid for water will be increasingly used to improve the risk-return ratio for private investments into public infrastructure on the back of these reforms. International aid for urban water supply will also increasingly be used to help governments in developing economies mobilize credit through local markets for private investments into public water infrastructure, on the back of policy reform.

Desalination is one key urban water market for wealthier countries that will attract the attention of the private sector in particular, as discussed in Chapter 2.

Implications

According to Andrew Liveris, Chairman and CEO of the Dow Chemical Company, "We believe that providing sustainable resolution to the global water challenge requires a collaborative approach from governments, businesses, and humanitarian organizations. Technology enables purification and distribution of water, but technology alone—without a sound strategy that includes water management, infrastructure, investment, agricultural/industrial/consumer use, and education—has limited power to address the crisis."[20] Governments will have to implement reforms in how city water supplies are financed and managed in order to attract in the private capital that will be required for investment. This will require a political discussion that makes it clear that the role of managing water remains in public hands, but that more private capital and expertise will be required to help fund the investment.

A wide range of public-private partnerships will emerge as different ways to arrange the relationship between the state, the private sector, and civil society partners are explored, in order to find new approaches to build and deliver urban water services. The public-private discourse about water services will become much more nuanced than it has been in the past.

The role of the city as a major consumer of water will also have economic and political implications. As cities start to seek water from farther away, the debate will arise about whether it is, in fact, economical to bring water to cities. Which will be the first inland city to instead move closer to its water?

The Way Forward

An explosion of new models for public-private partnerships in water service management and delivery have been explored over the past decade or so, across small towns and large cities in Latin America, sub-Saharan Africa, and Asia. Much work is in development that can offer potential for meeting the water and wastewater needs of urban consumers at both the small and the large scale.

For example, NGOs and organizations such as WaterAid, the International Rescue Committee, the United Nations Development Programme's Water and Sanitation Programme, and the Gates Foundation have been creating and testing a wide range of innovative models for localized pro-poor delivery of water and sanitation services in urban and peri-urban areas, creating new understandings about public-private-civil partnership arrangements as a result. Discussions at annual events such as Stockholm's World Water Week abound with new ideas for urban and peri-urban water service delivery models. Organizations such as Building Partnerships for Development in Water and Sanitation work to chart and explore these discoveries, disseminating best practices for water professionals. The OECD and World Bank invest time and effort into helping to develop pro-poor regulatory structures and institutional frameworks for these new kinds of service delivery options.

For example, successful private-sector participation tenders at the local level have targeted local private operators in small towns, with populations between ten thousand to fifty thousand residents. Experiences in Colombia and Paraguay[21] have been positive in this regard, whereby local firms were hired through long-term contracts to operate water supply services among poor populations. Private operators contribute a fifth of capital costs, with the rest financed by World Bank–secured grants channeled through national and local governments. The contracts included service targets, monitored by a national regulator who specified formulas and rules for setting tariffs. Previously unserved neighborhoods got connections.

Brazil has also pioneered low-cost "condominium" sewerage networks. These systems connect individual dwellings in neighborhoods through small-bore pipes for water and shallow trenches for sewerage. Communities invest "sweat equity" to get the system in place and also help manage collection, recovering a third of the capital used to set up the networks.[22]

At a broader level, new forms of public-private partnerships aim to work at scale on the issue, across whole cities or urban areas. Water and Sanitation for the Urban Poor (WSUP) is one example of an innovative and successful partnership that helps local service providers to deliver affordable and sustainable water and sanitation services to the urban poor. Working with the government and development agencies to achieve practical and sustainable solutions, the WSUP partnership has worked in Maputo, Mozambique, for example, to expand tertiary water supply networks among informal communities around the city in coordination with the asset owner (reaching out to seventeen thousand end users), while also improving basic sanitation (latrines and sanitation blocks) in coordination with the municipal council. WSUP also works to support national regulators to engage more with consumers and test alternatives for the management of bulk water sellers, such as developing pro-poor public-private partnerships.[23]

There is consequently much activity within the pro-poor urban and peri-urban water supply and sanitation agenda, and many new configurations of public-private-civil society arrangements being trialed. A further interesting development is the arrival of more private-sector-driven social entrepreneurialism into the space, to see if scalable micro-business models can be identified. The ideas contained in David Kuria's contribution at the end of this chapter—a social entrepreneur in sanitation—are interesting in this regard.

Despite all of this activity, however, one overriding structural problem remains. Given the sheer speed and scale of urbanization around the world, and the size of the urban water and wastewater investment challenge, how will financing get to scale in the next two decades to start addressing the urban water services problem in its entirety? Can the new public-private partnerships and new business models for service delivery currently being explored be rapidly scaled up? At the same time, can a step change in private capital flow be attracted into the urban water market, especially in developing countries?

Perspectives

The following personal perspectives amplify the main themes touched on by this chapter. They help to illustrate the range of current viewpoints on the water-urbanization nexus. The views expressed do not necessarily represent those of the World Economic Forum, nor do they necessarily represent the views of the other individual contributors or the various contributing companies or institutions.

- Arjun Thapan, Special Senior Adviser in Infrastructure and Water, Asian Development Bank; and Chair, Global Agenda Council on Water Security, explores the socioeconomic breakdown that inadequate water and sanitation services creates, especially in Asian cities.
- Richard Harpin, Senior Vice-President and Head of Water Scarcity, Halcrow Group, draws attention to the real challenge of urban flooding facing many cities in developing countries, as well as water and wastewater management issues.

- Margaret Catley-Carlson, Patron, Global Water Partnership; Member, United Nations Secretary-General's Advisory Board on Water and Sanitation; and Chair, Global Agenda Council on Water Security, 2007–2010, suggests ways that innovations in planning and design can revolutionize the wastewater management challenge facing many cities, especially in Asia.
- David Kuria, Founder and CEO of Ecotact, 2010 African Social Entrepreneur of the Year; a Schwab Fellow and an Ashoka-Lemelson Fellow sets out a social enterprise solution for water and sanitation services in Kenya's slums.
- Craig Fenton, Partner and Head of Water Sector Advisory Practice, PricewaterhouseCoopers, Australia, looks at the potential for desalination to provide urban water supply security.

A Socioeconomic Breakdown

ARJUN THAPAN, SPECIAL SENIOR ADVISER IN INFRASTRUCTURE AND WATER, ASIAN DEVELOPMENT BANK; CHAIR, GLOBAL AGENDA COUNCIL ON WATER SECURITY, 2010/2011

"People without water and sanitation"—the title alone suggests an impending social and economic breakdown. Yet how else should one describe 360 million urban dwellers of India with access to varying qualities of water for an average of 2.9 hours a day? Or 780 million South Asians forced to defecate in the open? Or how Asia's urban utilities leak and lose most of the water they first paid to clean? Or how nine out of ten liters of untreated sewage and wastewater that leaches into our rivers, streams, lakes, and aquifers?

If the water is cloudy, the trends are clear: a dangerous spiral of less water and more pollution for more and sicker people.

The poor quench their thirst at an increasingly high cost. Low incomes buy increasingly smaller amounts of unsafe water. As Asia urbanizes more rapidly than expected, big city slum dwellers will scavenge for water. Since water prices bear no relationship to economic end use values, industry will continue its profligate water use. Untreated wastewater will worsen as a consequence of additional consumers. Water quality will deteriorate. Fecal coliform will plague our water bodies on a more or less permanent basis. Sickness will increase. Asia's water world is witnessing a new dynamic—that of diminishing returns.

The implications of this doomsday scenario go beyond the non-attainment of MDGs and the unlikely imagery of "stimulus packages" bankrolling the water sector. With towns and cities going further afield to secure water, and with public irrigation systems becoming increasingly unreliable, Asia will see massive monetary shifts in capital. Just as energy and transport infrastructure determine today's investment decisions in industry and agriculture, soon those investments will follow the availability of assured water supplies. Before that can happen, however, assured water supplies will require significant investments. If that doesn't happen soon, the economy will slam into limits imposed by lack of water.

In water is the absence of equity. Yet people rarely just "learn to accept" what they lack. To the contrary, empowerment and education breeds restless agitation and a hunger for more. An assertive lower income group will demand redress, as is now happening in India and China. When you lack water, you have little to lose and everything to gain. Entrenched poverty will provide a ready spark for this disruption in cities and irrigated farms.

Urban public-private partnerships are a sign of hope, exemplified in Manila and Jakarta. The Phnom Penh state-owned enterprise model in Cambodia performs as well and, perhaps, better in some respects. Water companies in Laos and Vietnam are rapidly adopting a business outlook, where full cost recovery is more the rule than the exception. Numerous small-scale providers admirably fill the gaps caused by stretched large providers.

Sanitation is increasingly addressed in differentiated ways. Some fifty-four million people in India already use a twin-pit, pour-flush toilet, developed by Dr. Bindeshwar Pathak. In Vietnam, towns and cities are adopting common sanitation standards and local governments are helping residents and businesses meet them. At the other end of the scale, the concessionaires in Manila are preparing to invest large sums in collecting and treating the megacity's wastewater in a bid to promote a healthier environment, attract investment, and revive sick and dying water bodies.

There's no shortage of bright ideas. Investments in the recently launched water operators' partnership are yielding early payback. Expert utilities are partnering with weaker ones in India, the Philippines, Vietnam, Sri Lanka, and Cambodia, helping to improve utility performance in critical operational areas. If performance improvement contracts follow, and financial performance improves, local governments are more likely to be persuaded to permit badly needed structural reform. And that will lead to better resource utilization, a postponing of investments in developing new water sources, and consumer satisfaction. It can, potentially, alter the politics of urban water in positive and enduring ways.

The quality of Asia's socioeconomic growth over the next twenty-five years is likely to be determined predominantly by people and cities with quality water and sanitation services. That is probably less moot a point today than at any time in the past.

Fatal Flooding in Modern Cities

RICHARD HARPIN, SENIOR VICE-PRESIDENT AND HEAD OF WATER SCARCITY, HALCROW GROUP

Heatwaves and drought are not the only natural and unpredictable forces haunting our cities. Urban water security effects come from across the spectrum. At the other end of the scale from drought is the failure to cope with or prepare for extreme deluge, as the floods in Pakistan in 2010 have so devastatingly illustrated.

Flood hazards are natural phenomena, but damage and losses from floods, especially within cities, are the consequence of human action. Urbanization aggravates flooding by restricting where floodwaters can go, such as by covering large parts of the ground with roofs, roads, and pavements; by obstructing sections of natural channels; and by building drains that enable water to move to rivers faster than it did under natural conditions. As more people crowd into cities and the urban environment, these effects intensify. As a result, even quite moderate storms produce high flows in rivers because there are more hard surfaces and drains.

Intense rain events can prove fatal to cities already suffering from uncontrolled urban growth, unplanned physical development, a lack of access to basic services, a lack of or substandard infrastructure, land scarcity, poor health and sanitation conditions, poverty, and a lack of proper drainage systems. When the city floods, fecal and other hazardous materials contaminate standing waters and spill into open wells, elevating the risks of waterborne disease.

Already many of the urban poor are forced to live in hazardous places, building their homes and growing their food on floodplains in towns and cities, and sometimes dwelling on riverbanks. Others construct their shelters on steep, unstable hillsides, or along the foreshore on former mangrove swamps or tidal flats vulnerable to destructive floods, damaging landslides, or storm surges.

While every deluge is unique, the underlying reasons for why urban flooding can affect poor countries so greatly are often similar: loss of wetlands, marshes, and natural buffers in the hinterland; unplanned expanses of hard impermeable surfaces that accelerate water runoff; a lack of parks and other green spaces to absorb hard storms; and crude drainage systems too often clogged by waste.

Consider Mumbai, a key city for India's economy. It generates one-sixth of the country's income tax revenues and more than a third of its corporate tax. But in 2005, for several weeks, floods brought the metropolis to a halt. As floodwaters rose, the drainage system collapsed, affecting twenty million people and taking seven weeks to recede. In that time, floodwaters destroyed 1,200 human lives, 26,000 cattle, 14,000 homes, half a million hectares of crops, made domestic refugees out of 200,000, people and caused US$ 200 million damage to roads and bridges.

Consider Jakarta, Indonesia's key urban center. The city is located within a swampy floodplain where thirteen rivers empty into the sea. During monsoon season, the city's natural floods are worsened by human activity, such as groundwater extraction and the fact that weight of the concrete built area creates a high subsidence rate. In February 2007, historic floods rose a record 11.2 meters high, damaging three out of every five urban acres, affecting four hundred thousand people.

Consider Manila. There has been a tenfold population increase in Greater Manila between 1940 and 2000, creating considerable pressure on resources. This, in turn, has intensified both the severity and duration of floods. Most of the expanding population in Manila is made up of migrants from rural areas who cannot afford the rapidly increasing housing costs. The majority have to then find accommodation in the informal housing sector on the urban fringes, or on the banks of rivers, canals, and drains. The resultant makeshift housing encroaches onto waterways, blocking maintenance access and narrowing their capacity to handle discharge. This creates great potential for the human impact of any flood event to be amplified significantly.

Consider Buenos Aires. Here, significant expansion and development has occurred in the city over the last few decades and present systems now have inadequate hydraulic capacity to convey flood flows from across the enlarged urban areas. Inundations are frequent, disrupting and damaging the economy. In March 1985, several people were drowned when a major storm event caused serious flooding. But a sophisticated model was subsequently used to develop a master plan. The model covered not only the drainage networks but also road networks along which excess water travels, so that integrated solutions could be investigated. Solutions developed included major parallel "high-level" reinforcement sewers, major "low-level" storage tunneled sewers with terminal pumping stations, major storage tank facilities, and the use of real-time control to retain flows in the upper catchments.

In vulnerable cities, the increasingly common disaster phenomenon of urban flooding can cripple not only a city but also the surrounding province and even the entire country.[24] Management tools exist and can help to improve the ability of cities to cope with floods. If flood events are likely to occur on a more regular basis against the backdrop of continued urbanization trends, then it would seem sensible to enhance urban flood management programmes across the developing world to protect both human lives and the environment, and to improve the resilience of the national economy to such events.

Creating a Wastewater Revolution in Asian Cities: The Concept of Cascading Use

MARGARET CATLEY-CARLSON, PATRON, GLOBAL WATER PARTNERSHIP; MEMBER, UNITED NATIONS SECRETARY-GENERAL'S ADVISORY BOARD ON WATER AND SANITATION; CHAIR, GLOBAL AGENDA COUNCIL ON WATER SECURITY, 2007–2010

The current approach to safeguarding Asian water is philosophically flawed. Attitudes of policy makers, planners, and investors are notoriously rooted in the logic of "no return, no investment." Environmental sanitation is considered an investment dead end. This flaw needs redressing.

A major factor contributing to investment delay is the exorbitant cost of building or extending new systems, especially in major cities. Applying traditional concepts means that miles of pipe are needed to collect, carry away, and process the water wastes. Significant energy is required to deliver water and to process waste (often 30–40% of municipal energy bills), so change can bring significant energy savings.

With a system revision it is possible to harvest energy and resources in the waste. Current techniques and designs render these less accessible through wholesale collection from highly differentiated sources and massive dilution. New technology creates new possibilities. Membranes, for example, create an extraordinary range of possibilities, especially with new system designs.

The promotion and acceptance of "cascading use" has much potential— clean water for drinking and personal use, cascading down to gray water, which can be "cleaned enough" for agricultural, urban, and industrial use, which can be "cleaned enough" for recycling or environmental recharge, and so forth. Sewage, either harvested for energy or nutrients, then can be "cleaned enough" for agricultural or environmental use.

New city installations of wastewater facilities and the refits of older systems could be designed around a cascading, modular system. This modular approach to city wastewater design could use a series of interconnecting "clean enough for next use" technologies for a finite number of households/ entities.

But there is no international organization for water as there is for health, agriculture, or weather. This means that new ideas must percolate to scale through informal, professional networks. Often, key political and financial players are not aware of the new possibilities being created by new technologies. Engineers tend to talk to engineers, city managers to elected officials, and so forth. Some creative cross-hatching is needed.

What is required is a programme of targeted outreach to achieve the widest possible dissemination and adoption of new core water management concepts across Asia, which is home to about 62% of the world's population. Lessons learned from the Asian experience could then move to eastern Europe, Africa, and Central and Latin America. This programme would include stakeholders from governments, the private sector, and aid agencies.

The technological pieces exist, but a shift in the existing paradigm of city wastewater design and planning is needed. Champions of the cause are essential. System managers tend not to be sufficiently aware of change possibilities; financial institutions work from current concepts of what a wastewater system is; and politicians tend to shy away from programmes related to sanitation and wastewater. That 90% of Asian wastewater is untreated, however, reduces the absolute volumes of clean water available for consumption. Moreover, current treatment methods are energy-intensive, expensive, and very often poorly adapted to local situations in terms of technology and maintenance.

Social Enterprise Solution for Water and Sanitation Facilities in Kenya's Slums

David Kuria, CEO and Founder, Ecotact

Africa is not only failing to reach the Millennium Development Goals for water supply and sanitation, it is falling even further behind. To meet MDG targets, in five years 404 million more people will need to gain access to improved sanitation, and 294 million additional people require safe water. How can that happen, given the mounting threats? Let's explore one route.

In Kenya, water resources are polluted, degraded, and overexploited. In 2005, 39% of Kenya's thirty-two million people lacked access to safe drinking water and 62% lacked safe sanitation. Overcrowded slums have few means of disposing excreta, let alone garbage. The situation in schools and health facilities is arguably worse: three hundred children may share one outhouse. This spreads disease, affects school attendance, and undermines educational performance. On Nairobi's periphery, a lucky quarter of all residents have access to a private ventilated improved pit latrine, an ordinary pit latrine, or a flush toilet. The rest have nothing, or share with neighbors. At night, women risk being raped while seeking a distant outhouse.

As Africa's cities swell from rural influx, the traditional water, sewer, and sanitation infrastructure can't keep up with escalating pressures. But rather than collapse, Africa may tap into a creative social enterprise revolution. Through innovative micro-financing mechanisms and public-private partnerships on social services, new initiatives focus on providing sustainable solutions to socioeconomic problems that affect poor and marginalized populations.

One of those is Ecotact, a social enterprise that helps establish water and sanitation facilities in Kenya's urban slums through its Ikotoilet initiative.

The Ikotoilet project aims to provide convenient, hygienic, and sustainable safe water and sanitation services in twenty urban centers, which currently serve ten million residents annually. It is creating more than two hundred jobs for targeted youth and influencing a shift in municipal water and sanitation policies and priorities. In short, it aims to transform, restore, and ensure continued dignity of the growing urban population and revolutionize public attitudes towards toilets.

Ecotact strives to develop innovative answers to the growing cry for environmental sanitation. In addition to clean toilets, showers, and potable water, the Ikotoilet "malls" include micro-vendors selling beverages, newspapers, prepaid phone cards, and shoe shines, attracting users to the facilities and helping to cover operational costs.

To achieve this goal, Ecotact collaborates with local authorities through pioneering Built-Operate-Transfer (BOT) agreements. This model has been adopted from large-scale infrastructure projects and applied to a dispersed sanitation service delivery system. It shares risks, ensures capital recovery, strengthens operations and maintenance, and includes a margin for cost recovery. It emphasizes innovative revenue streams in order to complement use and to ensure that sanitation and water vending is not a once-off delivery, but rather is owned and managed for long-term health and productivity.

Urban Water Supply Security and Desalination

CRAIG FENTON, PARTNER AND HEAD OF WATER SECTOR ADVISORY PRACTICE, PRICEWATERHOUSECOOPERS, AUSTRALIA

Confronted by the deteriorating performance of existing rainfall-dependant supply options, and in many cases much more rapid demand growth than anticipated, urban water planning now requires that decisions of a greater scale and consequence be made on a more rapid basis than ever before.

This presents challenges and opportunities for water utilities and planning agencies. New water supply options are oftentimes a multiple of the cost of incumbent supply schemes. Water utilities traditionally have struggled to adopt pricing strategies that fully recover existing costs. Introducing new, higher cost sources will make cost-reflective user pricing even harder to achieve.

At the same time, technological advances are creating more novel options to meet or manage water demand. These include desalination, wastewater recycling, and "decentralized" options such as demand management, rainwater tanks, and local-level integrated urban water cycle management solutions. Many of these move away from conventional, centralized utility network planning and operating paradigms.

The potential for desalination technologies, in particular, has received much prominence in the last decade. Much of this can be attributed to the threat of climate change and the emerging risks to existing or new rainfall-dependant supply options. Also important are technological improvements that have brought desalination costs down substantially, in some cases to levels comparable with other supply options.

DESALINATION: A CLIMATE CHANGE CURE-ALL FOR THE WATER SECTOR?

Twenty years ago, desalination was predominantly seen in the energy-rich-though-water-scarce Gulf States, and in other isolated and remote areas with few alternative supply options. Compared to conventional large-scale supply options like dams and groundwater, desalination was horrendously expensive. Few water utilities had plans to develop desalination as a "normal" supply option. Fast-forward to the present and desalination has become a mainstay of many water utility supply strategies. Desalination facilities are now operating in every continent, with significant plants in the US, the Asia-Pacific, Africa, the Middle East, Europe, and the Caribbean.

Globally, there are now more than thirteen thousand desalination plants in operation, though many are still comparatively small. These plants produce more than forty-five million cubic meters of potable water each day—a sizeable quantity, to be sure, though it accounts for less than half of 1% of total global freshwater extraction.

In Australia, where water management frameworks are perhaps the most advanced, the cumulative impact of drought and what widely is viewed as the early impact of climate change has led to development of large-scale seawater reverse osmosis desalination plants in nearly every mainland city. Wonthaggi, a small coastal town near Melbourne, the capital of Victoria, is to be the site of one of the world's largest desalination facilities. Capable of producing more than four hundred thousand cubic meters per day, the plant will be developed through a public-private procurement approach, involving a consortium of domestic and international investment, construction, and desalination technology companies contracting with the state government.

Improvements in membrane technology have brought desalination costs down significantly, to the point where medium- to large-scale desalination is quite often cost-competitive with alternative supply options. Desalination can produce potable water for around $US 0.60–0.80/m^3, though plant costs do vary significantly depending on scale, energy costs, and local factors such as raw water quality, infrastructure needed to connect to existing/proposed water distribution networks, and the complexity of required raw water inlet and saline water outflow structures. For example, a recent study of more than three hundred desalination plants worldwide, of differing scales and treatment technologies, suggested a cost range on the order of $US 0.50–2.00/m^3.[25]

Critically, cost comparisons need to pay attention to the different assumptions implicit in the way costs are presented—as desalination is highly capital-intensive, even small differences in the target capital return between two otherwise similar projects can result in large apparent differences in unit-rate desalination costs. Perhaps more important, desalination is seen as a climate-independent supply option, allowing water utilities to insulate themselves from the risks of climate change and drought. For some, this makes desalination a first-choice option for water utility future supply strategies.

Desalination has many attractive features, but it also has some important limitations. For this reason, it is important for planners and water utilities to objectively assess all potential options and strategies. First, desalination requires a saline or brackish raw water source. For coastal locations, the sea is an obvious choice. Particular consideration needs to be given to the appropriate siting of the plant with respect to inlet and brine discharge facilities. In some cases, these "connecting" structures can account for a significant proportion of overall plant costs. Potential environmental risks associated with hypersaline water discharge need to be managed. Away from the coast there may still be suitable raw water supply options—for instance, the El Paso desalination plant in Texas draws raw water from a brackish groundwater source—but clearly desalination cannot be applied everywhere.

Second, scale is still an important variable in overall plant costs. Some estimates suggest there are significant economies of scale in plant size up to

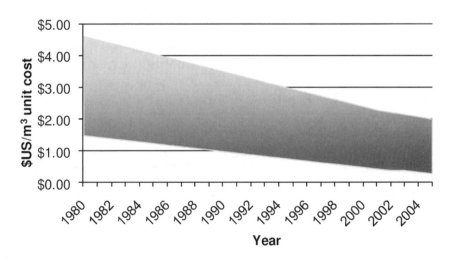

Source: adapted from Wittholz et at / Desalination 229 (2008) 10-20

Figure 5.1 Cost Reductions in Large Scale Desalination.

twenty thousand cubic meters per day, which is a sizeable capacity increment for even reasonably sized metropolitan centers. Larger plants may supply desalinated water at a cheaper unit rate, but if that capacity is not fully utilized, or is utilized only by substitution away from cheaper incumbent sources, then the effective cost per cubic meter may be very high. For example, a desalination plant may have a unit product cost of $US 0.60/m³, but two-thirds of its cost structure is fixed and independent of the volume of water produced. In this case, "effective" cost per cubic meter increases significantly once production volumes fall below an assumed plant capacity of twenty-thousand cubic meters per day (based on in-house PwC analysis).

Finally, desalination is energy-intensive, requiring a sizeable and reliable energy source. Energy costs typically account for around 35–40% of unit production costs for a seawater reverse osmosis plant, with benchmark energy consumption around four kilowatt hours for each cubic meter of water produced. Local energy systems need both the aggregate supply capacity—sufficient base-load power generation—and energy transmission/distribution capacity to support the power requirements of the desalination facility. The specter of tighter regulations in the next decades on greenhouse gas emissions will likely mean that fossil-fuel-based energy costs will increase, which will place upward pressure on desalination costs.

Partly to ameliorate this risk, a number of more recent desalination projects have specifically been partnered with renewable power supply options, such as wind generation. In Australia, each of the developed or under-

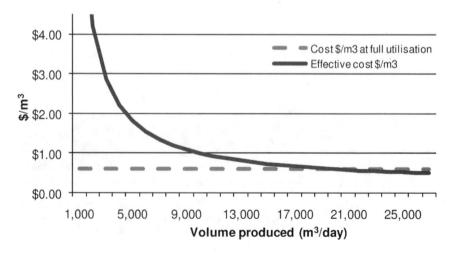

Source: PwC analysis

Figure 5.2 Impact of Scale on "Effective" Desalination Costs

construction desalination plants in Perth, Melbourne, Sydney, Adelaide, and the Gold Coast are powered by "green" energy sources. This creates an up-front energy price premium but removes the cost risk relating to any future carbon tax or cap-and-trade emissions scheme.

It seems clear that desalination will play an increasingly important role in water supply around the world. A robust evaluation of desalination projects will be important. This will give planners the confidence—and the information—to justify to their communities and to water users that a desalination strategy is indeed the preferred course.

Notes

1. UN-HABITAT, *State of the World's Cities, 2008/2009*, 2009.

2. Ibid.

3. Victor Hugo, *Les Misérables*, book II, chapter 1.

4. "China's Water Issues: Transition, Governance and Innovation," Prof Yi Wang, Deputy Director-General at the Institute of Policy and Management, Chinese Academy of Sciences, China. http://admin.cita-aragon.es/pub/documentos/documentos _WangYi_286d0ba6.pdf.

5. World Bank, *World Development Report, 1992: Development and the Environment*, 1992.

6. United Nations Development Programme, *Human Development Report, 2006: Beyond Scarcity*, 2006.

7. Ibid.

8. Ibid.

9. World Economic Forum Water Initiative, *The Bubble Is Close to Bursting*, 2009.

10. UN-HABITAT, *State of the World's Cities, 2008/2009*, 2009.

11. World Health Organization, *Costs and Benefits of Water and Sanitation Improvements at the Global Level*, 2004.

12. Goldman Sachs, *The Essentials of Investing in the Water Sector*, 2008.

13. Organisation for Economic Co-operation and Development, *Managing Water for All: An OECD Perspective on Pricing and Financing*, 2009.

14. See, for example, LeRoy W. Hooton Jr., "Clean Water Act Progress and Challenges," May 29, 2009, http://www.ci.slc.ut.us/utilities/NewsEvents/news2009/ news5292009.htm.

15. Organisation for Economic Co-operation and Development, *Managing Water for All: An OECD Perspective on Pricing and Financing*, 2009.

16. Organisation for Economic Co-operation and Development, "Development Aid at Its Highest Level Ever in 2008," March 3, 2009, http://www.oecd.org/document/ 13/0,3343,en_2649_34487_42458595_1_1_1_1,00.html.

17. United Nations, "Draft Decision: Copenhagen Accord," December 18, 2009, http://unfccc.int/resource/docs/2009/cop15/eng/l07.pdf.

18. Project Catalyst, *Project Catalyst Brief*, 2009.

19. International Food Policy Research Institute, *Global Water Outlook to 2025: Averting an Impending Crisis*, 2002.

20. World Economic Forum Water Initiative, *The Bubble Is Close to Bursting*, 2009.

21. World Bank, *Engaging Local Private Operators in Water Supply and Sanitation Services, Initial Lessons from Experience in Cambodia, Colombia, Paraguay, the Philippines, and Uganda*, 2006.

22. WaterAid, *Our Water, Our Waste, Our Town*, 2009.

23. For more information, see http://www.wsup.com/.

24. Asian Disaster Preparedness Center, Bangkok, *Effective Strategies for Urban Flood Risk Management*, 2008

25. Michelle K. Wittholz, Brian K. O'Neill, Chris B. Colby and David Lewis, "Estimating the Cost of Desalination Plants Using a Cost Database," *Desalination*, Vol. 229, Issues 1–3 (2008), pp. 10–20.

CHAPTER 6

People

This chapter explores the nexus between water and people, health, and livelihoods, especially in developing countries. It benefits greatly from the perspectives of many public, private, academic, and NGO representatives who have taken part in various Forum sessions and workshops on water issues over the last three years.

Background

"By means of water," says the Koran, "we give life to everything."
  Today, there are:

- 1.1 billion people who live without clean drinking water
- 2.6 billion people who lack adequate sanitation
- 1.8 million people who die every year from diarrheal diseases
- 3,900 children who die every day from waterborne diseases.[1]

The Millennium Development Goal (MDG) 7, Target 10, is the target that the international community has set itself to improve water conditions for the world's poor. The aim is to halve the proportion of the world population without sustainable access to safe drinking water and basic sanitation by 2015 against a 1990 baseline. There is consensus that improved water and sanitation conditions are essential for achieving each of the other Millennium Development Goals as well, including those regarding poverty, hunger, gender equality, health, education, and environmental degradation.

  The United Nations Development Programme's *Human Development Report* of 2006, which focused on the challenge of water and sanitation, said in quite blunt terms, "Not having access to water and sanitation is a polite euphemism for a form of deprivation that threatens life, destroys opportunity, and undermines human dignity."[2] Poor hygiene and sanitation kills more people in the world than HIV/AIDS and malaria combined, and more than any war claims through guns.[3] Dirty water and poor sanitation account for the vast majority of the 1.8 million child deaths each year from diarrhea—about five thousand a day. This makes poor access to water and sanitation the second largest cause of child mortality.

Diarrhea caused by unclean water is one of the world's greatest killers, claiming the lives of five times as many children as HIV/AIDS. Disease and productivity losses linked to poor water and sanitation amount to 2% of GDP, rising to 5% in sub-Saharan Africa, which is more than the region receives in official overseas assistance.[4] Ironically, the poor in developing countries generally pay more for their water than the affluent but receive poorer quality water.[5] The poorest people pay as much as ten times more than richer households for water.[6]

US$ 10 billion annually through 2015 would meet the MDGs for water and sanitation, according to the OECD. Current aid to the water and sanitation sector is less than 5% of the total aid budget, creating a gap to meet the MDGs of more than US$ 5 billion a year.[7] The problem is not only a developing country challenge; water infrastructure is aging in many developed countries. In 2009, failing water infrastructure caused more illnesses in the US than H1N1 did worldwide.

Trends

"Globally, our human pattern of water usage is unsustainable," says Maggie Catley-Carlson, Patron of the Global Water Partnership. "Why? Population, prosperity, and pollution. We have today the same basic amount of water as the Earth of the dinosaurs or Julius Caesar. But we have grown and grown from Caesar's world's population of about 400,000, to today's almost 6.5 billion people, headed to 8.5 billion. With increasing prosperity, people in many places use upwards of 2,500 liters of water a day. Do the math."[8]

In September 2010, a major meeting at the United Nations in New York assessed progress on the Millennium Development Goals, including the target for water and sanitation. The headline statement on the water target was that the world is on track to meet the MDG goal for improved water access, although much still needs to be done in some regions.[9] The 2010 assessment shows that if current trends continue, the world will meet or even exceed the MDG drinking water target by 2015. By that time, an estimated 86% of the population in developing regions will have gained access to improved sources of drinking water. Four regions—northern Africa, Latin America and the Caribbean, eastern Asia, and southeastern Asia—have already met the target.[10] This is a good-news story, which should be celebrated. Economic growth in many parts of the world, especially in China, has contributed towards this improvement in the aggregate numbers of people now with access to improved water services.

The latest assessment has also picked out a growing gap, however, in access to improved water services between rural and urban dwellers. Globally, eight out of ten people who are still without access to an improved drinking water source now live in rural areas. Significant differences between urban and rural areas were found, even in regions that have achieved relatively high coverage, such as western Asia and Latin America and the Caribbean. In particular, the 2010 assessment noted that the rural-urban gap seems to be much wider when only households that have a piped drinking water supply on premises are considered. For example, it found that the proportion of people who enjoy the health and economic benefits of piped water is more than twice as high in urban areas than in rural areas—79% versus 34%.[11]

It seems that the trend of rapid urbanization, as described in the previous chapter, has helped deliver these kinds of improvements since 1990, as rural dwellers moved to the city and gained closer access to a piped water supply of some description. The more potent challenge however, will likely come in the next decades if urban services do not improve for these new arrivals.

Against this context of a general improvement in water access through urbanization, the issue of water *quality* is also starting to gain more attention, especially through the nexus that links water for people to water used for agriculture and industry. For example, the latest MDG assessment concludes that during the last decade, expanded activity in agriculture and manufacturing has not only increased the demand for water, but has also contributed to the pollution of surface and groundwater.[12] When set alongside the challenge of contamination of naturally occurring inorganic arsenic in Bangladesh and other parts of southern Asia, the issue of tracking and measuring water pollution and water quality and its impact on people, especially in the urban and peri-urban context, is a trend that will likely gather pace over the coming decade.

For example, the MDG assessment suggests that in the future, water quality criteria will need to be considered when setting targets for access to safe water. Yet, despite efforts to compile global water quality data, the assessment observes that measuring the safety of water can be difficult in developing regions, and it has been attempted so far only in pilot surveys. The 2010 MDG report concludes that rapid, reliable, and cost-effective ways of measuring water quality locally and reporting findings at the global level will need to be identified to overcome the current technical and logistic constraints, along with the high cost.[13] A trend in innovation to find cost-effective and accurate ways to monitor and track water quality issues is likely.

The issue of sanitation, however, is much less rosy in terms of progress against the MDG goal. The September 2010 assessment has concluded rather bluntly that with half the population of developing regions without sanitation, the 2015 target appears to be out of reach.[14] Again, the challenge to make gains on improving sanitation seems closely linked to rapid urbanization trends. As explained in the previous chapter, this could be related to the high cost of investing adequately in the urban wastewater infrastructure that is required.

The 2010 MDG assessment found that between 1990 and 2008, sanitation coverage for the *whole* of the developing world increased by only 5% in urban areas (compared to 43% in rural areas). In southern Asia, coverage rose from 56% to 57% of the urban population—just a 1% increase.[15] Consequently, it seems that sanitation and wastewater management in the urban environments of southern Asia in particular will be a key "battleground" area for the MDG goal on sanitation moving forward.

Among sanitation practices in general, the 2010 MDG assessment picks the practice of open defecation as the one that poses the greatest threat to human health. While the practice has declined in all developing regions against the1990 baseline, southern Asia still has the highest rate of open defecation in the world (44% of the population). The report suggests that indiscriminate defecation is the root cause of fecal-oral transmission of disease, which can have lethal consequences for the most vulnerable members of society—such as young children, the already sick, and the elderly. Consequently, a decline in open defecation rates could have a huge impact on reducing child deaths, primarily by preventing diarrheal diseases and the stunting and undernutrition that tend to follow.[16]

The challenge of mobilizing resources and political will and developing scalable, bankable projects in the urban sanitation and wastewater treatment sector—which can attract significant flows of private finance to help meet the infrastructure investment gap that exists in developing countries, especially in Southern Asia—stands out as a core issue.

Forecast

With urbanization continuing apace for the next two decades at least, it seems likely in the aggregate that the MDG for improved access to freshwater services will be achieved by 2015. The greater problem to 2030, however, will be to improve on service delivery within the urban setting. It is likely that once the first jump in experiencing improved access has been made (broadly, from rural unconnected to urban connected services of some sort), there could be a significant risk of stagnation in improvement if urban infrastructure remains chronically underfunded and as more people arrive in the city.

The same forecast applied to the sanitation goal. Due to the large numbers of people arriving into cities, and the lack of wastewater facilities, it is highly likely that the MDG for sanitation will not be met by 2015. Worse still, sanitary conditions in cities around the world in developing countries could decline still further without a dimensional change in investment flow into the whole value chain of urban sanitation and wastewater infrastructure. The picture by 2030 could be grim indeed. This is probably the most urgent issue that will affect people's health, wealth, and livelihoods that emerges. Geographically, cities across southern Asia will likely bear the social, economic, and political brunt of this challenge if business as usual continues.

Implications

Meeting the MDG target for water and particularly for sanitation makes economic as well as social sense. Calculations suggest that meeting the targets would provide US$ 38 billion in economic benefits annually. Studies suggest that every US$ 1 spent in the water and sanitation sector creates on average of another US$ 8 in costs averted and productivity gained (e.g., school attendance, time savings).[17] This then is question of combining political will and financial innovation.

Political desire to meet the MDGs for sanitation is low, as the 2010 assessment highlights. If the powerful have running water and a toilet, then there is little political imperative to do more. But the politics of this issue may rapidly change as economic development continues. A restless second-generation urban populous across southern Asia, with access to the Internet and mobile phones but no adequate toilets, will be a potent political force for tomorrow's Asian leaders to deal with. One or two outbreaks of disease due to poor sanitation and wastewater facilities that affects both the poor and the middle class across a suite of Asian cities could provide a dramatic political trigger for change. Investors from overseas could also be key influencers when they start avoiding or disinvesting in certain cities and industrial parks due to poor wastewater services.

The huge investment challenge to fix the problem is the other major implication to consider. This is where history can offer some clues. In richer countries in the 19th century, large amounts of investment were spent on sanitation, as a growing awareness of the human cost of urban industrial life forced water and wastewater treatment onto the political agenda. An 1842 Report on the Sanitary Condition of the Labouring Population of Great

Britain reported that "the annual cost of life from filth is greater than the loss of death or wounds from any war in which the country has been engaged in modern times."[18] This report went on to recommend a private tap and a latrine connected to a sewer for every household, and municipal responsibility for providing clean water.

The analogue of how the money was raised to pay for these investments is also interesting. Then, like now, government finances were stretched. New approaches to financing the required new infrastructure played a critical role. The challenge of how to fund large up-front payments from a limited revenue base without raising taxes was met by cities in the 19th century by supplementing low-interest loans from central government with municipal borrowing on bond markets. In fact, at the end of the 19th century, water and sanitation accounted for about one-quarter of local government debt in Great Britain.[19] But the cost-benefit equation was seen to be worth the debt burden. The political, economic, and social benefit of the laboring poor being healthy outweighed the equivalent political, economic, and social costs to the state if they were sick. It simply made sense to make the investment, if the financial markets could be tapped and if government could underwrite the risk.

The resonance of this story, almost two hundred years later, is clear. If political will for improved water and sanitation services is forced to increase, especially among decision-makers in cities across southern Asia, then how to help national and local governments raise revenue from the international capital markets? What role can international finance organizations play in this regard? Could elements of enhanced aid commitments in the run-up to the MDG target date of 2015 be combined with national government initiatives to create financial innovations focused on raising the capital to deliver a "blue new deal" for the urban poor?

Underpinning these ideas is, of course, the implication that better data are needed, as the 2010 MDG assessment highlighted. This is a particularly important issue for political leaders embarking on any major investment programme. They need to be able to communicate to the populous where we are now and therefore why we need the programme, where we aim to be by when and how we will know when we get there. Simultaneously, better technical analysis will be required to help governments identify the most cost-effective investment and technological options open to them in the wastewater sector to take this journey (e.g., initiatives that can help fix what exists rather than simply build new facilities).

Across all these cases, which touch upon finance, data and technical analysis, the important role that the private sector and private capital markets will have to play to support the government's investment agenda is becoming clear.

The Way Forward

Government leadership can emerge and government reforms can work. Uganda reformed water policy in the 1990s; budget allocations increased from 0.5% of public expenditure in 1997 to 2.8% in 2002, and coverage levels increased from 39% in 2003 to 51% in 2006. Similarly, in Morocco, a rural water reform programme since 1995 has boosted coverage to 50% with many economic multiplier effects.[20] Local leadership is also possible. A well-documented success story relates to the Phnom Penh Water Supply Authority, in which a decrepit and war-torn water supply system with missing water and missing customers was transformed into a model public sector water utility that provides around-the-clock drinking water.[21] Many other local success cases exist, too. Change is possible.

International aid can help government leaders in developing economies to make these changes by providing credit through local capital markets for private investments into public water infrastructure, or through a wide range of other public finance mechanisms. Almost a decade ago, Michel Camdessus, the former head of the IMF, chaired a world panel to look into financing for water. The group's report contained many prescient recommendations on blending public and private finance to raise the investment that is required in the water and sanitation sector. Ten years on, the wider political agenda may now be catching up with much of the thinking the report captured. Decision-makers across the public and private sectors may be becoming ready to try and put some of these innovations into practice.[22]

New technologies and new business models also abound. New membrane technologies mean that wastewater treatment plants can be local, small-scale, and safe. The market for toilets in the developing world, for example, is an opportunity possibly worth billions of dollars. The market for clean-energy/zero-water energy sources to power desalination or wastewater treatment plants could also be huge. "Public goods like clean water and sanitation will not be provided solely by the market," says Jacqueline Novogratz, Founder and CEO of the Acumen Fund. "What is needed in social and economic development is the equivalent of venture capital in the marketplace. The field is witnessing an explosion of new ideas."[23]

Innovations are also emerging within and between development aid agencies, foundations, charities, and the private sector on how best to use official development assistance or other grants; on how best to focus on providing water services to the rural as well as the urban poor; and on how best to work within new partnerships with governments to help unlock new markets and new opportunities for water service and sanitation delivery. While the role for overseas aid, charity, and private donations is undisputed, a more substantive interaction between the public-private and civil society sectors is required to help support governments that choose to lead in this space innovate, both in terms of financing and in terms of new business models for water and sanitation services. Arguably, these interactions are beginning to deepen and blossom, as activities within the World Economic Forum (and this publication) indicate.

But to accelerate the innovation that the agenda needs, so that a wide range of new public-private-civil arrangements are tried out and helped to get to scale, new approaches are required. More official development assistance and philanthropic capital could be invested in "higher-risk" innovations at the onset to test new ideas. If successful, increasing levels of concessional loans or patient private capital could then be gradually drawn in, to enable successful enterprises and projects to start getting to scale effectively. It is clear that the water and sanitation field is witnessing an explosion of new ideas, but iconic breakthroughs are needed—an innovative but scalable urban wastewater programme focused on Asian cities, for example. For the next two decades, what is needed in the water and sanitation sector is perhaps the equivalent of what venture and private equity capital does in the marketplace—to drive new ideas to scale and then to drive the new organization to scale to deliver them widely into the marketplace. With this kind of focus, many more of the people who suffer the burden of poor water access, poor water quality, and poor sanitation and wastewater services will be reached.

Perspectives

The following personal perspectives amplify the main themes touched on by this chapter. They help to illustrate the range of current viewpoints on the nexus between water and people, health and livelihoods. The views expressed do not necessarily represent those of the World Economic Forum, nor do they necessarily represent the views of the other individual contributors or the various contributing companies or institutions.

- Barbara Frost, Chief Executive, WaterAid, sets out the challenge of water and sanitation, its links to people's health and livelihoods in the developing world, and the importance of the Millennium Development Goal Targets for Water and Sanitation. The water crisis is now, she argues.
- Ajit Gulabchand, Chairman and Managing Director, Hindustan Construction Company, points out the challenge of overcoming poor government capacity and weak governance in helping to improve the health and livelihoods of the poor through improved water and sanitation services.

- Thabo Makgoba, Anglican Archbishop of Southern Africa, reflects on the human and spiritual importance of access to clean water, arguing for free access to the water nexus.
- Jack Sim, Founder and Director, World Toilet Organization, presents a social entrepreneur's approach to not only tackling the sanitation crisis facing the world's poor, but also turning it into a market opportunity.

The Water Crisis Is Now

Barbara Frost, Chief Executive, WaterAid

This insert is taken from a speech made to the UN General Assembly on March 22, 2010.

WaterAid is an international NGO that works in some of the world's poorest countries of Africa, Asia, and the Pacific, with some of the poorest and most marginalized communities, where many of the MDGs are unlikely to be met.

When poor people are asked about their priorities, water is invariably number one. Women know that it is dirty water that makes their children sick, and that if safe water was closer to their homes they could be able to earn a living rather than spending hours each day collecting it. When disasters strike, a lack of drinking water and sanitation can become especially acute. In Haiti, safe drinking water was critical in the first hours and days of the relief work.

From the perspective of the people we work with, who live without drinking water in unhygienic situations with nowhere to wash and defecate, there is a world "crisis" now. We all know that climate change is likely to make this crisis worse and have the greatest impact on some of the world's poorest countries, bringing further hardship to people already dealing with lack of the absolute basics of life—the right to safe water to drink and a decent place to go to the toilet.

It cannot be right that in 2010, 2.6 billion people do not have anywhere safe to defecate and thus risk ill health—children die an untimely death and women have to deal with the lack of privacy and indignity. That is 40% of the world's population lacking this most basic right. However, with the political will and commitment and the right investment, we know change can happen.

In South Korea, child mortality halved between 1960 and 1970, partly as a result of investment in sanitation—a shining example of what can be done. The number of medical staff hardly changed over that decade. In South Africa, the government is committed to the right of families to have safe water and has made huge strides forward to ensure that there is a basic minimum quantity available for all.

Despite considerable political commitment, the people we work with in countries such as Bangladesh or Mali struggle with a falling water table, saline and arsenic contamination, increasing numbers of floods, cyclones, and droughts, and erratic rainfall. This poses serious health hazards and livelihood constraints. With increasing floods, pit latrines overflow and pollute the wells, and it is always women and children who suffer the most.

However, we have seen the amazing fortitude shown by communities when they decide through self-help to take action—they take control to manage the standpipe in their area or the well they will maintain, or to ensure improved health and hygiene of their families through the use of pit latrines and improved hygiene practices.

We have seen global compacts work before—we witnessed the success of the Education for All initiative, which set out to end user fees in primary education. Ending water poverty is also possible.

We agree with UN-Water that climate change adaptation is mainly about water. Furthermore, migration, urbanization, changing levels of consumption, and pollution compound this and pose significant threats to future water resources. Water is such a precious commodity; as our African partners say, "Water is life."

However, as we know, this is not a crisis of scarcity. It is about equitable distribution. One in eight people still live without safe water today.

While the crisis in domestic water is holding back development, it is the sanitation MDG that is one of the most lagging sectors. If current trends continue, the sanitation target will be missed by one billion people. Four thousand children continue to die every day from diseases caused by unsafe water and poor sanitation. Diarrhea is the second biggest killer of children under five in the developing world and kills more children than AIDS, TB, and malaria combined.

Without improved sanitation, children will not get to school—they will get sick or they will die, and hospitals will continue to be treating people with waterborne diseases that could so easily be prevented. This is a daily disaster that can be solved. Solved through investment and good governance—through governments, the private sector, and NGOs like WaterAid working together. We have seen the dramatic change to people's lives that safe water makes. Yet despite this, only 32% of the aid allocated for water and sanitation goes to the low-income countries where the need is greatest.

Investment in sanitation and water will also enable the other MDGs to be met. Girls will stay at school after puberty if there are decent toilets, and women and girls will be healthy, freed from the burden of water carrying, indignity, and disease.

Drinking water supplies and sanitation are critical to ensuring the MDGs are met, and climate change and increasing natural disasters highlight their importance. At the current rate, the MDG for sanitation will not be met in sub-Saharan Africa until 2206, almost two hundred years too late. We look to governments and the UN to galvanize world leadership and bring to an end this crisis.

We also urge world leaders to commit to investing more in sanitation as well as water. Investment in sanitation brings economic and social return ($US 1 invested brings a $US 9 return, according to the WHO). Failure to invest will lead to the failure of other MDGs.

Water for People: The Capacity Constraint of Governments Hinders Action

AJIT GULABCHAND, CHAIRMAN AND MANAGING DIRECTOR, HINDUSTAN CONSTRUCTION COMPANY

What leaves people without water and sanitation? It is not always the case that the shortfall of water sanitation services is linked solely to water scarcity. The lack of capacity within governments to adequately invest in and maintain good public water sanitation assets can also contribute to many in the population failing to receive adequate water and sanitation services.

This "capacity poverty" of governments can manifest itself through failures in financial, institutional, and political effectiveness, as well as through solely technical constraints. To address these weaknesses, large aid programmes for water and sanitation are apportioned to the (relatively) poor countries. Despite aid being an empathetic approach from richer countries to support the poor nations, concessional loans and borrowings for water and sanitation seems to be ever increasing. Why is this?

Although it is known that poverty and environmental degradation are synonymous, little has been done to understand or establish the cause-consequence relationship between the deterioration of overall economic conditions due to a shortfall in water and sanitation services. For example, the impact of poor quality water and sanitation services can manifest itself in degraded health and environmental conditions, leading to a weaker economy. A weaker economy results in a diminished availability to leverage investments for water and sanitation, resulting in poor quality services—in other words, a downward spiral.

If it can be made clear to governments where and how they find themselves positioned on such a spiral of economic and environmental degradation, through better analysis and a clearer fact base of the current situation and what the future might hold under a business-as-usual trajectory through 2030, for example, this is likely to trigger action to prevent a further slide down into the poverty trap. Consequently, a stronger focus on forecasts and trends, on the potential effects of inaction, and on understanding the political and economic implications of leaving people without water and sanitation would help encourage government action. This in turn would help address one of the key challenges for the water and sanitation sector—the lack of government action.

Free Access to the Water Nexus

THABO MAKGOBA, ANGLICAN ARCHBISHOP OF SOUTHERN AFRICA

In January 2009, I visited the impoverished Diocese of Lebombo in Mozambique to bless the new water supply of the village of Chihunzuine. It was a simple service, but it conveyed to me, in a powerful way, why water is rightly such a potent symbol within Christian tradition. The physical, cultural, and religious significance of water is interwoven from Genesis's story of Creation through to Revelation's river of the water of life flowing from the throne of God through the heavenly city. Water is, and has always been, the fundamental stuff of life.

People and flocks really were in danger of dying of thirst in the wilderness when Moses struck the rock with his staff at God's command and water came forth: a sign of his providential care. The Psalmist describes a righteous person as prospering like a tree planted by streams of water, green-leaved and yielding fruit in season. Jesus, conversing with the Samaritan woman as she draws water from a well for him to drink, speaks of himself as the source of living water, which will "well up into eternal life."

Water signifies birth into new life. From Noah's Ark to the Exodus across the Red or Reed Sea, from Jacob's crossing of the River Jabbok to Joshua's of the Jordan, passing through water communicates leaving the old and beginning afresh. Jesus is baptized as the initiation into his active ministry as the Messiah; and Christians understand our baptism as uniting us with our Savior, in both his burial and his rising to new life, something that is particularly powerfully conveyed when the rite is performed by total immersion.

With these images in mind I came to Chihunzuine, where the Bishop had raised funds to pump and pipe water from a distant reservoir to a communal tap. The joy and celebration this single tap engendered went far beyond what a Westernized mind might easily comprehend. The tap stood in the village square, close to the church—humanity's spiritual and physical needs side by side, where people meet and gather and weave the fabric of society. The tap unlocked safety and protection: now women could fetch water without fear of being assaulted or raped on a long, isolated journey. The tap truly was a source of life and health and nourishment, providing water to drink, for hygiene, and for irrigating garden plots that would now produce better crops: a true security-food-energy-water nexus.

Yet water is not unalloyed good news. Noah's deluge also destroyed. Chihunzuine is vulnerable to torrential downpours and flash floods that sweep away houses and erode fertile topsoil. In dry seasons, water is scarce, reducing harvests, killing livestock, and undermining food security. Urbanization, often a consequence of worsening rural poverty exacerbated by environmental issues, brings its own tensions, over both supply and sanitation. Conflicts over water, whether between pastoralists, or pastoralists and farmers, or nomads and the settled, is as old as the civilizations recorded in Scripture—and still plague the lands where Jesus walked.

We should not sentimentally allegorize every aspect of water, but some parallels from Christian tradition can inform and energize our attitudes towards its use. Jesus says that streams of living water will flow from those who have faith. Therefore our blessings, of whatever sort, are meant to be shared; Christ's spiritual well, said to be bottomless, nourishes our commitment to act responsibly in response to the risks of, for example, climate change, pollution, urban and peri-urban construction, and the safeguarding and sharing of our finite supplies.

Right stewardship of creation is a central spiritual value, as is ensuring justice, especially for the poorest of the poor. And while faith communities generally do not share all the presuppositions that underlie the language of human rights, we nonetheless would concur that access—free access—to adequate clean water is something that should be guaranteed for every single person on our planet.

For not only did Jesus say that whoever is spiritually thirsty should come to him and drink, he also cautioned that we shall all be judged on whether we have fed the hungry, welcomed the stranger, sheltered the homeless, tended the sick, clothed the naked, visited the imprisoned—and given the thirsty something to drink. It is a warning none of us, whatever our beliefs, are at liberty to ignore.

SaniShop: Transforming the Sanitation Crisis into a Massive Business Opportunity for All

JACK SIM, FOUNDER AND DIRECTOR, WORLD TOILET ORGANIZATION

Water is a key source of life. In fact, it is so important that it often overshadows another equally important agenda, sanitation, which remains a key global challenge for humanity. With excreta polluting so much of our surface water, we cannot ignore the impact of poor sanitation on clean water. Prevention is always cheaper than a cure.

More than 2.6 billion people—almost 40% of the world population—are without access to toilets or latrines that allow them to defecate in safety, privacy, and dignity. Unsafe disposal of human excreta can cause the transmission of oral-fecal diseases, like diarrhea and intestinal worm infections such as hookworm and roundworm. Its economic burdens—through morbidity and mortality (1.5 million kids die annually from diarrhea alone), and through school dropouts, especially by girls who have reached the age of puberty—fuel the poverty cycle and attack basic human decency.

Despite its overwhelming effects, the sanitation crisis remains a "taboo topic" among politicians, investors, media, and the general public in both developed and developing countries. With sanitation lagging behind water, fresh thinking and innovative approaches are desperately required.

Since 2001, the World Toilet Organization (WTO) has used a unique mix of humor and serious facts to engage the global media to bring focus to the sanitation agenda, and along the way the WTO has become a media darling. Its World Toilet Summit series and World Toilet Day (November 19) are followed and celebrated all over the world.

Having built media legitimacy, the WTO is now demonstrating that market-based approaches, as compared to donor-based approaches, have the potential to bring about that innovative change. According to the Monitor Group, the approach promises self-sustaining efforts to harness markets and the discipline of demand-led activities to improve services to the poor and better engage them in supply chains and activities that improve their livelihoods.[24] The pressing challenge now is to scale up these market-based approaches. WTO firmly believes that its social franchising model, which WTO has branded as SaniShop, is one of the cornerstones of harnessing market forces to propel developmental efforts to meet the MDGs and provide access to proper sanitation for all.

ADVANTAGES OF A MARKET-BASED APPROACH OVER A DONOR-BASED APPROACH TO SANITATION

Below are common aspects of the historic donor-based approach:

- It treats the poor as helpless and powerless
- It distorts the marketplace by creating dependency
- Toilets are often abandoned due to lack of maintenance
- High overhead costs make it unsustainable beyond donor funding
- It is unable to go to scale due to low local participation
- Current trends point to donor fatigue
- Supply-driven products tend to look "drab" and lack appeal to the poor
- It is impossible to solve a 2.6 billion people problem through donation.

The new SaniShop market-based approach uses a combination of promotional strategies and supply-chain strengthening to create an ecosystem where affordable sanitation options are available. This approach:

- Treats the poor as enterprising and capable of self-help
- Improves health through access to proper sanitation and creation of local enterprises/jobs
- Means that the user pays for the product and service
- Creates product designs that are "sexy" and appeal to the aspirations of the buyer
- Enables grand economy of scale, meaning we can combine high tech, good design, and large volume at low cost and extreme affordability
- Builds local capacity to help the poor to help themselves
- Uses natural market forces to serve the poor with innovation and sustainability
- Possesses visual branding and franchising for fast market penetration leveraging on existing distribution channels across other sectors and geography.

WTO's Experience in Kg Speu, Cambodia

WTO has started to develop such a model in Cambodia. Its features include:

- Engagement of sales agent, typically government officials, in direct sales activities such as village meetings, door-to-door sales, and follow-up at the village level.
- Training sales agents to develop sales area planning and monthly targets in coordination with their local concrete producer.
- Distribution of brochures through schools and factories.
- Banner display at supplier sites and sales promotion meetings.

The first product, an easy latrine model designed by IDEO, has been selling well to Cambodians for as low as US$ 32 per unit for the squat pan, chamber, and pits, with the option to buy the external shelter for an additional US$ 33 per unit.

To Scale This Solution, SaniShop Is the Next Stage

SaniShop is a free franchise distribution model, designed for rapid replication using modern marketing tools and best practices. It is a departure from the traditional charity approach. Below are listed the three elements of SaniShop's value proposition.

1. Global Engagement
WTO's objective is to bring sanitation onto the global stage with a specific

aim of engaging global commercial organizations in the technological, mass-manufacturing, and business advancement of the sanitation marketplace. In tapping into this global pool of resources and expertise, WTO aims to accelerate the scaling up of sanitation marketing through the engagement of different stakeholders.

WTO's supporters and resources include Index Award for Design That Improves Life, Technical University Hamburg, Xavier University, Sustainable Sanitation Alliance technology members, Rockefeller Foundation, Clorox, CLSA, Unilever, Ashoka, BoP Hub, Grameen Creative Lab, World Entrepreneurship Forum, and the World Economic Forum connectivity into its Schwab Foundation, Technology Pioneers, Young Global Leaders, Sustainability Initiatives, civil society groups, and corporate members. Although still at its nascent stage, a number of potential partners are attracted to the Sani-Shop mission of synergies, creative capitalism, and scalability of the model.

2. Aspiration as Drivers

The last mile in sanitation is people-centric, not technology-centric. The rapid adoption of mobile phones by the poor has taught us that aspiration is a high-level demand driver. Beyond health, sanitation would be positioned as a status symbol, a bridge to a better future and an enabler of children's education. Appealing toilet designs, creative marketing such as cartoons, and branding are powerful enablers to elevate the perception of toilets. Further, SaniShop provides a brand to deliver an assurance of quality control and trust.

3. Empowerment and Aspiration

By teaching a man how to fish, he can eat for a lifetime. The SaniShop franchise will create jobs and ignite the entrepreneurial spirit of the poor by triggering a vision of a better future. Without many resources, a person can become a sales agent or a supplier. Her customers will similarly be inspired by what the health improvement means to her family's future.

To raise the status of sanitation, WTO has developed a very powerful and positive visual brand: "Door to Dreams" for SaniShop. It pictures each toilet door opening to a better future for the user:

- Healthy kids laughing
- Teenage daughters going to school
- Healthy people working and earning more money
- Farmers having better crops (great fertilizers from toilets)
- Healthy elders smiling and giving the thumbs-up to toilets
- Earning enough money to buy other things
- Sanitation as an engine for growth and better quality of life
- No more pictures of sad and pathetic conditions. Our new positive

message will inspire all people across the globe to join hands to help the poor get out of poverty. And the door to dreams is now in their hands.

Notes

1. United Nations Development Programme, *Human Development Report, 2006: Beyond Scarcity*, 2006.
2. Ibid., p. 5.
3. Ibid.
4. Ibid.
5. World Wide Fund for Nature, *Water at Risk*, 2009.
6. United Nations Development Programme, *Human Development Report, 2006: Beyond Scarcity*, 2006.
7. Ibid.
8. World Economic Forum Water Initiative, *The Bubble Is Close to Bursting*, 2009.
9. United Nations, *The Millennium Development Goals Report, 2010*, 2010.
10. Ibid.
11. Ibid.
12. Ibid.
13. Ibid.
14. Ibid.
15. Ibid.
16. Ibid.
17. United Nations Development Programme, *Human Development Report, 2006: Beyond Scarcity*, 2006.
18. Her Majesty's Stationery Office, *Report on the Sanitary Conditions of the Labouring Population of Great Britain*, 1842, p. 369.
19. United Nations Development Programme, *Human Development Report, 2006: Beyond Scarcity*, 2006.
20. Ibid.
21. Asian Development Bank, "Country Water Action: Cambodia," August 2007, http://www.adb.org/water/actions/CAM/PPWSA.asp. In recognition of its world-class performance in water supply and self-sufficiency, the Cambodian Phnom Penh Water Supply Authority (PPWSA) won the Stockholm Industry Water Award in 2010.
22. World Panel on Financing Water Infrastructure, *Financing Water for All*, 2003.
23. World Economic Forum Water Initiative, *The Bubble Is Close to Bursting*, 2009.
24. Monitor Group, *Emerging Markets, Emerging Models. Market Based Solutions to the Challenges of Global Poverty*. Executive Summary, 2009.

CHAPTER 7

Business

This chapter explores the water-business nexus. It benefits greatly from the perspectives of many public, private, academic, and NGO representatives who have taken part in various Forum sessions and workshops on water issues over the last three years, as well as from the contributions of members of the Forum's Water Initiative Industry Project Board.

Background

It was at the Annual Meeting of the World Economic Forum in Davos-Klosters, January 2008, where the agenda of viewing water as a strategic issue for business really took off. A series of discussions and roundtables culminated in a CEO panel with the United Nations Secretary-General Ban Ki-moon. The head of the UN praised increasing levels of private-sector engagement with the global water challenge, saying to the audience of five hundred senior business, government, and civil society representatives that "business is becoming part of the solution, not part of the problem."

At this session, the Secretary-General also introduced the new UN Global Compact CEO Water Mandate to the Davos-Klosters community. Beside him were the then CEO and Chairmen of four global companies from the food, beverage, chemical, and engineering sectors: Peter Brabeck-Letmathe of Nestlé, Neville Isdell of the Coca-Cola Company, Andrew Liveris of the Dow Chemical Company, and the late Ralph Peterson of the engineering company CH2M HILL. Fred Krupp, President of the Environmental Defense Fund, was also with them. For many in the audience, this was the first time they had heard senior business peers sit alongside UN and NGO heads and speak passionately and with concern about the interlinked economic, social, environmental, and geopolitical challenges that they felt water now posed to growth, both for their own businesses and for the world system at large—and equally important, about the key role that governments must play to help set fair frameworks for all.

Trends

Over the last few years since that Davos-Klosters discussion, a plethora of activity and reports have now taken off, involving more and more business associations, financial analysts, and companies looking at the strategic importance of water security to their operations or investments. Water is now a fast-moving space for those at the forefront of the business risk agenda.

The UN Global Compact CEO Water Mandate is a good early example of such activity.[1] The CEO Water Mandate is a unique public-private initiative designed to assist companies in the development, implementation, and disclosure of water sustainability policies and practices. It recognizes that the business sector, through the production of goods and services, affects water resources—both directly and through supply chains. As of September 2010, nearly seventy CEOs from around the world have now endorsed the mandate (see fig. 7.1).

Endorsing CEOs acknowledge that in order to operate in a more sustainable manner and contribute to the vision of the UN Global Compact and the realization of the Millennium Development Goals, they have a responsibility to make water resources management a priority, and to work with governments, UN agencies, nongovernmental organizations, and other stakeholders to address this global water challenge. The CEO Water Mandate covers six areas: direct operations; supply chain and watershed management; collective action; public policy; community engagement; and transparency.

At about the same time as the CEO Water Mandate, the World Economic Forum's Water Initiative was relaunched, gaining considerable traction following the 2008 Davos-Klosters discussions.[2] Working on raising awareness, helping the development of new analytics, and trialing new forms of practical public-private-expert partnerships in water, thirteen companies formed the leader group. These included CH2M HILL, Cisco Systems, the Dow Chemical Company, Halcrow Group, Hindustan Construction Company, Nestlé SA, PepsiCo, Rio Tinto, SABMiller, Standard Chartered Bank, Syngenta, the Coca-Cola Company, and Unilever. As a multistakeholder platform, the Forum's Water Initiative was supported by several governmental organizations, including the International Finance Corporation, the US Agency for International Development, and the Swiss Agency for Development and Cooperation. It also created links with the International Federation of Agricultural Producers and the World Wide Fund for Nature. A major new phase to the Forum's water initiative has begun in 2010. More details on the next stage to the Forum's Water Initiative can be found in the concluding chapter to this book.

• Agbar (Spain)	• Compagnie de Saint-Gobain (France)	• Levi Strauss & Co. (USA)	• Siemens AG (Germany)
• Akzo Nobel nv (The Netherlands)	• Cool House (Thailand)	• Metito Ltd (United Arab Emirates)	• Stora Enso (Finland)
• Allergan, Inc. (USA)	• Daegu Bank (Republic of Korea)	• Molson Coors Brewing Company (USA)	• SUEZ (France)
• Aluminum Corporation of China (China)	• De Beers (South Africa)	• Nalco Holding Company (USA)	• SunOpta Inc. (Canada)
• Anheuser-Busch InBev (Belgium)	• Diageo plc (UK)	• Nestlé S.A. (Switzerland)	• Sustainable Living Fabrics (Australia)
• Athens Water and Sewerage Company - EYDAP S.A. (Greece)	• Dow Chemical Company (USA)	• Netafim (Israel)	• Syngenta International AG (Switzerland)
• Avon Metals Ltd (UK)	• DSM NV (The Netherlands)	• Nike, Inc. (USA)	• Talal Abu-Ghazaleh Organization (Egypt)
• Banco do Brasil (Brazil)	• Euro Mec S.r.l. (Italy)	• PepsiCo, Inc. (USA)	• The Coca-Cola Company (USA)
• Banesto Bank (Spain)	• Finlay International (Bangladesh)	• PricewaterhouseCoopers (USA)	• Unified Technologies Group, Inc. (USA)
• Baosteel Group Corporation (China)	• Firmenich SA (Switzerland)	• Progressive Asset Management (USA)	• Unilever (UK)
• Bayer AG (Germany)	• GlaxoSmithKline plc (UK)	• Ranhill Berhad (Malaysia)	• UPM-Kymmene Corporation (Finland)
• Cadbury (UK)	• Groupe DANONE (France)	• Reed Elsevier (UK)	• Veolia Water.(France)
• Calvert Asset Management Company, Inc. (USA)	• Grupo Via Delphi (Mexico)	• Royal Dutch Shell plc (The Netherlands)	• Westpac Banking Corporation (Australia)
• Carlsberg Group (Denmark)	• H&M Hennes & Mauritz (Sweden)	• Royal Philips Electronics N.V. (The Netherlands)	• Wilmar International Limited (Singapore)
• CH2M HILL, Inc. (USA)	• Hayleys Limited (Sri Lanka)	• SABMiller (South Africa)	• Woongjin Coway Co., Ltd (Republic of Korea)
• Coca-Cola Enterprises Inc. (USA)	• Heineken NV (The Netherlands)	• SAM Group (Switzerland)	• Xstrata PLC (Switzerland)
• Coca-Cola Hellenic Bottling Company (Greece)	• Hindustan Construction Co. (India)	• Sasol Ltd. (South Africa)	
	• Hong Kong Beijing Air Catering (China)	• SEKEM Holding (Egypt)	

Source: **www.unglobalcompact.org**

Figure 7.1 The CEO Water Mandate—Signatories.

Also inspired by the 2008 water discussions at Davos-Klosters were McKinsey & Company, who then started the development of new analytics to help government and business better understand the water challenge through 2030. McKinsey reached out to others and later in 2008 formed the 2030 Water Resources Group (WRG) with the objective of contributing new insights to the increasingly critical issue of water resource scarcity. Initial members of the WRG included the Barilla Group, the Coca-Cola Company, Nestlé SA, New Holland Agriculture, SABMiller, Standard Chartered Bank, and Syngenta. Veolia Environment and Firmenich later joined the group, and Halcrow Group acted as an adviser. The WRG produced their first report in October 2009, titled *Charting Our Water Future: Economic Frameworks to Inform Decision-Making*. Using case studies, the report's methodology identified supply- and demand-side measures that could constitute a more cost-effective approach to closing the water gap and achieving savings. Chapter 10 of this book provides more detail on this analytical methodology and its potential.

The World Business Council for Sustainable Development (WBCSD) has been working on water issues for more than ten years, much longer than some of these more recent initiatives.[3] In this time it has produced an important series of facts and trends on water for business and a set of water scenarios through 2025. One of its key outputs has been the extremely successful Global Water Risk Mapping Tool, which is detailed at the end of this chapter. In 2010, WBCSD has just begun a major new water programme, the Water Programme Leadership Group, which consists of Accenture, BASF, Bayer CropScience, Borealis, DSM, DuPont, Holcim, IBM, ITT, Kimberly-Clark, PepsiCo, PricewaterhouseCoopers, Rio Tinto, Royal Dutch Shell, Siemens, Suncor Energy, Swarovski, and Unilever.

A suite of other reports from business and financial analysts on water security and the risks it poses to business and investors has also emerged since 2008. Some notable examples that focus on the business implications of water security include the following:

- *Watching Water: A Guide to Evaluating Corporate Risks in a Thirsty World,* released by JPMorgan Global Equity Research in March 2008, with support from the World Resources Institute (WRI). In this report, JPMorgan equity analysts, with help from the expertise of WRI, lay out the water-related risks and opportunities they see facing companies in specific sectors, and they provide criteria for examining these issues. Their main points include the following:
  - Exposure to water scarcity and pollution is not limited to on-site production processes and may actually be greater in companies' supply chains than in their own operations.
  - Power generation, mining, semiconductor manufacturing, and food and beverage sectors are particularly exposed to water-related risk.
  - Corporate disclosure of water-related risks is seriously inadequate and is typically included in environmental statements prepared for public relations purposes, rather than in the regulator filings on which most investors rely.
  - They recommend that investors assess the reliance of their portfolios on water resources and their vulnerability to problems of water availability and pollution.

- *Understanding Water Risks: A Primer on the Consequences of Water Scarcity for Government and Business,* released by WWF International, March 2009. Some of the key messages this report contains include the following:
  - Water scarcity risks can be classified in terms of insufficient water to meet basic needs and in terms of the consequences that arise from this situation, such as political and business instability or lost economic opportunities.

- Water scarcity normally arises due to a complex interaction of social, economic, and environmental factors. It is seldom the product solely of a lack of precipitation.
- Companies will come under greater pressure to reduce water use and increase efficiency. Where such actions are not enough to guarantee a social license to operate, the company may need to become involved in supporting better water policy for all users.
- Risk from water scarcity is often shared between government and business; consequently, the need for better public policy, stronger institutions, and broad stakeholder engagement can be shared principles between business and government.
- Ultimately, government is always responsible for putting better water management in place, but businesses have a key role to play in helping to implement better management.
- Healthy ecosystems underpin sustainable water use. A key step in reducing water scarcity risks is to understand freshwater ecosystems better, ensuring that the basic water needs of people and ecosystems are met first and foremost, and then ensuring that remaining water is allocated for economic use on a rational, equitable, and transparent basis.

- *Global Water Scarcity: Risks and Challenges for Business*, released by Lloyd's in association with World Wide Fund for Nature (WWF) as part of their 360 Risk Insight series, 2010. This report identifies the following key issue areas:
  - Business needs to consider how governments and the international community will manage water scarcity over the medium to long term. How can business work with the public and nongovernmental sector, not simply to influence the debate but also to broker solutions?
  - Different types of business face different threat levels. Agriculture or beverages face a direct challenge in identifying sufficient and reliable water sources. Manufacturers need water for their operations but can be viewed by governments as a lower priority. Some retailers are investigating the sustainability and ethics of how their suppliers use water, in part to combat possible reputational damage. And some parts of the financial services sector are looking at how their clients are managing their water risks.
  - Companies working on water management strategies need to look at very local issues, as well as the implications for the wider basin. They also need to consider strategies for engaging with national

governments, or even in some cases international initiatives on corporate best practices around water.

- Tools and approaches that can help companies understand and manage their water-related risks are important. These include methods developed by the Water Footprint Network and the World Business Council for Sustainable Development; forums for the development of water stewardship standards, potentially leading to some kind of certification scheme (such as that being developed by the Alliance for Water Stewardship); and forums within which companies can exchange best practices and address shared risk issues (such as the World Economic Forum or the UN Global Compact CEO Water Mandate).

- A number of NGOs and think tanks are beginning to partner with companies to address risks that also affect the environment and local communities, including WWF, the Nature Conservancy, and the Pacific Institute.

Another notable and recent development in the business-water nexus is the CDP Water Disclosure project, which began in 2010.[4] CDP Water Disclosure plans to provide critical water-related data from the world's largest corporations to inform the global marketplace on investment risk and commercial opportunity with regard to business and water issues. To do this, CDP Water Disclosure will request information on the risks and opportunities companies face in relation to water; on water use and exposure to water stress in companies' own operations and in their supply chains; and on companies' water management plans and governance. The aim is for this data to provide valuable insight into the strategies deployed by many of the largest companies in the world on water, and for it to be used to help drive investment towards sustainable water use. The lead sponsor for the CDP Water Disclosure project is Molson Coors, with Norges Bank Investment Management and IRBARIS also sponsoring the work. The Ford Motor Company, L'Oreal, PepsiCo, and Reed Elsevier demonstrated their leadership on transparency around water, according to CDP, by committing to report to CDP Water Disclosure in 2010.

Across all these various business-related activities in water (and for the many more that are not mentioned here), some common themes emerge. A leading group of business chiefs are becoming much more aware of the exposure to the water security risks they face (note how many of the same multinational companies are involved in several of the activities listed above). They are deploying tools and techniques to identify, measure, and manage these risks. Investors, too, are becoming interested in how the businesses they invest in are addressing their exposure to water risk. But the various reports and initiatives all stress that the water problem is complex—that it is both a local and a global issue for a multinational business.

Keith Weed, Unilever's Chief Marketing, Communications, and Sustainability Officer, provides an interesting perspective: "Unilever's water strategy reduces total water use across the entire value chain. By working with farmers on drip irrigation and water harvesting technologies, we have reduced water in our own manufacturing by 65% in the past 10 years. Innovative R&D which designs products that require less water when used by the consumer can also save them time and money as well as positively impacting the environmental. We're also rolling out Pureit, our sustainable water filtration system that eliminates all bacteria, viruses, parasites, and cysts without needing electricity or pressurized water, making safe drinking water available to millions."[5]

It seems that many of the structural answers to improved water management lie well beyond the limits of any one company's own influence. Multi-company partnerships with governments and other agencies therefore become important if the business is truly to help take a lead in the water reform agenda. Consequently, and aside from the issue of more formalized water risk disclosure for investors, the issue of public-private partnerships (PPP) is an emergent theme that permeates many of the most recent business and water reports. This is particularly the case when forward-thinking water strategies for large corporations to engage in are being recommended. Importantly, these partnerships are not the same sort of public-private partnership that became popular in the 1990s in the water sector, whereby a private firm works on a water service delivery contract for a public-sector utility. Instead, these new forms of PPP seem to engender more of a sense of partnership at the strategic level between multiple private sector, civil society, and government players—an action dialogue, if you will, to help key stakeholders share thoughts on how best to tackle a common resource problem facing them all, and which is ultimately the responsibility of the host government to create a framework for. Yet, at the moment, these ideas seem rather theoretical. There is less information available to business leaders on how to actually develop and engage in the sorts of multi-company activities being broadly described, or what such partnerships might look like, or indeed what they could realistically set out to achieve. There are not too many significant case studies out there to learn from, yet much of the analysis on offer points towards the fact that logic dictates these are the sorts of activity that will be required once a critical mass of companies choose to go beyond their fence or immediate value chain, in terms of developing a robust water management strategy for a given country or region. This, then, is where the business and water agenda seems to be for those companies most exposed to water-related risks.

At the same time, for those businesses engaged in providing water supply and wastewater services, or associated goods and services, business seems to be blossoming. Water funds (which invest in a range of technology and engineering companies with a focus on the water space) are suggested by analysts to be good long-run picks (see the following chapter on finance).

Quoted recently in the *Wall Street Journal* for Europe, Jean-Louis Chaussade, CEO of Suez Environnement (the world's second largest water utility by revenue, supplying up to ninety million people around the world with drinking water), noted that "waste and water businesses typically expand about two to three percentage points above a country's growth in gross domestic product," which is why he targets China as such an important market for his business. "What's more," he adds, "after years of rapid industrialization the Chinese are more concerned about the quality of their environment."[6]

Forecast

For those companies with risk exposure to water, the type and range of business-related activities in the water agenda listed above will grow over the next several years, especially among those companies in the power generation, mining, semiconductor manufacturing, and food and beverage sectors. As well as being a sound risk management strategy, there is an element of tangibility, both in terms of local impact and in terms of visible results, for these companies in addressing water use and water management issues. This differentiates the water agenda from the climate change agenda, and will likely engender increasing levels of business engagement.

The increasing level of investor interest in business exposure to water risk is interesting, too. CDP has put the issue of business' "water disclosure" on par with their breakthrough "carbon disclosure" work, recognizing the concern that increasing water security issues around the world is giving to company shareholders, especially institutional investors. This is a material issue, said the CDP Water Disclosure leader, Marcus Norton: "It matters because long-term investors in particular see that water scarcity is going to impact companies' operations and supply chains."[7]

According to the *New York Times*, Norges Bank Investment Management in Oslo (a sponsor of the CDP Water Project) has identified 1,100 companies in its portfolio facing water risks. Anne Kvam, the global head of ownership strategies for NBIM, which manages $US 441 billion, said in the interview, "As investors, we need to know if companies are in industry sectors or regions where water supplies are scarce and how they are managing those supplies. It's a challenging thing to get good information about water management."[8]

For those active in the water supply, wastewater, wastewater reuse, and desalination business, the market will continue to expand, especially across Asia. Challenges will be less related to business opportunity and more to project financing issues, given the softness that still exists in international and many domestic capital markets.

From the viewpoint of a CEO with operations in a water-stressed country, if water security issues within a particular country of operation do not improve there will be mounting financial losses across the value chain—loss of revenue due to the disruption of production process or higher input costs from a tightening of the water supply. A first reaction may be to find platforms that enable the company to work alongside others to help support the government in water reform processes.

But if no reform agenda is forthcoming, and pressure from investors on exposure to water risk mounts, then multinational companies could start to relocate en masse from poorly managed countries (in terms of water resources) to better managed countries. A broad analogue could be a similarity to the situation in the last twenty years where lower wages in emerging countries such as China and India made them much more attractive locations for manufacturing.

Conversely, which provinces in China, which states in India, and which countries in Asia will see the market gap first and position themselves through forward-thinking reform agendas to become blue leaders, attracting the most water-efficient investors and technology pioneers into their clean and well-serviced "blue development zones"?

Implications

Corporate executives and investors will become smarter about water risks. They are already starting to share more knowledge and develop new tools to benchmark public and private performance on water efficiency while putting pressure on governments to reform.

From a government perspective in this equation, it becomes more likely that stable economies with clear economic instruments to manage the potential national or regional water challenge will attract investment; unstable, water-stressed nations with poor policy frameworks and haphazard planning for water stress will experience disinvestment. Indeed, the issue of water management could tip the scale between competing risks when it comes to business or investor engagement with many countries over the next two decades. Blue-green development zones (water and energy efficient development regions) could emerge as attractive locations for international companies and investors, especially across Asia where water and wastewater challenges in urban areas are becoming more acute.

This suggests an important implication in relation to governments and water policy, especially for those nations facing water security issues. It seems that those governments and regions in water-scarce areas who take a lead in progressive water policy reform will likely enjoy an economic triple win: they will retain and attract companies; they will attract more inward investment into their water infrastructure; and their economy will be strengthened as a result of improved water management. While laggards will lose, which country in Asia will position itself for business as the first Turquoise Tiger?

The Way Forward

"Leading businesses have put in place water strategies with challenging efficiency targets," says Graham Mackay, Chief Executive, SABMiller. "However, water scarcity is a complex issue and acting alone is not enough. That's why we are working with NGOs and other stakeholders to gain improved insight into local water resource risks and developing new partnership models to provide solutions."[9] There is a network of CEOs, senior executives, and content professionals across a group of multinational companies, mostly from those sectors with greatest exposure to water risk, who are now at work ensuring that not only do their own companies keep ahead of the curve on the water security agenda, but that they are also helping to lead the wider agenda on water. They engage in specific internal corporate activities to improve performance, they strike particular partnerships to get things done, and they also engage in multiple platforms and activities, often with one another, including many of those initiatives mentioned above, so as to keep abreast of and influence the wider water agenda. Some standout members of this leading multinational business group include (but of course are not limited to) those listed in the appendix to this chapter, which also provides some examples of their various activities in the water space.

Although they come from different sectors of the economy, each of these companies has undertaken investigations or has developed longer-term strategies to not only anticipate water security risks, but also to turn them into core business opportunities where possible. They are investing in water efficiency. By using water footprinting methodologies and tools from organizations like the World Business Council for Sustainable Development, many of them are developing a comprehensive understanding of where their water comes from and how best they can ensure a reliable and sustainable supply. Through engaging in platforms such as the CEO Water Mandate, they work to mitigate their future water risks through transparent, ongoing dialogue with UN agencies, governments, communities, and other key stakeholders. Through their investment to develop new analytics such as those of the Water Resources Group, some of them are creating new insights into the economic frameworks required for decision-making. And by engaging with governments in new forms of coalition building and public-private collaboration on water through the work of the World Economic Forum, they are now engaging in the practical business of supporting, nurturing, and assisting governments to undertake meaningful water reform and transformation processes to benefit all stakeholders in society, as well as the environment.

Perspectives

The following personal perspectives amplify the main themes touched on by this chapter. They help to illustrate the range of current viewpoints from the business community on the water-business nexus. The views expressed do not necessarily represent those of the World Economic Forum, nor do they necessarily represent the views of the other individual contributors or the various contributing companies or institutions.

- The World Business Council for Sustainable Development provides an overview of their hugely successful Global Water Tool.
- Graham Mackay, Chief Executive, SABMiller, explains why understanding and managing water in the value chain is of such importance to a company like his and others.
- Jeff Seabright, Vice-President of Environment and Water Resources, The Coca-Cola Company, explains why water resource management and sustainability is of such importance to Coca-Cola.

Global Water Tool

WORLD BUSINESS COUNCIL FOR SUSTAINABLE DEVELOPMENT

When multinational companies want to make water-informed decisions, the first step is to ask the right five questions:

1. How many of your sites are in extremely water-scarce areas?
2. Where are those at greatest risk now?
3. When will the others cross the threshold of scarcity?
4. Who of your employees lives in countries that lack access to improved water and sanitation?
5. Which of your suppliers are now constrained by water, or might be in 2025?

The Global Water Tool provides the answers to these questions. It helps companies and organizations map their water use and assess levels of corporate risk across their global operations and supply chains.

A company needs water for its own operations, employees, and supply chain, and ultimately its customers. In order to manage risk related to global water issues now and in the future, companies have to understand their water needs in relation to local externalities such as: water availability (current and projected), water quality, water "stress" (relating to people, environment, and agriculture), access to safe drinking water sources and sanitation, as well as population and industrial growth. To manage your water globally, you need to understand the water situation locally—which is increasingly unpredictable as climate change unfolds.

The tool is easy to use. It can compare a company's water uses with external data, or create key water indicators, inventories, and risk and performance metrics. A company may use it to establish relative water risks in its own portfolio to prioritize action, or to view its facilities spatially through Google Earth, with detailed geographic information, including surface water. The Global Reporting Initiative (GRI) Indicators on total water withdrawals, water recycled/reused, and total water discharge are calculated for each site, country, region, and in total. The GRI has endorsed the use of the Global Water Tool as a method for compiling this information.

The tool's external water data sets provide recent and globally credible coverage in the public domain. But because the tool is limited by the poor quality of local background water data sets, it does not aim to provide specific guidance on specific situations; these require more in-depth, systematic analysis. Other tools may be more targeted towards this outcome, such as the Global Environmental Management Initiative Water Sustainability Planner.

The Global Water Tool's rate of uptake is increasing, and more than three hundred companies now use it to measure their water use, mitigate their effect, and communicate their performance. The tool's Excel file had been downloaded more than 8,300 times since its launch in August 2007. Anyone can access the tool for free at http://www.wbscd.org/web/watertool.htm. There is no need to register to use it, and the information input into the tool is saved on the company's own IT system and cannot be accessed by outside parties. The WBCSD regularly revises the tool as new data become available.

Water in the Value Chain

Graham Mackay, Chief Executive, SABMiller plc

Since all markets depend on freshwater, growing scarcity will constrain economic growth, inhibit job creation, constrict trade, and may even spark mass migration. Yet most countries do not prioritize water management; even fewer properly value, conserve, and govern their precious liquid assets. If governments don't sense the widespread risks of water scarcity, the private sector certainly does—and some sectors are undoubtedly more exposed than others.

As a founding signatory of the United Nations CEO Water Mandate, SABMiller recognizes our responsibility to promote responsible water use throughout our operations, and to encourage our suppliers to do the same. The brewing industry relies on water-intensive raw materials, and because several of our operations are in water-stressed regions, the scarcity of water—and its quality—are increasingly critical business issues for us.

In response to these urgent pressures, in November 2008 SABMiller announced plans to cut the amount of water used per hectoliter of beer produced to an average of 3.5 hectoliters by 2015—a 25% reduction from 2008. This target boosts efficiency of water use within breweries, an important first step. Arguably more important is to understand and evaluate the way water is used throughout the value chain.

Working with WWF, SABMiller has pioneered the use of "water footprinting" as a tool to understand where future water risk lies in the value chain, and then identify potential hot spots where partners can reduce this risk. Transparency is critical. In 2009, SABMiller and WWF together published the water footprints of its beers in South Africa and the Czech Republic, along with insights into the specific risks identified in these markets. In both cases, agricultural water use accounts for more than 95% of the total footprint. By using the same approach, we are exploring the risk of long-term water scarcity in Peru, Tanzania, Ukraine, and other markets.

Water issues are by nature cross-community and cross-boundary, and therefore cannot be managed simply within the fence lines of our own brewing operations. Rather, they must be tackled as part of a broader approach, working in partnership with local stakeholders. Shared responsibility for water also means sharing the exposure to risks among all those who depend on a particular watershed for their sustenance, livelihoods, and growth. These risks can include both direct scarcity of supply, and also decline in quality due to overabstraction or pollution. By engaging in local dialogues on water issues, we contribute to public policy discussions and help ensure that governments do manage water resources as efficiently, sustainably, and transparently as their private-sector partners.

What's next? The findings of the water footprinting exercise led SAB Ltd in South Africa towards ways to include water efficiency in barley farming, to better understand the risk of climate change on water availability, and to better see how this may affect crop growth in the future. In addition, we are reviewing how legislative risks may affect its crop-growing areas, with particular reference to groundwater, nitrate limits, and engaging with suppliers in the process. In September 2010, we published the first report of the Water Futures partnership, a new collaboration with WWF and GTZ (German Society for Technical Cooperation) to understand and manage the shared risks faced by businesses, communities, and ecology in some of our most water-scarce markets.

The complex challenges surrounding water will only grow. Companies must not only do what is necessary in our own operations, but also engage outside our traditional, fenced-in comfort zone to ensure the long-term viability of this critical resource.

Water Resource Management and Sustainability

JEFF SEABRIGHT, VICE-PRESIDENT, ENVIRONMENT AND WATER RESOURCES, THE COCA-COLA COMPANY

Water is critical to business for The Coca-Cola Company and our bottling partners, not only as a direct ingredient in our products, but also in our manufacturing processes and as an ingredient vital to the sustainability of much of our supply chain (e.g., juices, teas, nutritive sweeteners). Water also is a fundamental resource for sustainable communities as well as the ecosystems we all rely on. Our business thrives in sustainable communities, and we therefore recognize that our stewardship of water is a critical priority.

Throughout our 124-year history, the quality of the water we use has been paramount. In some one thousand production plants in more than two hundred countries and territories, we source water from the surrounding environment and serve the local market. Our employees, customers, and consumers also are colocated, as are many of our business partners and suppliers. With increasing stressors on water, we realized we needed to understand water in its totality.

The past decade can be viewed as a seminal period in our history and our relationship with water. By the early 1990s, we had already matured beyond a focus solely on water quality; we had begun to incorporate water efficiency and wastewater management into our operations. We began tracking system-wide water use and efficiency in the mid-1990s and, over time, harvested better management practices to drive improvements. From 2004 through 2008, we improved water efficiency by 9%; since 2002, our efficiency has improved by more than 22%. In 2008, we announced a public goal to further improve water efficiency in our plants by 20% by 2012, compared to a base year of 2004. Along the way, we codeveloped with our water conservation partner, WWF, a world-class tool to help operations learn from others in our system and within our peer industry group.

Realizing the potentially negative ecological impacts of discharging untreated industrial wastewater, in 1992 we issued requirements for processing wastewater. Global operations are given the choice of discharge to municipal systems that have fully functioning secondary treatment capability, or building a treatment plant on-site; both options are to treat the water to "fish life quality" standards prior to discharge into the environment. By the end of 2010, 100% of operations will treat all wastewater from production-related operations to a standard capable of supporting aquatic life and return that water back to the environment. It is important to note that we are requiring our plants to treat their wastewater as described above even where applicable law or custom does not require such treatment; with 70% of global, industrial wastewater untreated, we believe this is a strong demonstration of our dedication to water stewardship.

A key turning point in our evolution on water stewardship came in 2003, when we first cited water quality and quantity as a material risk to our business in our Form 10-K, which is required for publicly traded companies by the US Securities and Exchange Commission. In the atmosphere of growing awareness of global water challenges, we began the process of educating ourselves on how the global water challenge affected our business. We formed relationships with leaders across government, civil society, academia, and conservation to evaluate water risks to our business and the markets of which we are a part. This work culminated, in part, in a qualitative risk assessment at the regional level, which verified these issues were real and growing. This process also sensitized our system and unleashed a latent desire to expand our stewardship of water.

Building on the engagement with our business system in understanding these issues, in 2005 we executed a plant-level, comprehensive, quantitative water risk assessment to quantify the many water risks we face and to inform strategic responses across six categories: efficiency, compliance, watersheds, supply reliability, the social context, and supply economics. This data-driven, bottom-up approach was married to a top-down stewardship commitment from senior management across our system. Armed with this understanding, we developed an integrated water strategy that has been activated across our global operations.

Outside our plants, we are committed to engaging with local communities, governments, and NGOs in protecting watersheds and enabling access to safe water and sanitation for communities in need. Partnering with communities and stakeholder organizations to improve water stewardship is sound business practice for us as well as good corporate citizenship. Our goal in communities is to balance the water used in our finished beverage products through projects in watershed conservation, reforestation, and community water and sanitation access. We have more than 210 projects in sixty countries that, when all are fully implemented, will help conserve watersheds and provide safe drinking water to more than two million people.

To build on these existing water stewardship initiatives, we are putting additional guidelines in place to ensure that Coca-Cola bottling plants take a rights-based approach to water for the siting of new plants and the operation of existing plants. We are requiring our global bottling system's management to consider the following:

- Has the plant engaged in routine community and stakeholder engagement in order to understand the water needs and challenges of the local community and environment?
- Will the plant's use of water limit the availability or quality of sufficient water for the people in the local community? If yes, what mitigation steps will be taken, in consultation with community stakeholders?
- Is the plant adjusting its operations to effectively address identified issues?

We also require each plant to map the source of water it shares with the surrounding community and environment, assess vulnerabilities to the quality and quantity of that water, and then work with local communities and the relevant government agencies to develop and implement a source water protection plan.

We see two critical areas that will define our future maturity on water. The first is a continuation and acceleration of the capacity building for our system and partners. This will include new and expanded tools and training coupled with a new analysis of measuring the benefits of such support. The second is the translation of effective water stewardship into our supply chain, especially our agricultural ingredient supplies.

We believe that water resources can be managed effectively to support sustainable agricultural, industrial, environmental, and community uses. But no single group can solve this challenge. To drive meaningful progress on water, public-private alliances are needed along with more effective government investment and many other efforts. Our mutual capacity for cooperation will serve as a critical litmus test for effective water management around the globe. We look forward to working with all organizations—public and private—in helping make progress on this critical issue.

Appendix: A Snapshot of Business Water Leadership

CH2M HILL

The company devotes a section in their sustainability report to water and runs a blog/Facebook site on the topic: "As a leader in the industry and one of the first engineering and construction companies to publish a sustainability report in 2005, CH2M HILL continues a tradition of excellence and transparency in reporting on internal operations related to sustainability. Our goal is to both manage the impacts of our own operations and apply our company's portfolio of services to help our clients' organizations become more sustainable—whether dealing in master planning, land use, programme management, water, wastewater, environmental work, energy, transportation, industrial systems, ecosystems, or waste management."[10]

Cisco Systems, Inc.

The company devotes a section in their 2009 sustainability report to water.[11]
   Climate change, increasing global population, and polluting human practices underscore the reality that water is a precious and limited resource. With headquarter offices in drought-prone northern California, Cisco has always been conscientious about water use in their operations.
   Key objectives of Cisco's water management program are to:

- Identify and respond to site-level water conservation opportunities for our operations
- Work with partners such as local governments, water utilities, and owners of our leased buildings to pursue and replicate best practices in our operations and beyond.

Program highlights are as follow:

- In FY09 we began to lay the groundwork for the development of a Global Water Management System. Water use is currently tracked by some campuses, with each local site owning its information. Using our GHG emissions tracking system as a model, we are developing a robust and standardized reporting system for collecting water data, measuring impacts, and designing a global water strategy.
- In FY09, Cisco selected eleven of our largest sites, representing 61 percent of employees, for a study of water usages and local water availability. Total water consumption for the sites in FY09 was 1,654,030 m^3 and reflected an increase over FY08 due to expansion of Cisco's San Jose campus.

- Cisco landscaping was a focus area for reducing water consumption in FY09. Key activities at our San Jose campus included using recycled water, installing irrigation controls, changing groundcover, and taking fountains offline or converting them to landscaped beds with California native and drought-resistant plants.
- Cisco proactively mitigates impacts in water-scarce areas by incorporating resource constraints into our local office building and data center development plans.

The Coca-Cola Company

An important recent document is *Product Water Footprint Assessments: Practical Application in Corporate Water Stewardship*, published in collaboration with the Nature Conservancy in September 2010. This report contains details pilot studies that were conducted on Coca-Cola products and ingredients. The Company and the Conservancy found that the largest portion of the product water footprints comes from the field, not the factory.

Another key recent report is *A Transformative Partnership to Conserve Water: Annual Review, 2009*:

When it comes to big issues such as safeguarding our global water supply, no individual sector—government, NGO, or business—can make as big a difference alone as we can make by working together. For this reason, we have embarked on a transformative partnership with WWF to conserve freshwater resources around the world. Our work together focuses on five goals:

1. Conserve seven of the world's most important freshwater basins
2. Improve water efficiency within the company's operations
3. Reduce the company's carbon emissions
4. Promote sustainable agriculture
5. Inspire a global movement to conserve water

In 2009, our partnership achieved significant progress and notable success in each of these areas. This report summarizes our accomplishments over the last year, outlined by goal."[12]

The Dow Chemical Company

As a world leader in chemistry, Dow is combining the creativity of its employees with its technological expertise to provide innovative solutions to help supply cleaner and safer water to those in need—breakthroughs like lower cost desalination technologies, more effective ultra filtration systems, materials to improve the sustainability of water infrastructure, sustainable business models for small community water systems, and innovative ways to increase awareness of the issue, starting with the Blue Planet Run.

Dow will lead the charge in helping to address the global water crisis by setting the standard for sustainable water use and management. Through the application of innovative chemistry, Dow is committed to ensuring greater access to water by addressing challenges including fresh water scarcity and inefficient water use for irrigation. Dow will develop innovative technologies and business models that lower the cost of water purification, set new levels for efficient water use at Dow's manufacturing facilities, and use creative partnerships to increase the global sense of urgency to solve this problem.[13]

Halcrow Group

Halcrow is major contributor to the Engineering the Future Alliance's 2010 report *Global Water Security: An Engineering Perspective*. According to Halcrow's website:

> The report is the culmination of six months' research into the worldwide issues of increasing water scarcity. It concludes that the security of the world's water resources is under severe pressure from many sources—a world population explosion, rapid shifts of people from rural to urban areas, the impact of dietary change as countries develop, increasing pollution of water resources, the over-abstraction of groundwater, and the not insignificant issues created by climate change. Key recommendations include that the global water sector needs to have an integrated water resource management and sustainability policy at its core; that the World Trade Organization should address water security issue in its strategy; and that water security should become a core component of UK policy-making—with government assessing the interrelationship between water, food and energy security in United Kingdom, with a view to achieving an optimal balance of aligned national policy.[14]

Halcrow became a member of the UN Global Compact CEO Water Mandate in 2010. As one of the leading global water engineering companies, Halcrow is meeting many engineering challenges associated with water scarcity in many countries, including the United States, Chile, Argentina, Jordan, UK, UAE, India, Philippines and Australia.

Hindustan Construction Company (HCC)

HCC contributed to the Leadership Group on Water Security in Asia's 2009 report *Asia's Next Challenge: Securing the Region's Water Future*. As detailed in HCC's *CEO Water Mandate* report:

> In April 2009, as a member of The Leadership Group on Water Security in Asia, Mr. Ajit Gulabchand Chairman [of HCC] put forth the concept of the private sector and governments partnering in developing the "Water Infrastructure Preparedness Index." The Leadership Group arrived at recommendations for the relevant policy-making processes to ensure adequate public and political support for water security in Asia. . . . HCC has taken up projects with a focus on water management, sanitation, and solid waste management to promote economical use of water, improved sanitation, and garbage disposal systems in rural areas. The Company has also become the only Indian signatory member of the UN Global Compact's CEO Water Mandate, a special initiative of the UN Global Compact, which recognizes the twin problems of water availability and sanitation that tend to pose a range of challenges and risks.[15]

Nestlé

Water is not a new concern for the Nestlé Group—the first wastewater treatment plant in our factories dates from the early 1930s. Today, water is our key environmental priority and effective water management is a core focus area of Creating Shared Value. We have been taking a leading role in the 2030 Water Resources Group—in a perspective of Corporate Global Citizenship—and we are among the first signatories of the UN Global Compact CEO Water Mandate. Our Water Resources Review monitors and manages local water criteria, such as quantity and quality and regulatory compliance. This, along with rigorous management, has helped us to reduce water withdrawals by 3.2 percent to 143 million m³ of water or 3.47 m³ per tonne of product in 2009. This equates to a 33 percent reduction since 2000, while our production volume increased by 63 percent. Our goal is to improve water efficiency by a further 10–15 percent over the next five years.[16]

PepsiCo

A key recent water document for PepsiCo is *Water Stewardship: Good for Business. Good for Society*, released in September 2010:

> As this report makes clear, many in the public and private sectors recognize the seriousness of the global water crisis and are taking steps to address it. This report

also emphasizes the enormity of the task ahead. Much work remains to be done, and only an ongoing, productive partnership between governments, NGOs, businesses, and other stakeholders will ensure significant progress. PepsiCo has come a long way over the last decade, by partnering with numerous global and local organizations to help solve this problem in ways large and small; by constantly looking within its operations to identify solutions to make it a more water-efficient company; and then reaching out into our value chain by seeking ways to help our business, suppliers, and community partners find ways to use less water more effectively.[17] A recent PepsiCo supported audio podcast on sustainable water practices for a global corporation can be found at http://sic.conversationsnetwork .org/shows/detail4551.html.

Rio Tinto

A key report for Rio Tinto is *Rio Tinto and Water*, released in April 2009:

> This booklet provides information about Rio Tinto's water strategy and the programmes and tools that our businesses have implemented to help manage water responsibly. . . . Companies, including Rio Tinto, cannot afford to regard water as an inexpensive commodity; rather it is a shared resource and we must collaborate to ensure society uses it to the greatest benefit. In the past, we focused on managing the operational impacts of our water use on the environment. Since 2005, we have adopted a more strategic approach that accounts for the social, environmental, and economic aspects of water management. Such an approach requires us to research and adopt the best water management practices, to engage with others on sustainable water management, and to understand better the value of water in our business decisions. Tough economic times reinforce the need to recognize there is a cost to using water. Beyond the broader social and environmental benefits of conserving our water resources, it makes good business sense not to waste water and to reduce our water use.[18]

SABMiller

A recent important document for SABMiller was *Water Footprinting: Identifying and Addressing Water Risks in the Water Value Chain*, released 2009: "The report provides a detailed insight into the learning of WWF and SABMiller, who worked together with consultancy URS Corporation to undertake water footprints of the beer value chain in South Africa and the Czech Republic. It discusses what the water footprint results in both countries mean for SAB-Miller's businesses and their action plans in response to the findings. This study looks beyond the basic water footprint numbers and considers where the resource is used and the context of its use—in particular by considering water use for different agricultural crops in the context of specific water catchments."[19]

A more recent document is *Water Futures: Working Together for a Secure Water Future*, released in September 2010 in partnership with the WWF. According to the *Environmental Leader* website:

> The report, "Water Futures," which mapped water footprints in Peru, Tanzania, Ukraine, and South Africa, identifies the critical water challenges in each country and how they impact SABMiller's operations. A key finding of the report shows that the largest part of SABMiller's water footprint is from crop cultivation. In each country, more than 90 percent of water used in the production of SABMiller's brands relates to the cultivation of the raw materials such as hops and barley. However, the water used in agriculture varies from around 150 liters per liter of beer in South Africa to 55 liters in Peru.[20]

On the SABMiller website, Head of Sustainable Development Andy Wales explains, "Water footprinting enables SABMiller to understand which parts of our supply chain might face water scarcity, or poor water quality, in the future, and means that we can plan now to deal with these future challenges."[21]

Standard Chartered Bank

A key water document for Standard Chartered Bank is *Water: The Real Liquidity Crisis*, released in March 2009: "Freshwater is fundamental to human life and economic growth. Parts of Asia, Africa, and the Middle East face particularly acute water shortages. Population growth, economic development, pollution, and climate change are all exacerbating the problems. Solutions require investment, economic return, and political will. The current economic turmoil and fiscal stimulus provide a great opportunity to tackle those water-related problems."[22]

Syngenta

The Syngenta website has a specific section devoted to water called "The High Stakes for Water": "Syngenta believes that agricultural policies will have to make water efficiency a priority if we are to manage water scarcity. Growers need incentives to implement better water management. They need infrastructure and financial support to explore innovative solutions that produce crops with greater water efficiency."[23] For Syngenta's latest work on "peak water," refer to the following: http://www2.syngenta.com/en/media/pdf/inthemedia/20101021-tefr-oct-nov-2010-peakwater.pdf.

Unilever

An important water document for Unilever is *Unilever and Sustainable Agriculture: Water*, released in 2009. According to the Unilever website, "Our latest water booklet showcases the expertise on water management that the Unilever Sustainable Agriculture team has built up through more than ten pilot projects in 15 countries since 1997. This includes working with suppliers and partners to use water more efficiently and protecting the quality of water resources."[24] According to the report, "For Unilever's food products, the majority of water use is upstream in the growing of agricultural raw materials. We also use water in the factories that process agricultural products and manufacture our products, and our consumers use water in the preparation and consumption of both food and home and personal care products. Unilever's future success will rely on the ability of many of the farmers that supply us to produce agricultural raw materials with higher water efficiency. Scarcity strengthens the business case for water efficiency just as rising oil prices mean companies need to become more energy-efficient."[25]

Notes

1. See "The CEO Water Mandate," http://www.unglobalcompact.org/issues/Environment/CEO_Water_Mandate/.

2. See "World Economic Forum Water Initiative," http://www.weforum.org/water/.

3. See "World Business Council for Sustainable Development," http://www.wbcsd.org/.

4. See "CDP [Carbon Disclosure Project] Water Disclosure," https://www.cdproject.net/water-disclosure.

5. Keith Weed, personal communication.

6. "Taking Hold of Liquid Assets, *Wall Street Journal*, European Edition, September 27, 2010, p. 10.

7. Todd Woody, "Nonprofit Group Will Prod Companies to Report Their Water Use," *New York Times*, April 6, 2010, http://www.nytimes.com/2010/04/07/business/energy-environment/07water.html.

8. Ibid.

9. World Economic Forum Water Initiative, *The Bubble Is Close to Bursting*, 2009.

10. CH2M HILL, *Sustainability Report, 2009*, 2009, http://www.ch2m.com/corporate/about_us/assets/Sustainability_Report_2009.pdf.

11. https://www.cisco.com/web/about/ac227/csr2009/the-environment/water-supplies/index.html.

12. The Coca-Cola Company and the World Wide Fund for Nature, *A Transformative Partnership to Conserve Water: Annual Review, 2009*, 2009, http://www.thecoca-colacompany.com/citizenship/pdf/partnership_2009_annual_review.pdf.

13. "Dow Sustainability: Dow's Commitment to Water," 2010, http://www.dow.com/commitments/goals/water.htm.

14. "Halcrow Experts Contribute to Global Water Security Report," April 2010, http://www.halcrow.com/News/Latest-news/Halcrow-experts-contribute-to-global-water-security-report/.

15. HCC, *The CEO Water Mandate*, 2009, http://www.unglobalcompact.org/docs/issues_doc/Environment/ceo_water_mandate/water_mandate_cops/Hindustan_Construction.pdf.

16. Nestlé Creating Shared Value Summary Report 2009. http://www.nestle.com/Resource.axd?Id=1BE93BE6-BFA1-4414-9C71-CFB246B55D22.

17. PepsiCo, *Water Stewardship: Good for Business. Good for Society*, 2010, http://www.pepsico.com/Download/PepsiCo_Water_Report_FNL.pdf.

18. Rio Tinto, *Rio Tinto and Water*, 2009, http://www.riotinto.com/documents/RTandWater.pdf.

19. SABMiller and World Wide Fund for Nature, *Water Footprinting: Identifying and Addressing Water Risks in the Water Value Chain*, 2009, http://assets.panda.org/downloads/sabmiller_water_footprinting_report_final_.pdf.

20. "Crop Cultivation Drinks Most of SABMiller's Water Use," *Environmental Leader*, September 13, 2010, http://www.environmentalleader.com/2010/09/13/crop-cultivation-drinks-most-of-sabmillers-water-use/.

21. "WWF and SABMiller Unveil Water Footprint of Beer," August 18, 2009, http://www.sabmiller.com/index.asp?pageid=149&newsid=1034.

22. Standard Chartered Bank, *Water: The Real Liquidity Crisis*, 2009, http://research.standardchartered.com/researchdocuments/Pages/ResearchArticle.aspx?&R=60899.

23. "The High Stakes for Water," 2010, http://www2.syngenta.com/en/grow-more-from-less/the-high-stakes-for-water.html.

24. "Water Use in Agriculture," 2010, http://www.unilever.com/sustainability/environment/water/agriculture/index.aspx.

25. Unilever, *Unilever and Sustainable Agriculture: Water*, 2009, http://www.unilever.com/images/sd_Unilever_and_Sustainable_Agriculture%20-%20Water_tcm13-179363.pdf.

CHAPTER 8

Finance

This chapter explores the water-finance nexus. It benefits greatly from the perspectives of many public, private, academic, and NGO representatives who have taken part in various Forum sessions and workshops on water issues over the last three years.

Background

Of all the sectors in the world economy, the one that might seem to have a negligible interdependence with water would be finance. In reality, the finance-water nexus is both old and intricate. To appreciate the inextricable linkages, consider just one pivotal example from two centuries ago.

For now, the dominant world currency is still the US dollar. The foundation for that currency's value was established by Alexander Hamilton, a widely acknowledged financial genius and pioneer of a strong federal monetary system. Less appreciated was Hamilton's role as a controlling investor in one of the United States' first water supply and sanitation companies, among the earliest pioneering public-private partnerships.

In 1799, New York City resembled most cities in today's developing world. It was a fast-growing metropolis on a mostly undeveloped island surrounded by saltwater. As disease spread and demand grew, a business proposition presented itself to Hamilton, who was then the US Treasury Secretary, and Aaron Burr, who was then Vice-President of the US. They saw an opportunity to corner a lucrative market in providing water for the new city, and as partners they formed a venture they called the Manhattan Water Company.

Burr and Hamilton gained the exclusive right to a water source and to divert it via aqueduct to the city's thirsty population. They arranged a "natural monopoly" by not allowing any competition and gaining rights to tap the water source into perpetuity. This enabled them to raise the up-front capital expenditure they required to develop a delivery infrastructure. They were allowed to reinvest profits as they saw fit.

Once up and running, they cut costs at every opportunity. With no competition, the company reaped considerable profits, and Burr leveraged the company equity, capital, and income into making further secured loans, with which he established an entirely new bank—now Chase Manhattan—to rival Hamilton's Bank of New York.[1]

Then, as now, water was a unique commodity with no substitute or alternative, with a high future demand and low price volatility. Given the challenge set out in the previous sections of meeting our future water needs, can today's investors, like Hamilton and Burr before them, make their money in water over the next two decades? How is the nexus of water and finance interlinked, and what trends and effect might we see emerging through 2030 as a result?

Trends

Investing in the Business of Water

There are now a wide number of water index and hedge funds that track performance in both the water manufacturing industry (producers of pipes, pumps, desalination, new hydro-tech, etc.) and those companies that are involved in the delivery of water and wastewater services around the world. An increasing number of analysts view the high future demand for water- and sanitation-related infrastructure in both the developed and developing worlds as an attractive investment opportunity.[2] Pension funds also embrace water stocks because they involve secure, multiyear contracts that will yield in line with their own liabilities, while private bankers see water as a safe pick, offering steady, low-volatility returns for their demanding clients.[3]

The raw economics driving the opinions of these various financial analysts are compelling. Water is a commodity with no alternative and no substitute, which all human activities require and for which analysis suggests we will face a 40% global shortfall between demand and supply by 2030. As the previous chapters have shown, whether it is needed for agricultural, energy, urban, business, or domestic requirements, all the trend lines for water point upward.

As a consequence of the scale of the challenge, new technologies and new business models in the water sector abound. New membrane technologies mean that wastewater treatment plants can be local, small-scale, and safe. If a new business model can be found, the market for toilets in the developing world is possibly worth billions of dollars. Innovations in leakage control, in water quality improvement, even in turning water vapor into rain are in development. Significant investments are also being made to scale up and bring down the costs of new water sources such as desalination and in the important area of water reuse, which may offer significant opportunities, straddling as it does the agricultural-energy-urban nexus of water.

Consequently, over the next decade or so, it is not unreasonable to predict a blue-tech water efficiency theme emerging from the financial sector as strong as the recent green-wave new energy theme has been, as the venture capital community herd to support these various new technologies and their service innovations. The Technology Pioneer community of the World Economic Forum is already recognizing a growth in water-related innovation companies. Could Australia, Israel, or Singapore house cutting-edge "blue business technology parks" to promote this innovation wave, creating significant opportunities from their chronic water security challenges?

Goldman Sachs estimates a total global market for water services at US$ 400 billion a year, and set to grow.[4] The OECD aims higher, estimating that by 2015 an average annual investment of US$ 772 billion will be required for water and wastewater services around the world.[5]

As the previous chapters to this book have set out, the fundamentals for these assertions of market strength and depth seem sound, especially across Asia. Waste and water businesses typically expand about two to three percentage points above a country's growth in gross domestic product, according to a leading CEO in the water service sector.[6] This points investors towards the high-growth markets in Asia, at least for the next decade. Recall that of China's 669 cities, 60% suffer water shortages; and in 2005, nearly half of them lacked wastewater treatment facilities.

Predictions for the desalination market are also bullish, for 20% or more annual growth in China, India, Australia, and the US through 2015, and then for an acceleration. Total investment in new desalination plants could top US$ 30 billion by 2015.[7] Interbasin transfers are also being considered (and reconsidered) on an unprecedented scale, such as the south-north transfer in China, the interlinking rivers initiative in India, and various large canal projects across North Africa, sub-Saharan Africa, and the Middle East. As water security challenges start to bite during the next decade, it will be hard for governments to resist going to the market for big hydro-infrastructure projects.

Meanwhile, the interplay between water use and energy efficiency is an innovation space worth watching. Service companies that operate as Water Service Companies (or WATCOs—businesses that offer services to companies or organizations to improve their water use efficiency, detect and fix leaks, etc., saving them money as a result) could use the same business models as they do for their Energy Service Company (or ESCOs—businesses that offer services to companies or organizations to improve their energy efficiency, saving them money as a result) business lines, undertaking water use efficiency activities for major industrial clients with multiple plants, saving them significant costs from their future water charges and avoiding risk, with the WATCO taking a slice of the future savings to the client for itself. Could ESCO and WATCO services become bundled together for clients perhaps? As regulations tighten and prices rise, especially across Asia and the Pacific, it is likely that this interplay between energy and water use efficiency will be a takeoff area for new business growth, in particular within and across the agricultural and urban sectors.

Against this context, consider the venture capital pitch to encourage a fund manager to invest in new blue-tech activities. It will likely be quite compelling: dwindling supply; soaring demand; no alternative or substitute goods; limited competition; and a relative lack of price volatility on revenues due to public-sector regulations on price, making it easy to model the returns and identify key risks.

Investing in Water Funds Compared to Other Commodities

Some commentators now see water funds as a better pick than oil. Both oil and water as commodities have seen their prices increase at a similar pace. But water prices have remained much less volatile. Since 1989, the annual price increase of oil has been 6.2% versus 6.3% for water. On the other hand, price volatility during the same period rose by 43% for oil versus only 4.2% for water. Water price volatility is capped because the water market for the most part, unlike oil, is publicly run.

Investing in Water as a Commodity in Its Own Right

The raw economics of property rights attached to water are also compelling from an investment point of view. While reliable data are patchy, during the housing bubble years the historic price of water rights in the Middle Rio Grande in New Mexico, for example, rose from approximately US$ 1,000 per acre/foot in 1993 to over US$ 5,500 per acre/foot by 2006. Some innovative investors are selecting opportunities today in water, which may be both a sign of a possible future market for water as a commodity in its own right, and— importantly—a signal for clearer government rules in the water market.

According to a 2008 article by *Bloomberg Businessweek*, the businessman T. Boone Pickens has spent over US$ 100 million over the past eight years purchasing land and associated water rights in Texas, with the hope of selling them in the future at a higher price each year to Dallas–Fort Worth. Since Mr. Pickens began to purchase water rights, the price of water in some places has doubled (to US$ 600 per acre/foot).[8]

Thinking about water as a commodity in its own right, but within a very different context, at a recent World Economic Forum meeting in China, in a public plenary discussion on water, the President of Iceland noted how his country, which was particularly hard-hit by the recent financial crisis, is now filling converted oil tankers with freshwater and selling them to Saudi Arabia.

Finding the Finance for Water Infrastructure

The perennial challenge for water infrastructure is raising the project finance. Against the billions of dollars of market potential that Goldman Sachs, the OECD, and others identify for water investment around the world, a large gap between what is financed and what is built remains. Even to meet just the Millennium Development Goals (MDG) challenge will require an additional $US 10 billion a year into the sector, according to United Nations Development Programme.

Given current budgetary challenges in many developed countries and competing pressures for government spending, it is unlikely that a step change in official development assistance (ODA) will fill the gap. Besides, the track record of pledge versus disbursement of ODA is not strong. Inevitably, governments and project planners will have to look to the private capital markets to attract the scale of investment they need. Private capital is unsympathetic to the moral argument regarding the need for water and sanitation and water resource management investment. Rather, a combination of good national policy, forward-thinking international finance institutions who can work to improve the risk/return ratio that private investors face in water infrastructure in developing countries, and a scaled deal flow of investible project opportunities will be the ingredients required to help fill the financing gap for water infrastructure.

The most comprehensive investigation into these issues was undertaken between 2001 and 2003 by a panel chaired by the former head of the International Monetary Fund, Michel Camdessus, which explored the ways and means of attracting new financial resources to the water field. Concretely, members of the panel tried to answer the question, "How to find appropriate financial resources for the achievement of the two Millennium Development Goals for water access and sanitation?" The panel reported its findings through a report, *Financing Water for All*, to the 3rd World Water Forum in Kyoto in 2003.[9] In some ways, it was both a forerunner and an analogue to the recent 2010 High Level Panel on Finance set up by the UN Secretary-General to explore ways to meet the finance for addressing climate change, required for developing countries under the Copenhagen Accord. The findings of *Financing Water for All* have become more resonant since they were published eight years ago.

The panel calculated that current spending on new water infrastructure in developing and emerging countries was roughly $US 80 billion a year and that this would have to more than double through 2025, to around $US 180 billion. Much of the increase will be needed for household sanitation, wastewater treatment, and treatment of industrial effluents, irrigation, and multipurpose schemes.[10] Much of it would have to come from private capital markets, domestic and international. To help catalyse the additional investment required, the panel came up with a cluster of recommendations:

- Each country should produce a national water policy and plan, including specific programmes to meet the MDGs and beyond, as part of an agreement for additional ODA for water.
- Finance ministries should give sub-sovereign bodies (e.g., local governments, water authorities) enough financial freedom to carry out their tasks. Municipalities should cooperate in credit pools to raise finance. Well-run national development banks could be considered as suitable channels for funding local bodies. Sub-sovereign bodies should be given credit ratings. Donors and multilateral financial institutions should target sub-sovereign bodies with their technical support, aid, and loans, and remove unnecessary constraints to lending to them.
- Both public and private water providers should be able to borrow more of their capital locally, reducing the foreign exchange risk. Governments and central banks should encourage the growth of local capital markets and attract more local savings (from pension funds, mutual funds, and other institutional investors) into suitable local outlets. Multilateral financial institutions should make greater use of guarantees and other instruments to encourage more long-term local lending and raise more resources in local currency markets.
- Water service providers should aim for revenues sufficient to cover their recurrent costs and develop sustainable long-term cost recovery policies, anticipating all future cash flow needs. Sustainable cost recovery includes operating and financing costs as well as the cost of renewing existing infrastructure. Users as a group should cover revenues arising from charges. Under sustainable cost recovery, not all users need pay the same price. Individual affordability of water charges should be ensured by appropriate tariff structures, including local cross-subsidization (e.g., by setting a rising block tariff structure). The part of recurrent revenues provided by taxpayers from public budgets should be secured by agreeing to the allocation of sufficient fiscal transfers a long time in advance. Sufficient fiscal transfers

should then be earmarked as appropriate to meet central support commitments.

- The panel recommended the creation of a revolving fund consisting of grant money to finance the public costs of preparation and structuring of complex projects, including private-sector participation and other innovative structures, and more partnership arrangements to provide expert help from developing countries.
- In view of the capital intensity of water investments, the panel suggested that developed-country governments should create a special national or international facility to prefinance ODA disbursements to water budgeted for a later period.
- The panel identified that the main obstacles to increased international flows of finance into water infrastructure in developing countries (debt and equity from foreign banks) were sovereign risk, foreign exchange risk, the heavy preparation costs of project finance, and the minimum threshold size of project financings, caused by the specific costs of structuring and the restrictive OECD consensus rules on export credit. The panel recognized the benefits of banks developing a track record and creating a market precedent in water projects—and of developing local capital markets and enhancing and extending sovereign risk coverage from both MFIs (multilateral finance institutions, such as the World Bank and the International Finance Corporation) and export credit agencies.
- The role of the MFIs was seen as crucial. MFIs should revise their policies on capital provisioning where these act as constraints or disincentives to the use of guarantees. MFIs subject to the participation requirement should consider amending their articles to enable them to have the freedom to issue guarantees on a stand-alone basis, unrelated to actual loans made.

These findings were a decade or so ahead of their time. Interestingly, the current finance debate on climate change is reaching broadly the same conclusion on how to find the finance for low-carbon infrastructure, even given the delicate state of current international capital markets compared to 2003.[11] A step change in investment flow from private capital markets into water (or low-carbon) infrastructure has not yet happened, but it will be required if these various financing challenges are to be met at scale within the next two decades. An opportunity exists for the multilateral finance institutions, investors from the private capital markets, project implementers, and governments with their development agencies to come together and devise a new breed of public-private funds for both blue and green infrastructure. In many cases, the domestic governance requirements to attract improved flows of finance into a country will be broadly similar within a climate-related Nationally Appropriate Mitigation Action (NAMA) plan and an equivalent national water plan.

Consequently, the financing and governance nexus between the water and the low-carbon investment agendas for developing countries can be pulled closer together. This can achieve more coherent policy reform to develop broader public-private fund mechanisms to address both sets of issue (creating both coherence and a spreading of risk through a wider portfolio). Building on both the Camdessus panel's findings and the recommendations of the High Level Panel on Climate Finance offers a robust platform on which to build a new set of public-private blue-green infrastructure fund arrangements for developing countries.

Forecast

It will be beneficial for managing future water security if investments from venture capital, private equity, and investment banks in water technologies were able to reach a critical mass over the next two decades, ensuring scale-up and market liquidity. But this investment interest will likely only be channeled to clear business opportunities in those economies or regions where there is sound water management and, consequently, perceived low levels of risk. Therefore, the role of government in undertaking reforms to attract these investments becomes of central importance, especially within the developing world; otherwise, private capital will be attracted into water investments only in the richer countries, where the problem may not be quite as urgent.

It is unlikely that by 2030 water will emerge as a globally tradable commodity in its own right to a significant scale. Water does not have a global trading platform of its own. This means that investors cannot trade water like other commodities, because it cannot yet be priced within the context of a global market. Water is also very heavy and transporting costs would always be higher by multiples than its market value, so a literal global trade of water is highly unlikely. All this lends water to being traded much more in local, regional, or national markets.

But some argue that a global market in water *rights*, rather than physical water allocations per se, is certainly feasible (a "virtual water market" perhaps?). Some investors speculate that with increased water insecurity, virtual exchanges for water rights could emerge, which may lead to a quasi-global market platform for water futures and possibly derivatives—such that the value of traded virtual water rights could start to climb significantly over the next decade or so as speculation took hold. This may be particularly the case in the sale of agrarian water rights to hoarders, who may buy low and then wait, selling instead on the futures of their rights to others. Underpinning this virtual financial world would be a recognized web of actual water trading markets, including existing and emergent schemes in Australia, China, India, and the US. If left unregulated, the social implications of such a scenario would be worrisome.

In terms of financing of water infrastructure, without any concerted push from a coalition of governments and others to stimulate public-private fund design and an initial slew of project deals to help catalyse the capital markets, it is unlikely that the ideas of the Camdessus panel will become implemented in a widespread fashion. Piecemeal innovation is more likely, as is currently the trend.

Implications

Governments and regions in water-scarce areas that take a lead in progressive water policy reform will enjoy an economic triple win: they will retain and attract companies; they will attract more inward investment into their water infrastructure; and their economy will be strengthened as a result of improved water management. Laggards will lose.

The role of international aid and multilateral finance institutions would then be nudged to evolve, with the market requiring development agencies away from investing their own debt and equity into water projects, and towards helping governments in developing economies attract private finance into their water sectors by creating instruments to buy down risks on the back of national policy reforms. But without either a few national governments taking the lead in policy reform, or a concerted push from developed-country governments in collaboration with investors to create new financing arrangements, the political and economic imperative to act will remain low. The "invisible" water crisis will likely continue, with investments occurring on more of an ad-hoc basis in reaction to events.

Regional and international financial regulators must also become aware of the potential for water rights exchanges and futures markets to emerge within the coming decade; they should think about the economic and political implications of what this might mean, and how, therefore, to develop rules and regulations to manage the virtual trade of water.

The Way Forward

At a local, regional, or national level, market mechanisms can be developed to more efficiently allocate water while at the same time attracting investments to the sector. The establishment of water rights and trading mechanisms for the Murray Darling basin, for example, created the price signals needed to incentivize major shifts to high-value crops. This market improved agricultural productivity in Australia by 36% from 2000 to 2005, protected and created industries, and developed a large financial water market (worth $US 1.7 billion in 2007/8).[12]

Based on the Australian experience, one important step to unlocking water markets is establishing defined, defensible, and divestible rights to water. To achieve efficiencies in optimizing water allocation and use, equitable markets must grow within the framework of effective government intervention. Research has demonstrated how water and wastewater are good businesses in and of themselves, and, more important, how they allow other businesses to take root and thrive in an atmosphere of health, stability, and water security. Experience suggests that this is not simply about raising the price of water. A more complex reform agenda is required, including the following:

- Clearly establish the amount of surface and groundwater available and the current and future requirements to cover ecological, social, agricultural, and industrial demands
- Put in place a structure that allows effective intervention across all aspects of the water issue, including energy, industry, agriculture, and so forth
- Promote the development and adoption of efficient water technology, as with clean energy
- Establish and maintain stable and transparent water allocations, including a property rights regime, so individuals know how much water they have to use or negotiate
- Establish cost recovery to pay for operations, maintenance, and renewal costs of the assets
- Empower water trading between individuals (willing sellers and willing buyers), which will enable the transfer of water and set the true marginal value of the resource (this will normally be much higher than government is prepared to charge).[13]

Another opportunity lies in the potential to codesign new funds for water infrastructure investment involving multilateral finance institutions and investors. Some new pilot funds could be developed (perhaps in concert with the climate finance agenda) such that they could offer both green (low-carbon) and blue (water) infrastructure project portfolios to developing countries. This would scale the investment opportunities for investors and would likely add coherence to funding and project design across many levels, including for the recipient government.

From discussions the World Economic Forum has had with investors, there *is* appetite among a significant minority of the investment community to take a leadership position and explore investment opportunities in low-carbon infrastructure in developing countries. They would likely be amenable to explore investment opportunities in water as well, perhaps as part of the Fund portfolios discussed above. But to justify their engagement, these leaders within the investment community require a concrete and sustained dialogue with the public sector (domestic and internationally), in particular regarding the role that MFIs can play to mitigate risks and augment returns at the margin.

There are now a sufficient number of specific public-private fund models, instruments, and mechanisms on the table or under development, within the low-carbon space at least, that can provide a focus for such dialogue. Private investors, however, also want to get concrete and specific. Another Camdessus style report is not needed. They are looking for active participation by the intergovernmental community in international platforms that foster discussions around specific "live" transaction opportunities with scalable potential. Consequently, if such a public-private investment initiative, based on real opportunities, could be constructed, the potential to pilot a significant new public-private financing arrangement could be realized. Is the agenda now ready for the development of a pilot entity along these lines?

Perspectives

The following personal perspectives amplify the main themes touched on by this chapter. They help to illustrate some current viewpoints on the water-finance nexus. The views expressed do not necessarily represent those of the World Economic Forum, nor do they necessarily represent the views of the other individual contributors or the various contributing companies or institutions.

- Usha Rao-Monari, Global Head of Water, Global Infrastructure and Natural Resources Department, International Finance Corporation, sets out some key issues surrounding the challenges and opportunities of project financing in the water sector, especially in developing countries.
- Alex Barrett, Global Head of Client Research, Standard Chartered Bank, offers a perspective on why water is important to a financial organization such as his.

- Stuart Orr, Freshwater Manager, WWF International; and Guy Pegram, WWF Adviser, South Africa, suggest that water pricing is difficult to implement in practice, especially in agriculture, if one wants to change behavior rather than simply raise revenue; rather, they argue, why not look instead to pricing and market regulations for the embedded water in traded goods?
- David Zetland, Professor at University of California, Berkeley, looks outside the box at the potential, financial and otherwise, of creating the ability to trade water property rights for all.
- The award-winning journalist James G. Workman explores the case study of innovation in a local water market in Sonoma County, California, where water rights were actually allocated to the population and were allowed to be traded, accumulated, banked, or sold.

Financing Water

Usha Rao-Monari, Global Head of Water, Global Infrastructure and Natural Resources Department, International Finance Corporation

The management of the water resource and its use is critical to economic growth and poverty reduction. Over the past five decades, as the world's population increased from 3 billion to 6.5 billion, water use has tripled. Population growth, in conjunction with urbanization, economic development, and industrialization, has pushed water use to unsustainable levels. Population growth means increasing food demand, which is pushing the expansion of irrigated agriculture, one of the most inefficient users of water. Economic development and energy needs require new industrial and power plants, which use significant amounts of water. The sector and the resource are further affected by worsening water quality and the effects of climate change.

The lack of available finance is widely regarded as the main constraint on the development of the water sector and is typically linked to risks specific to the sector: commercial (tariffs, cash flows, credit risk), political (expropriation, political interference, devaluation), legal, regulatory and contractual, water resource–related (scarcity, flooding, pollution, reallocation), and reputational. More important, the water sector has certain characteristics that make it unique:

- Governance in the water sector is poor, and until recently, few countries have recognized water to be a scarce resource.

- Decision-making in the water sector is fragmented and pushed down to the lowest political level.
- Water is rarely priced to reflect supply and demand.
- Basic quantitative information about water supply and use is lacking.

The size and complexity of water-sector financing required, and the risks peculiar to the sector, imply not only the need for both public and private sector finance, but also the need to invest on both the demand and supply sides. Adapting to climate change will mean even greater investments, particularly in the parts of the sector that tend to remain underfunded, such as environmental flows. An absence of required investment will not only mean limited reach and access, but more fundamentally, a scarcity in the resource itself.

Future financing of water cannot be based on past practices and historical measures; there is a need for a transformational change in the approach to financing water, and this could be considered in terms of the following principles:

- *Demand- and supply-side management and financing*: The management and financing of water and sanitation should take into account its different and competing uses. Management and financing of the sector has traditionally focused on the physical supply of water, with an emphasis on supply-side infrastructure. An integrated view of the water sector would place equal emphasis on demand- and supply-side solutions to ensure more sustainable use of water. Future financing approaches would take into account the demand and supply sides of the sector and support market-based allocation mechanisms.
- *Quantitative information base*: Historical assessments of investment needs in the sector have been based on inadequate information, resulting in inaccuracies and inexact decision-making. Future water financing should rely on a rigorous and comprehensive database of information at the country level.
- *Cost-based analytical framework*: Investment and financing decisions should not only be based on accurate quantitative information, but should be made within a least-cost analytical framework. Cost, as defined, should not only take into account economic costs, but also costs related to "ease of implementation" and required regulatory and behavioral change. This would result in an optimization of investment and financing decisions, which may, for example, result in efficiency-related investments as opposed to supply infrastructure.
- *Essential nature of private participation*: While public finance will continue to be vital to achieve water security, private finance and

private sector participation will become increasingly essential if the sector is to become more efficient and continue to evolve towards long-term water security. Financing models may change, however, to accommodate the new demand- and supply-side approach, and to recognize the risks inherent in the sector. While direct financial returns from investment in the sector can sometimes be limited, the total return includes substantial benefits to health, development, and economic growth.

- *Impact of climate change*: Adapting to climate change requires more investment in infrastructure, as climates are expected to become more variable, and drought and flooding are likely to become more frequent. Climate change also has substantial effects on environmental flows, thereby necessitating financial structures that take these into account.

- *Need for substantially better governance*: Enhanced governance of the sector would not only enhance efficiency and service delivery, but would provide a vital basis for better investment and financing decisions. For example, efficient utilities would require less financing due to increased cash generation.

- *Sustainability through appropriate cost recovery and pricing*: Long-term sustainability of the sector is possible only through an appropriate balance between tariffs and other inflows to achieve sustainable cost recovery. Pricing of the service and the resource is necessary to ensure a balanced allocation between uses, while keeping in mind the need to ensure water and sanitation services to the poor.

- *Decision-making at a higher political level*: Future financing decisions should be taken at political levels substantially higher than the local government unit which may have current responsibility for the provision of water and sanitation services. Finance ministers, for example, should be integrally involved in the investment and financing of the sector, along with their counterparts in the urban, agriculture, power, regional development, environment, and public health ministries.

- *Innovation is key*: The future sustainability of the sector is entirely dependent on innovation—in service-delivery models, in technologies, and in finance. Delivery models such as distributed or off-network services could reduce financing requirements, as would newer desalination technologies. Importantly, financial products that take into consideration new sources of financing will play a substantial role in the future—the use of directed levies (e.g., pollution taxes), traded water-use rights markets, and farmers' subsidies to incentivize water-saving irrigation methods are examples of innovations that have a direct impact on investment and financing in the sector.

Meeting the Water Challenge

ALEX BARRETT, GLOBAL HEAD OF CLIENT RESEARCH, STANDARD CHARTERED BANK

Given the ubiquitous demand for water in all human enterprise, it is hardly a coincidence that the world's fastest growing economies are also the most vulnerable to water scarcity. Consider China and India. Their huge populations, breakneck growth, and severely constrained water resources are about to come under even more pressure through climate change. Three decades of rapid industrialization leaves China with a legacy of severe water pollution.

Yet the Chinese character for "crisis" resembles the symbol for "opportunity." The perfect opportunity to tackle the water issue arose during the recent financial and economic crisis, when nations began to prepare enormous fiscal stimulus packages for investment. If nations could secure freshwater availability, they would also secure the basis for economic growth.

Meeting the challenge will come in several political stages by national governments. First, governments will have to accurately quantify the demand and supply situation within the level of each river basin, and identify local solutions. Next, they must elevate water scarcity to the highest level and set out to tackle it across all sectors and between countries. Finally, they will have to set up a reliable and consistent framework that will encourage investment, provide incentives that reward innovation, and harness the financial sector to help allocate capital in the most sustainable way.

This won't happen overnight. But the prize for such a transformation will be incalculable: continued sound and rapid economic growth; enough food to feed growing and wealthier populations; and improved health and quality of life for rich and poor citizens alike.

Water, Agriculture, and the Pricing of Sustenance

STUART ORR, FRESHWATER MANAGER, WWF INTERNATIONAL; AND GUY PEGRAM, WWF ADVISER, SOUTH AFRICA

Many argue that agricultural productivity and security will emerge only through water pricing. They assume that irrigation pricing or markets will efficiently allocate water, bring technically efficient use, eliminate scarcity, and ensure that those able to afford water will guarantee their supply.

The theory makes sense on paper. But it is not backed up by existing evidence.

The central dimension to consider is that water is more than just another economic input to production; water forms the ecological foundation of all economic activity. A water-based economy varies by the dynamics in each basin. The nature of water's pulse, its flow through the environment, makes the location, volume, and timing of water abstraction absolutely vital. By definition, "free markets" are indifferent to the local ecology and social network of unique users with diverse water requirements. Once again, without strong regulatory mechanisms, the rural poor and healthy ecosystem would have most to lose from a purely economic approach to allocation.

Moreover, to really promote water efficiency, price increases must rise exponentially. Yet seeking efficiency may undermine equity. Water pricing for agricultural productivity pits smallholder farmers against large commercial interests. Farmers rarely can compete for water against more affluent urban and industrial users. Economic efficiency has consequences for food security and rural development. South Africa considered those real political risks, against the unambiguous benefits of irrigation pricing, and instead chose regulatory interventions to allocate water efficiency.

Scale and location matter immensely. Informal markets have evolved in most agricultural regions of the world and enable reallocation between farmers within a local area during a specific season. Effective formal markets have depended on strong institutional and regulatory frameworks that protect noneconomic users, like aquatic invertebrates, and ensure that the information and related conditions for effective trading are in place. In most situations this leads to the administration of water pricing, but mainly as a tool for cost recovery.

The principles for water pricing are generally well understood, yet the realities, socially and hydrologically, of implementing these principles remain significant. What also remains missing is market regulation and prices for the commodities in which water is embedded. This may become water's most contested domain. As water markets restrain speculation and significant profit margins in bulk water, investment focus will largely shift to where water remains exploitable: trade in commodities with significant amounts of embedded water, as well as the means of their production.

Property Rights to Water for All

DAVID ZETLAND, PROFESSOR, UNIVERSITY OF CALIFORNIA, BERKELEY

What if everyone were given a property right in water that they could use to secure their human right in water and generate income sufficient to pay for its delivery? That's right: endow each citizen with his or her fair share of their own nation's water wealth. Ownership not only makes it more likely that people will get water; it will also provide them with an asset that they can then sell in markets. As a useful side effect, the markets will increase transparency and improve efficiency in water allocation.

Sound radical? Actually, the UN has implicitly recognized such reasoning. While the Universal Declaration of Human Rights does not mention water, Article 17 states, "Everyone has the right to own property alone as well as in association with others."[14] Moreover, though at times we may forget it, water is owned by "the people." The state merely distributes the usufruct rights to use citizens' water to maximize its social value for the greater common good through the production of food, energy, ecosystems, and healthy populations.

One objection to owning water is that few of us can actually use "our fair share" of water—most of us are not farmers. That objection goes away if we are allowed to *sell* our water to others who will use it. But that raises a second concern: we should not sell the water we need to survive.

We can address this concern by dividing ownership rights into two types. "Lifeline rights" would be inalienable, fixed, and equal for every person, at approximately 135 liters per capita per day (lcd), for example.[15] "Tradable rights" would be alienable, would vary with supply, and would be subject to changes in population. Tradable water rights could be rented but not sold. The ban on sales would protect owners from sharp dealing and communities from drying out.

So, how much water would fall into each category? Using the definition and data for renewable water supplied by the United Nations Environment Programme,[16] we find that Canadians would get 135 lcd as an inalienable lifeline right and still have 239,265 lcd to allocate as they please. Although that number seems preposterously large, the numbers in water-scarce Israel (with 611 lcd of renewable water) would be 135 lcd for lifeline water and 476 lcd for trade water. Total renewable supplies are 64,100 lcd in Australia, 4,300 lcd in Haiti, 4,200 lcd in Somalia, and 27,500 lcd in the US.

Owning water means little without delivery.[17] But local, private, or public delivery organizations could buy the tradable water in markets and deliver it to customers (who pay for service with the money they earn as sellers). Market prices will clarify the value of water and increase the competition to deliver efficiently. This competition will not just take place among existing delivery organizations; the transparency of markets will encourage nontraditional organizations to get into water management, which has been one of the most conservative and non-innovative business sectors. New people, ideas, and management techniques could benefit customers in the same way that deregulation of US air transport sparked massive improvements in service and pricing.

To be sure, ideologues may raise horror stories about "socialized" or, alternately, "privatized" water. Yet the evidence suggests that public or private ownership matters far less than community oversight in ensuring efficient and equitable water management. And trade incentivizes community oversight because it alters the way that we value our water.

This system could also have a big impact on reducing poverty, even in the most water-poor nations. Not only are the poor protected from thirst or poor hygiene in this tradable water market (with the inalienable right to 135 lcd for all), but they would also most likely prefer higher prices, since they have the most extra water to sell above their inalienable right (they do not use as much as rich people). A property-rights allocation increases both equity and efficiency, the former by the allocation of rights (and their value) to every person, the latter by trading water from owners to users.

An Example of Local-Level Water Market Innovation in Sonoma, California

JAMES G. WORKMAN, AUTHOR AND COFOUNDER, SMARTMARKETS, SAN FRANCISCO, CALIFORNIA

It may be the world's eighth largest economy, but few populations face more volatile water supplies: California is like a nation unto itself. From its birth, the Golden State's history has hinged on reliable access to water, which has grown unstable due to climate change, growth, and fierce competition. Water wars erupted during the 1849 Gold Rush and have continued to this day. Yet, while the government in Sacramento has called for conventional $US 11 billion water bond to finance top-down infrastructure and management projects, innovative bottom-up water coalitions may turn conflicts into collaboration.

Sonoma County's six hundred thousand people represent a microcosm of the state. They had traditionally increased supplies through hard infrastructure. Two dams and an interbasin transfer annually divert seventy-five thousand acre-feet from the Russian River. Then it hit a wall. Unchecked groundwater pumping undermined regional water tables, local streams, aquifer recharge, and the river itself, resulting in a 17,300-acre-foot deficit. Diversions are decreasing 25–50% due in part to climate change and protection of three endangered salmon species. For the next fifteen years, at a cost of $US 100 million, Federal and State Endangered Species Act requirements are forcing Sonoma to leave even more water for in-stream flows—right when people demand more. To complicate matters, some municipal contractors had filed lawsuits to get more water; others had to effectively "punish" water conservation with higher rates to make up lost revenue.

These are all classic water management headaches. Yet rather than close inward in a defensive crouch, Sonoma County Water Agency opened up to include collaborative partners. It launched "blue-tech" innovations, investing in soft water infrastructure to empower demand response and to improve shared decisions; these reduced negative effects on disenfranchised natural and human communities. Sonoma also recognized the water-energy nexus and invested with key partners to supply 90% of its peak demand from renewable power sources. Rather than crack down to regulate un-metered groundwater users, it has sought ways to engage them as voluntary partners, showing that their future is interdependent on a common resource. It has begun working with IBM to share transparent data from diverse sources so that traditional water managers can integrate strategies and coordinate efforts. Above all, it seeks to enlist end users to become water managers by giving them a vested interest in conservation.

One voluntary initiative, the Sonoma Water and Energy Efficiency Market, has launched a demonstration project to encourage efficiency through new and informed knowledge of individual consumption patterns, combined with a broad sense of egalitarian ownership. Those who find ways to use less water than a median threshold can save, accumulate, and bank virtual credits, or EcoShares, of water that can be bought and sold and donated within the watershed. Because people want their newly acquired assets to increase in value, the AquaJust exchange system may lead to an unprecedented situation whereby a majority of end users actually encourage the district to raise rates above the threshold. With more efficient use, conservation becomes both more challenging but also more rewarding; there are fewer EcoShares in circulation, but each is worth more. The equitable allocation also reduces conflict among residential, commercial, industrial, and agricultural users, because all parties can negotiate the value of that which once divided them. This project represents, albeit at a small scale, a classic example in which a public-private coalition formed a strategic alliance to increase efficiency, equity, and ecological benefits for all parties involved.

Notes

1. Koeppel, Gerald T. *Water for Gotham: A History.* Princeton, NJ: Princeton University Press, 2000. The key chapter is 7–8 starting with "Aaron's Water" pp. 70–101.

2. See, for example, Merrill Lynch, *Water Scarcity: A Bigger Problem Than Assumed*, 2007; Sustainable Asset Management, *Water: A Market of the Future*, 2007; Goldman Sachs, *The Essentials of Investing in the Water Sector*, 2008; Calvert, *Unparalleled Challenge and Opportunity in Water*, 2008; and Standard Chartered Bank, *Water: The Real Liquidity Crisis*, 2009.

3. See the water fund at Pictet Private Bankers, Switzerland, for example.

4. Goldman Sachs, *The Essentials of Investing in the Water Sector*, 2008.

5. Organisation for Economic Co-operation and Development, *Managing Water for All: An OECD Perspective on Pricing and Financing*, 2009.

6. Jean-Louis Chaussade, CEO of Suez Environnement, interviewed "Taking Hold of Liquid Assets, *Wall Street Journal*, European Edition, September 27, 2010, p. 10.

7. Environmental Technology Action Plan, *Water Desalination Market Acceleration*, April 2006.

8. Susan Berfield, "There Will Be Water," *Bloomberg Businessweek*, June 12, 2008, http://www.businessweek.com/magazine/content/08_25/b4089040017753.htm.

9. World Panel on Financing Water Infrastructure, *Financing Water for All*, 2003.

10. For reference, the 2009 Copenhagen Accord called for a similar amount, $US 100 billion a year by 2020, to help developing countries address climate change. UNFCcC, Copenhagen Accord, http://unfccc.int/resource/docs/2009/cop15/eng/l07.pdf.

11. See, for example, the recent proposals on climate finance from the UN High Level Panel on Climate Finance, November 2010. UN High-level Advisory Group on Climate Change Financing, Report of the Secretary-General's High-level Advisory Group on Climate Change Financing, 2010. http://www.un.org/wcm/webdav/site/climatechange/shared/Documents/AGF_reports/AGF_Final_Report.pdf

12. Water Resources Group (WRG), inhouse analysis.

13. Don Blackmore, Chair, eWater, Australia, personal communication.

14. See http://www.un.org/en/documents/udhr/ for a complete text of the Declaration.

15. Chenoweth (2008) estimates that 135 lcd is enough for human health and economic and social development. BAWSCA (2009) reports residential consumption ranging from 185 to 1,266 lcd (median 316 lcd) for communities of the San Francisco Bay Area. Zetland (2009) reports that municipal and industrial consumption ranges from 383 to 1,239 lcd in Southern California cities. Jonathan Chenoweth, Minimum Water Requirement for Social and Economic Development. *Desalination*, 229 (2008): 245–256. BAWSCA, Annual Survey FY 2007–08. Annual Survey, Bay Area Water Supply and Conservation Agency, 2009. David Zetland, Conflict and Cooperation Within an Organization: A Case Study of the Metropolitan Water District of Southern California, 2009.

16. "Total actual renewable water resources (TARWR): The sum of internal renewable water resources and incoming flow originating outside the country. The computation of TARWR takes into account upstream abstraction and quantity of flows reserved to upstream and downstream countries through formal or informal

agreements or treaties. It is a measure of the maximum theoretical amount of water actually available for the country" (UNEP, 2009).

17. Water delivery requires more than just pipes. Other fixed costs include the cost of drilling wells, building dams, installing treatment facilities, and so forth. Variable costs that change with operating volumes include the cost of energy for pumping and treating water, water quality control, customer service, and the like. Administrative and personnel costs are also important; they can be classified as fixed or variable.

CHAPTER 9

Climate

This chapter explores the water-climate nexus. It looks at climate variability, climate change, and water, including potential impacts and adaptation strategies. It is based on a text prepared by Professor Upmanu Lall, Director of the Columbia University Water Center, a leading expert on hydro-climatology and climate change adaptation, risk analysis, and mitigation. Professor Lall is a member of the Global Agenda Council on Water Security.

Background

Human activity (including but not limited to greenhouse gas emissions, deforestation, irrigation, and aerosol production) is systematically changing the earth's climate. The Intergovernmental Panel on Climate Change in its *Fourth Assessment Report* highlighted an accelerated change in average surface global temperature as well as in the sea-level rise since the mid-1980s. Growing scientific evidence suggests that failure to limit global warming to an increase of 2 degrees Celsius (3.6 degrees Fahrenheit) above preindustrial levels would make it impossible to avoid potentially irreversible changes to the earth's ability to sustain human development. According to the most advanced climate system models, there is a five in six chance of success in keeping below a 2°C increase in temperature if worldwide greenhouse gas output is reduced by 80% by 2050, relative to 1990.

Some of these factors are well understood. They project significant changes in the space and time distribution of water availability and floods across the globe over the current century (particularly 2050 and beyond). These changes will affect all aspects of water supply and demand, and hence increase the risk of supply-demand imbalances as well as the degradation of water quality and ecological functions. In particular, tropical and subtropical regions of the world, where more than 60% of the global population lives and where the vast majority of the water is used for agriculture, are especially susceptible to increasing risk of drought and floods.

But current climate models do not yet provide sufficient precision in generating rainfall statistics, either when used retrospectively for the 20th century or when projected forward into the 21st century. Consequently, there is still considerable uncertainty as to how rainfall patterns may actually change for specific locations, including for those where adaptation to changing risk is an issue. Therefore, broad statements about the type of changes one can expect are possible, but these are not precise enough to use with existing decision-making tools for water system capacity expansion and management.

For example, the United Nations Development Programme's *Human Development Report* of 2006, which focused on water, draws attention to climate models that project "marked reductions in water availability in East Africa, the Sahel, and Southern Africa as rainfall declines and temperature rises."[1] While valid as a general statement, the models that can help give confidence to such statements do not yet provide enough granular information for decision-makers in these regions to develop any specific adaptation strategy.

As a point of context, it is also important to note that all societies have historically faced risks due to climate variability. Persistent, multiyear droughts or wet spells dramatically affect all aspects of water availability and use, and can (as historical evidence suggests) translate into triggers for migration and conflict. In general terms, the longer such dry and wet cycles are, the greater their impact on society can be.

It is now better understood that long climate cycles are not necessarily random. In fact, they may be the rule rather than the exception and they may even have some short-term predictability. This may provide hope for developing adaptation strategies for the coming century, even if the climate change scenarios themselves (in particular how the frequency and strength of long cycles may change) are clouded by uncertainty.

In almost all places, but especially in developing countries, water storage capacity for surface water is limited to a few months or at most a few years. Conversely, groundwater corresponds to slower fill and drain cycles; it can therefore be seen as longer-term storage. But in many countries, groundwater stocks are being rapidly depleted as use rates exceed recharge rates. As one of the contributions at the end of this chapter also indicates, much freshwater is also stored in mountain glaciers around the world. The glaciers can also be viewed as a longer-term store of freshwater.

The key question global society faces with regard to climate variability and water is this: How should our water best be stored, and which stores should be used to minimize risks due to long-term climate variability and change? Answering this question becomes the important policy and technical issue to focus on if sensible and focused risk management and adaptation strategies are to be developed vis-à-vis water and climate change.

Trends

"A similar amount of water to what we have been used to in the past will be available for future generations? No more," says Don Blackmore, Chair, eWater, Australia. "Climate change with the increase in temperatures in the temperate and arid zones means that there will be less water for much of the heavily populated areas of the earth. Growth in food production must therefore come from more efficient use of the available water."[2]

Over the last century, statistical analyses reveal increases in the frequency of rainfall extremes (both wet and dry) in many parts of the world. But unlike the temperature trends, it is not clear that the rainfall trends lie outside the range of long-term climate variability in the vast majority of these places. In fact, where proxy data are available for the past thousand years, much wetter and drier periods can be noted in most places than for the last hundred years of data.

What is clear is that water use has increased exponentially over the last century in almost all regions of the world, in particular through agricultural intensification to meet the food needs of a global population that is now at least double what was projected as the potential carrying capacity of the planet at the beginning of the 20th century. This means that the margin between average water supply and demand has become much tighter globally, which is responsible in part for the groundwater depletion trends. Further, a changing climate implies changes in both the average water supply and its variability in a region. And increased variability tends to lead to water use through irrigation that is generally higher even than that implied by the difference between average supply and demand. Such trends are becoming evident, and in places like India are manifest even in the sociopolitical changes that provide subsidies for groundwater extraction to mitigate the risk in the short term.

Much of the increased agricultural productivity in the 20th century can be traced to the ability to store and provide water for reliable irrigation. Initially, this happened through large, centralized surface water storage such as dams and distribution projects such as canals; towards the end of the century, the widespread expansion of groundwater pumping also occurred. Social, management, and environmental factors have severely limited dam construction and utilization in the last thirty years or so. These include the issue of conflicts between upstream and downstream users. As a result, the spatial distribution of such large storage is largely restricted to the more developed nations.

A recent policy trend is the promotion of "watershed management" strategies that focus on smaller storage projects that potentially deliver irrigation benefits without the institutional and environmental issues associated with large projects. Unfortunately, such systems are not as effective in addressing the risk associated with persistent climate extremes, and may in some cases increase the vulnerability to climate variability and change. Water allocation strategies that are responsive to emerging and current climate conditions and demand management are being advocated, but other than in Australia, no large-scale changes in such management are yet evident.

Forecast and Implications

The average water supply-demand imbalance is expected to become critical in much of eastern, southern, central, and western Asia, in much of Africa and the Middle-East, in southern Europe, the American Southwest, Mexico, the Andean region, and northeastern Brazil by 2025/2030. Persistent, multiyear drought induced by either anthropogenic climate change or as part of a natural cycle could significantly exacerbate this situation in one or more of these regions. Significant food aid and other drought relief measures (including efforts to control migration and internal or external conflict) by the international community may be needed to help those affected in such a situation.

Continuing water abstractions for human use, coupled with climate variability and change, have the potential for negatively affecting water quality and wildlife in these regions. Species extinction may also emerge as a major threat. These problems will likely be accentuated by "adaptation" efforts that try to store more water for human use, either using small or large storage development. The depletion of high mountain glaciers in certain regions may also exacerbate these problems through changes in the seasonality of river flows (conversion of many perennial streams to ephemeral) and the associated reduction of flow in the dry season.

"The central dimension to consider is that water is more than just another economic input to production; water forms the ecological foundation of all economic activity," says Stuart Orr, Freshwater Manager, WWF International. "That water-based economy varies by the dynamics in each basin. The nature of water's pulse, its flow through the environment, makes the location, volume, and timing of water abstraction absolutely vital. By definition, 'free markets' are indifferent to the local ecology and social network of unique users with diverse water requirements. Once again, without strong regulatory mechanisms, the rural poor and healthy ecosystem would have most to lose from a purely economic approach to allocation."[3]

Climate exigencies may push populist governments to provide additional entitlements and subsidies related to water to the large rural, impoverished population base in developing countries. These may in turn exacerbate the problem, as inefficient use of water by agriculture will make access to water for other uses much more difficult. It is possible that some collective action on improving investment and efficiency in the agricultural sector may emerge, but at this point the urgency does not seem to be apparent. In this respect, the pain inflicted by a persistent climate exigency and the interest in climate change adaptation and mitigation may actually emerge as a useful political tool towards water-sector reform.

The Way Forward

Due to research on paleoclimatic and seasonal to interannual climate forecasting, a dramatically better database now exists on the nature of potential climate risks that we face. Thus there is an opportunity to focus on these challenges and develop strategies for addressing them through physical, policy, and financial tools. Recognizing that the range of climate-induced hydrologic variability over the previous several centuries is often dramatically larger than what we experienced in the 20th century, any success in better managing such future risks will clearly pay dividends as we are faced with a changing yet uncertain risk profile later in the century. Much needs to be done now to improve the reliability of water supply in the face of a highly variable climate, while recognizing social and environmental factors associated with development and management. This could be taken on as a grand challenge across industry and government.

The climate change debate itself is drawing unprecedented attention to the flash points of potential climate-induced crises. These are predominantly related to water issues over much of the world. This attention is systematically improving public access to data and information on both water supply and demand, and to the impacts of degraded water quality on health and ecology. Water is indeed at the center of much of the impact and adaptation story. Thus a *global* opportunity to dramatically address water management and development goals, through economic as well as physical means, is emerging as a result of the climate-water linkage, despite the fact that water is typically viewed as a state or national issue.

Unfortunately, the climate change debate can also be a distraction to the water challenge, and unless properly shepherded, it may not direct due attention to the specific nature of climate extremes as manifest through persistent multiyear and seasonal changes in rainfall and water availability through surface and groundwater reservoirs. Business involvement in sharpening this focus through appropriate advocacy related to investment in infrastructure, demand management, spatial optimization of use (in particular agricultural and other choices), and catastrophic risk management (insurance as well as planning and relief) will be important for timely action in the face of a grave climate- and population-induced risk of water supply-demand imbalances.

Perspectives

The following personal perspectives amplify the main themes touched on by this chapter. The viewpoints help to illustrate the range of current perspectives on the water-climate nexus. The views expressed do not necessarily represent those of the World Economic Forum, nor do they necessarily represent the views of the other individual contributors or the various contributing companies or institutions.

- Orville Schell, [Greater China] Director, Center on US–China Relations, The Asia Society, New York; Member, Global Agenda Council on Climate Change, writes on the effects of climatic variability on glaciers, water security, and Asia's rivers.
- Mark Smith, Head, International Union for Conservation of Nature, Water Programme, Switzerland, writes on combining the what and the how of building climate resilience through considering the use of water ecosystems and infrastructure.

Glaciers, Water Security, and Asia's Rivers

Orville Schell, [Greater China] Director, Center on US–China Relations, The Asia Society, New York; Member, Global Agenda Council on Climate Change

It has become commonplace for us to think in terms of a "food chain," that infinitely complex but elegant sequence of causes and effects that must take place in the natural world, if the food on which we all depend is to grow. One of the most critical elements in this "food chain," is, of course, water, which depends on its own infinitely complex, and equally elegant, chain of cause and effect.

In an endless cycle of evaporation and condensation, water is in constant motion, falling on the earth to nourish life, and then being taken up into the atmosphere through evaporation to be purified and redistributed around the world once again as rain and snow. During this delicately calibrated and never-ending process (which is reminiscent of the whole Buddhist/Hindu notion of life, death, and reincarnation), there is really only one link where water, whose very nature is fluid, finds itself in a state of suspended motion. This is when water freezes.

After it is precipitated to earth in colder alpine climes or during wintertime, water becomes frozen and immobilized in one of the planet's ice fields or glaciers. The largest ice masses on earth are situated in the Arctic, the Antarctic, and in the grand arc of mountains that stretches from Afghanistan and the Hindu Kush, through the Karakorum Range above Pakistan and India, to the Himalayan Range that rims Nepal, Bhutan, Bangladesh, and Burma, before lancing northward at Hengduan and Daxueshan Ranges to form the easternmost tier of the vast Tibetan Plateau. Because this high-altitude frozen reservoir sequesters the largest ice mass between the North and South Poles, it has come to be known as the "Third Pole." But, unlike the Arctic and the Antarctic, whose meltwaters flow into the oceans, the meltwaters of the Third Pole feed the 267 river systems of Asia. It is around these rivers that the great civilizations of the region have arisen, and on whose flows some two billion people continue to rely today.

The tens of thousands of glaciers in these mountains collect snowfall in their high-altitude "accumulation zones," which, as it compresses into ice, pushes the glacier slowly downhill until its "ablation zone" begins to melt during the warm summer months. It is just at this time during the "shoulder season"—before rains from the monsoons that arrive annually in the area and after they have ceased and ice starts to melt rapidly—that this "frozen water tower" begins to release critical supplemental flows that feed the Amu Darya, Indus, Tarim, Ganges, Brahmaputra, Irawaddy, Salween, Mekong, Yangtze, and Yellow Rivers.

These vast fields of ice and glaciers, known as a "cryosphere," have been nature's way of setting aside a reserve account of precious freshwater and then rationing it out at critical times. In this way, life-sustaining rivers are kept flowing at sufficient levels to support the civilizations, people, agriculture, and industry downstream that have grown dependent on them over the millennia.

The ability of a glacier to keep accumulating ice at a rate equal to, or greater than, its melt rate is known by glaciologist as "mass balance." And, over many tens of thousands of years, even as there have been temporary fluctuations in the climate caused by orbital wobbles of the earth, sunspots, volcanic eruptions, and the like, these glaciers have maintained their mass balance, without precipitous change.

Now, however, another great chain of cause and effect, "anthropomorphic climate change" (changes in the global climate patterns induced by man-made causes such as the burning of fossil fuels and the release of greenhouse gases into the atmosphere), has begun to intersect with the water cycle. Global warming has not only begun to trigger perturbations in historic rainfall patterns in many parts of the globe—causing floods, droughts, hurricanes, typhoons, blizzards, ice storms, and other kinds of aberrant weather—but it has also led to elevated temperatures and the increasingly rapid melting of the planet's ice fields. Indeed, in such mountain ranges as the Himalayas, temperature elevations have been rising at more than double global averages, because of the way in which latent heat from moisture-rich air from lower and more tropical climes is finally released at higher altitudes in the process of this air cooling, condensing, and then falling as rain or snow.

Of course, in the short run, flows in Asia's major rivers systems will increase, as we recently witnessed in the disastrous floods in Pakistan this year. And, during normal times, increased numbers of downstream users will become dependent on this added increment of flow as populations increase and urbanization continues with the growth of cities. But in the long run, as global warming causes the capital account of this critical frozen resource to become depleted, releases will not only be deranged, but will diminish. Since many of these river courses are transnational and are now relied on by hundreds of millions of users, and since there is as of yet no adequate body of international law governing riparian claims on such river systems, it is not unlikely that major struggles could erupt over decreasing flow volumes.

For example, the Mekong River rises on the southeastern tier of the Tibetan Plateau inside China as the Lancang River, but then flows down through Southeast Asia as the lifeline for four other countries. The Irawaddy River rises in the same region of China as the Nujiang and then flows down into Burma, where it becomes the most important waterway in this fertile, if presently misbegotten, land. And the Indus rises in western Tibet and Pakistan, in the shadow of the Karakorum Range, but then flows through Indian-controlled Kashmir before finally crossing the armed frontier back into Pakistan to become the key water source for much of that embattled land. So, for much of Asia, the water cycle and the carbon cycle intersect at the nexus of glaciers and rivers, and their interaction presents the world with a complex and potent cocktail of environmental, resource, and national security problems for which we do not yet have, nor are we likely soon to have, any remedy.

The best solution to these looming transnational water resource problems is a preemptive one: to keep the cryosphere of this once-remote and seemingly disconnected arc of mountains in its current frozen state. For once these glaciers waste away and seasonal flows diminish, states will inevitably begin to argue, compete, contend, and even fight for their shares of vital, but diminishing, river water that their people need to survive. By then, however, it may be too late to act.

Combining the What and How of Building Climate Resilience:
Water Ecosystems and Infrastructure

MARK SMITH, HEAD, INTERNATIONAL UNION FOR CONSERVATION OF NATURE
WATER PROGRAMME, SWITZERLAND

We live in an era of unfolding global change, with the resulting opportunities and dangers shaping our ability to address global and national priorities for economic and social development and for security. Among diverse drivers—such as growth in consumption, urbanization, population rise, and migration—the dangers of climate change are now better understood but, without credible action, increasingly stark. People's fears are multiple, relating to risks to health, food supply, biodiversity loss, employment, and infrastructure safety. The breadth of risks envisaged reflects the reality that we live in systems, where one thing is connected to another and people, economy, and nature are intertwined. Climate-change effects will play out across these "social-ecological systems" in complex ways, but the common thread propagating most impacts is familiar and simple: water.

Drought, floods, severe storms, melting glaciers, and sea-level rise are the headline issues in media, political, and popular understanding of climate change effects. Effectively adapting to each will begin with water management. Otherwise, economies and livelihoods will weaken as climate change intensifies, undercutting development in some of the most volatile or vulnerable regions of the world. Places like the Ganges or Indus basins of South Asia, drylands in Africa, hurricane-prone mountain watersheds in Central America, small islands in the Pacific, or the coastal megacities of Asia: using water management to adapt to climate change in these vulnerable "hot spots" will be elemental to sustainable futures.

Effective climate change adaptation will take place first and foremost locally—in villages, towns, and cities—supported by coordinated decision-making about how river basins and coastal zones are developed and managed. Yet these are the very scales where the inherent uncertainties of climate change are highest. Because of this, calls for action on adaptation increasingly stress the need to build climate resilience. This begs the question: what is resilience and what does it look like in practice?

Resilience is the capacity to withstand shocks and rebuild when necessary. In principle, we can imagine that climate-resilient communities, nations, or river basins will be able to cope with climate change effects, whether anticipated or unforeseen, avoiding collapse and renewing themselves according to needs created by the shifting climate. In a climate-changing world, the systems of people, economy, and nature in which we live will have to have characteristics that make them highly adaptive systems. Systems reality, where one thing is connected to another, means there are structural or engineered dimensions to climate resilience, but also social and ecosystem dimensions. Pretending that adaptation is a planning problem, to be solved by picking actions in one of these dimensions or another, will not be good enough.

We now better understand the characteristics of resilient, highly adaptive systems because of advances in the social and ecological sciences. This knowledge, combined with "learning by doing," led by the International Union for Conservation of Nature in demonstrations of river basin management in Latin America, Africa, and Asia, points to practical components of resilience. Ecosystems, economics, and social change are all important. Experience suggests then that resilience is built by integrating four components:

- *Diversity*—of the economy, livelihoods, and nature. Diverse markets—industry or farming systems, for example—give people the alternatives they need to be adaptive. Biodiversity ensures the availability of ecosystem services needed to buffer climate impacts—such as storage of water in upper-watershed forests—and sustain life and productivity.
- *Sustainable infrastructure and technology*—portfolios that combine both engineered and "natural infrastructure," as well as adaptable and sustainable technologies for their management that reduce vulnerabilities. This includes engineering responses (such as urban drainage or rainfall harvesting) as well as infrastructure management (e.g., application of "environmental flows" to allocate river flows within the limits of availability). Added to conventional infrastructure portfolios should be planning and investment in "natural infrastructure" such as wetlands, floodplains, and mangroves that store water, lower flood peaks, or protect coastal communities.
- *Self-organization*—a critical characteristic of resilient, highly adaptive systems that is implemented in practice through participatory governance and empowerment of people in adaptive institutions.
- *Learning*—ensuring that individuals and institutions can use new skills and technologies needed to adapt and make effective use of better climate information and adaptation strategies as they become available.

These four components of a "climate resilience framework" combine what action is needed and how it should be implemented. The test will be to use such resilience thinking to guide both practical action and the development of strategies and policies that are coherent across sectors. Experience from demonstrating water management has provided some clues that, by combining these components in river basins, brittleness and fragility can be replaced with resilience. In the Komadugu Yobe basin in northern Nigeria, part of the wider Lake Chad basin, for example, there is environmental degradation combined with severe poverty and conflict. Reform of water governance is building self-organization and promoting shared learning about climate, ecosystem services, and sustainable management of dams. Without these steps, climate change generates enormous fears for such regions, but new coping strengths are now emerging from implementing resilience in practice.

Notes

1. United Nations Development Programme, *Human Development Report, 2006: Beyond Scarcity*, 2006. p. 27.
2. World Economic Forum Water Initiative, *The Bubble Is Close to Bursting*, 2009.
3. Stuart Orr, personal communication.

CHAPTER 10

New Economic Frameworks for Decision-Making

This chapter sets out some new approaches that help provide a comprehensive economic analysis of the water challenge in a clearer, more concise manner than has been done previously. Through using these kinds of tools, it is hoped that decision-makers can develop common and agreed fact bases to better understand the magnitude of the water challenge they face, the options open to them to manage it, and the associated costs.

The chapter has been prepared by Martin Stuchtey, Director, and Giulio Boccaletti, Expert Associate Principal, of McKinsey & Company. They set out this new economic framework for analysis in general terms, referring to some country examples. The work is based on a global study undertaken for the first phase of the Water Resources Group (WRG, referred to in chap. 8).

Moving forward, the objective of the World Economic Forum's alignment of its Water Initiative with the Water Resources Group is to work closely with several governments to develop more focused national and subnational analysis and diagrams, building on those presented in the examples below. In this way, it is hoped that a suite of economic fact bases to look at various country's water challenges can be established.

In each case, this in-depth fact base can then enable focused conversation, debate, and action planning as governments use it to work with wider coalitions to develop their reform plans, create new integrated management systems, and design and implement sector transformation pathways for water. Contributions at the end of this section set out some of the decision support tools that can be utilized to help governments develop water resource management systems, once such a clear economic fact base exists for the nation or region. These examples illustrate not only the breadth of technical potential now on offer to develop smart and interlinked water management systems, but also the range of innovation that can be unlocked once a clear economic fact base is provided to work from.

Background

A lack of transparency on the economics of water resources makes it difficult to answer a series of fundamental questions, whether at a state, national, or regional level:

- What will the total demand for water be in the coming decades?
- How much supply will there still be?
- What technical options for supply and water productivity exist to close the "water gap"?
- What resources are needed to implement them?
- Do users have the right incentives to change their behaviors and invest in water saving?

As a result, many countries still struggle to shape implementable, fact-based water policies, and water resources face inefficient allocation and poor investment patterns because investors lack a consistent basis for economically rational decision-making.

This section describes how the Water Resources Group constructs a fact-based analysis on the economics of the water challenge, and how it can be used to support governments as they consider their water reform options and how best to choose and implement them.

Step 1: Identifying the Demand and Supply Gap through 2030

The analysis in figure 10.1 sets out in a simple way the global gap between supply and demand through 2030. This example is at the global level. Such analysis can be created for a state, a country, or a region.

The diagram can be read as follows: by 2030, under an average economic growth scenario and if no efficiency gains are assumed, global water requirements would grow from 4,500 billion cubic meters today to 6,900 billion cubic meters. The figure clearly shows that this is a full 40% above current accessible, reliable, and environmentally sustainable supply. In this way, a state, national, or regional government would be able to clearly see the overall water supply and demand challenge they face by 2030.

This global shortfall in supply is really the aggregation of a very large number of local gaps, some of which show an even worse situation: one-third of the population, concentrated in developing countries, will live in basins where this deficit is larger than 50%. A deeper-dive picture could also show for a particular state, national, or regional government what some of

Billion m³, 154 basins/regions

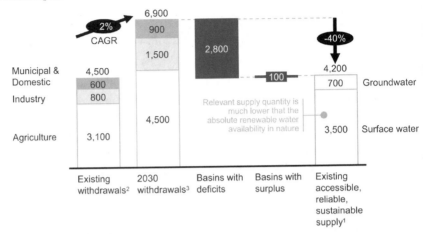

1   Existing supply which can be provided at 90% reliability, based on historical hydrology and infrastructure investments scheduled through 2010; net of environmental requirements
2   Based on 2010 agricultural production analyses from IFPRI
3   Based on GDP, population projections and agricultural production projections from IFPRI; considers no water productivity gains between 2005-2030

SOURCE: Water 2030 Global Water Supply and Demand model; agricultural production based on IFPRI IMPACT-WATER base case

Figure 10.1   Aggregated Global Gap Between Existing Accessible, Reliable, Sustainable Supply and 2030 Water Withdrawals, Assuming No Efficiency Gains

the more localized supply-demand gaps could be, which are hidden by the aggregation.

The drivers of this water resource challenge at the global level have been explained in the previous chapters. They are fundamentally tied to economic growth and development. An identification of the key economic drivers of the water resource challenge for a particular country through 2030 can be undertaken with the government.

Step 2: How Can the Gaps between Supply and Demand Be Closed?

The diagram in figure 10.2 shows how historic rates of efficiency improvements in different sectors will not close this gap. This is a global example. A diagram like this can be prepared for a state, a country, or a region.

Using the global example in figure 10.2, it can be seen that "business as usual" in the water sector will not land on an efficient solution that is environmentally sustainable and economically viable. The annual rate of efficiency

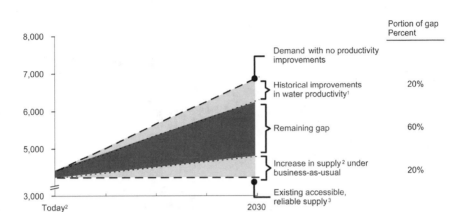

Based on historical agricultural yield growth rates from 1990-2004 from FAOSTAT, agricultural and industrial efficiency improvements from IFPRI
Total increased capture of raw water through infrastructure buildout, excluding unsustainable extraction
Supply shown at 90% reliability and includes infrastructure investments scheduled and funded through 2010. Current 90%-reliable supply does not meet average demand
SOURCE: 2030 Water Resources Group – Global Water Supply and Demand model; IFPRI; FAOSTAT

Figure 10.2 Business-as-usual Approaches Will Not Meet Demand for Raw Water

improvement in agricultural water use between 1990 and 2004 was approximately 1% across both rain-fed and irrigated areas, for example. A similar rate of improvement occurred in industry. Were agriculture and industry to sustain this rate through 2030, improvements in water efficiency would address only 20% of the supply-demand gap, leaving a large deficit to be filled. Similarly, a business-as-usual supply build-out, assuming constraints in infrastructure rather than in the raw resource, will address only a further 20% of the gap.

The global example used in figure 10.2 also shows that when some amount of the existing water supply is unsustainably "borrowed" (from non-replenishable aquifers or from environmental requirements of rivers and wetlands), this also slowly widens the demand-supply gap, as the volume of existing accessible reliable supply falls over time. Similar analysis can be created for a state, national, or regional government.

Step 3: What Technical Options for Supply and Water Productivity Exist to Close the "Water Gap"?

Figure 10.3 helps the government to see the relative costs of their current approaches to manage the demand-supply balance. In this example, the cost of desalination is set against other water options in agriculture and industry that can improve water use efficiency.

Cost of measure
$/m³

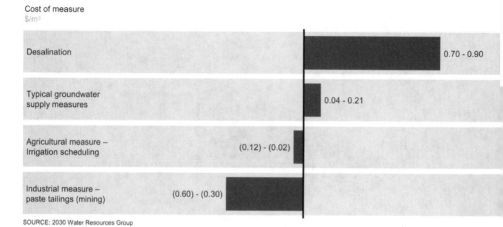

Desalination	0.70 - 0.90
Typical groundwater supply measures	0.04 - 0.21
Agricultural measure – Irrigation scheduling	(0.12) - (0.02)
Industrial measure – paste tailings (mining)	(0.60) - (0.30)

SOURCE: 2030 Water Resources Group

Figure 10.3 Representative Demand- and Supply-Side Measures

Often, the focus for most countries in addressing the water challenge has been to consider additional supply, such as desalination. In this case, desalination—even with expected efficiency improvements—is more expensive than traditional surface water supply infrastructure, which in turn is often much more expensive than efficiency measures, such as irrigation scheduling in agriculture. This analysis shows the differences very clearly (noting, of course, that the analysis does not take into account implementation and institutional barriers of improved irrigation scheduling in agriculture, which may involve the engagement of many small farmers).

The challenge is then to find a way of linking the various opportunities available to close the water gap, and in being able to compare the different options. A "water marginal cost curve," which provides a microeconomic analysis of the cost and potential of a range of existing technical measures to close the projected gap between demand and supply in a basin, can help provide such transparency.

Figure 10.4 provides an example of the cost curve for India. For a given level of withdrawals, the cost curve lays out the technical options to maintain water-dependent economic activities and close the gap, comparing on a like-for-like basis efficiency and productivity measures with additional supply. Each of these technical measures is represented as a block on the curve. The width of the block represents the amount of additional water that becomes available from adoption of the measure. The height of the block represents its unit cost.

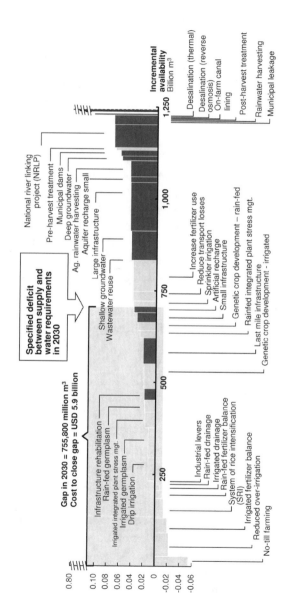

SOURCE: 2030 Water Resources Group

Figure 10.4 India: Cost of Additional Water Availability in 2030.

In this India example, the least-cost set of levers—those on the left-hand side of the cost curve—is dominated by agricultural measures, which can collectively close 80% of the gap. In combination with lower-cost supply measures, delivered mostly through the rehabilitation of existing irrigation districts and the "last-mile" completion of earlier projects such as canals, the total annual cost to close the gap is approximately US$ 6 billion per annum—just more than 0.1% of India's projected 2030 GDP.

This analysis does not take into account implementation and institutional barriers, or the impact on labor markets, GDP, or other economic metrics. It does however provide a clear economic starting point from which governments can begin to consider options and then to examine approaches to overcome the barrier to each option.

The analysis can come alive if a particular success story can be applied to it. For example, while capturing the potential of agricultural water efficiency improvements is difficult in India, as implementation needs to be pursued by hundreds of millions of smallholder farmers, the Indian government is already taking action. Through the Accelerated Irrigation Benefit Programme, for example, the Indian government has started supporting adoption of micro-irrigation systems (MIS) in the attempt to accelerate irrigation growth. MIS grew by 15% per year between 1999 and 2006. And drip irrigation for Indian agriculture has a technical potential to cover 37 million hectares by 2030, up from only around 2.5 million hectares in 2005. If the full potential were realized by 2030, drip irrigation would have an annual growth rate of 11%, leading to a market size of approximately US$ 2.4 billion per annum, up from some US$ 230 million today. At low payback periods, this forms a promising opportunity for farmers and investors alike if barriers to adoption like capital constraints and lack of awareness can be overcome.

Efficiency in industry and municipal systems is similarly critical. A similar marginal cost curve for China highlighted how rapid growth in industrial and urban water (at 3% per annum) can be mitigated in a cost-effective way by instituting aggressive, water-conscious, "new build" programmes and enacting water-saving regulatory reforms. If China pursued this path, the cost to fill the gap is negative, implying net annual savings of approximately US$ 22 billion. Most of the cost savings arise from industrial efficiency measures. They are distributed among the thermal power, wastewater reuse, pulp and paper, textile, and steel industries. Their savings potential derives from significant savings in energy and other operational expenditures, translating into overall productivity gains. Many of these solutions are readily available in China today. The largest capital need, for example, is in municipal leakage reduction, which has a technical potential of 9.2 billion cubic meters per year. With a 22% rate of return, the efficiency opportunity could become attractive for municipal utilities, if work is focused to develop the market.

Drawing on both of these cases, one can see how a marginal cost curve identifies a potential lever that could be cost-effective or even a cost saver, and then further work in the country on examples helps the government see what could be possible if enabling or scale-up policies were implemented. A good example of an NGO project that improved water use efficiency in agriculture to scale, thus offering potential to deliver on an important cost lever, might be something useful to discuss. Similarly, the results of a particular crop or leakage technology trial from a company or foundation may provide useful examples of what is possible to trigger a particular lever. In this way, the analysis can move from creating a clear fact-based understanding of the challenge into providing potential actions.

Most solutions identified on the cost curve also imply cross-sector trade-offs. For example, a curve prepared for South Africa indicated a balanced portfolio of solutions with cost-effective measures available across supply, agricultural efficiency and productivity improvements, and industrial and domestic levers. Seven river subbasins are almost entirely dependent on agricultural improvements, while the economic centers of Johannesburg and Cape Town are dominated by industrial and domestic solutions. Almost 50% of the levers involve significant savings of input costs. In the case of industrial levers (such as paste thickening and water recycling in mining, and dry cooling and pulverized beds in power), up to US$ 418 million in annual savings can be captured from the pursuit of efficiency.

In this way, a targeted approach can be taken, and for national policy-makers a clearer appreciation of the interlinkages between water-food-energy-climate policy levers emerges; blanket policies may not work and might create the wrong incentives, leading to poor outcomes. What works for Johannesburg will not work for a river subbasin elsewhere. A policy affecting water use in energy may have an impact on agriculture. This analysis, however, provides a clear understanding of what approaches to focus on, where, at what cost, and with what likely impact.

The Way Forward: A Fact-Based Analysis as a Platform for Action

"Quantitative indicators make it possible to spot problems, track trends, identify leaders and laggards, and highlight best management practices," says

Professor Daniel C. Esty, Director, Yale Center for Environmental Policy and Law, US. "What is shocking is how little water data is available on a methodologically consistent basis across countries."[1] Developing a fact-based vision for water resources at the country or state level is a critical first step to help the government make a reform agenda possible. This vision will help identify metrics, such as the supply-demand gap, or the potential of different measures, that can help to measure progress. It will link cost and economic data to water resource data—including environmental requirements—a step that is essential in order to manage the water challenge.

Having created the fact base and gone through the process of describing the options available, the next stage is for policy-makers, the private sector, and civil society to come together and put into practice a transformation towards sustainability.

The fact base can provide crucial guidance for this process at several levels. For example, an understanding of the economics of the chosen solution will help decision-makers come to a rational design of the economic regimes within which water is regulated. In this regard, there is considerable experience on the way market mechanisms can help the efficient use of water by businesses and cities.

Further, identifying the barriers to adoption, and the implementation challenges inherent in the measures described on the cost curve, will help leaders focus and improve the institutions needed to champion and implement reforms. The cost curve also provides a benchmark of existing technologies and their cost to deliver additional water, providing guidance for investment in technology hubs, research, and education to unlock future innovations in the water sector. Such innovation will be critical in generating new options and reducing costs of provision.

By demonstrating which measures have the greatest impact in delivering solutions, a robust fact base can also spur focused financial investments from the private sector as a key engine for transformation. A number of approaches exist, from public-private water financing facilities, to public projects that create the space for private financiers to scale up their investments, to innovative micro-finance solutions for end users. Policy-makers, financiers, conservationists, farmers, and the private sector need to cooperate to develop and promote innovative financial tools to ensure that those willing to improve their water footprint are given the opportunity—and capital—to do so.

In many cases large individual water users have a big role to play in managing demand. Government policy can help align industrial behavior with efficiency objectives, forming a key component of a reform programme. It is critical to ensure that incentive design emphasizes the value of water productivity—for example, through clearer ownership rights, appropriate tariffs, quotas, pricing, and standards—and at the same time recognizes the impacts such incentives can have on the companies' profitability. A fact base on the economics of adoption and on the real potential of efficiency measures in such sectors can help identify and prioritize the right regulatory tools for action.

Perspectives

Following a comment by Nestlé, one of the sponsors of the work described above, there are four further perspectives. Each set out decision support systems that can be developed to help governments manage future water trends, once a clear economic fact base exists for the nation or region. These examples illustrate not only the breadth of technical potential now on offer to develop smart and interlinked water management systems, but also the range of innovation that can be unlocked once a clear economic fact base is provided. The views do not necessarily represent those of the World Economic Forum, nor do they necessarily represent the views of the other individual contributors or the various contributing companies or institutions.

- Lee A. McIntire, Chairman and CEO, CH2M HILL; and Robert Bailey, President of the Water Group, CH2M HILL, describe Water Portfolio Management, which integrates stakeholder needs with technical support for water-sector decision making.
- Michael Norton, Managing Director of the Water and Power Division, Halcrow Group; and Roger Falconer, Halcrow Professor of Water Management, Cardiff University, present an innovative integrated water resource management framework called Cloud to Coast.
- Rabi H. Mohtar, Director, Global Engineering Program; Professor, Agricultural and Biological Engineering Department, Purdue University; Member, Global Agenda Council on Water Security, explains what will be required to develop an integrated system to manage the water, food, and energy interlinkages. He suggests that the creation of water knowledge hubs to assemble the required data would be a good place to start.
- Juan Carlos Castilla-Rubio, President, Planetary Skin Institute; Managing Director, Cisco Systems Sustainability and Resources Innovation Group, describes the innovative, information-driven partnership between Cisco Systems and NASA known as the Planetary Skin Institute, for which an interlinked, multi-scale Water Skin decision support system is planned.

The Work of the Water Resources Group

NESTLÉ

Nestlé has a major interest in water security for three reasons. First, because farmers supply our factories with basic raw materials; as the main users of water, they are also the most threatened by water shortage. Second, we need water for our industrial processes. These are modest amounts—less than two liters per US$ 1 of sales—but nonetheless essential. Finally, many of our products require access to good quality water by our consumers.

The Water Resources Group study helps bring water abstraction back into line with existing accessible, reliable, and sustainable supply. The cross-sectoral analysis per watershed provides new and improved sets of action-oriented data. This data, combined with the prospects of massive water overuse in a large number of countries and at the overall global level, show that the issue is much more urgent than previously thought.

We have to act now. The work offers the tools that identify and compare levers to close the gap from water overuse. It enables vigorous debate, discussions, and ultimately concerted efforts by all stakeholders. It also makes it possible to overcome the present piecemeal approach to solving the water problem. By showing these levers in one cost curve—from the most cost-effective to the least cost-effective measure—decisions on water management can also be integrated into the full set of economic choices a country needs to make.

We expect the report[2] to have a major impact on both national and regional water policies, and to lead to more focused and effective corporate efforts in water management. These necessary actions can ultimately reestablish water supply security in river basins where it is seriously threatened today.

Water Portfolio Management

LEE A. MCINTIRE, CHAIRMAN AND CEO, CH2M HILL; AND
ROBERT BAILEY, PRESIDENT OF THE WATER GROUP, CH2M HILL

Today, competition, pollution, threatened ecosystems, energy's thirst, and fast-paced population growth combine with the overarching effects of climate change to generate the most complex and multidimensional water management challenge of all time.

Complex water challenges require new and integrated solutions. These combine technical capacity with communication and trust among all parties throughout robust planning, design, implementation, and management phases. One leading approach is Water Portfolio Management (WPM).

WPM integrates stakeholder concerns with customized technical approaches in ways that are essential for system-specific needs. Best of all, WPM is scalable. Jurisdictions and governing bodies across geographies can assess their future water scenarios and pursue solutions.

WPM is integrating stakeholder considerations with technical options in multiple settings around the globe, including:

- *The Colorado River Basin.* The US federal government, seven western states, and environmental organizations are collaborating using WPM principles to understand gaps between supply and demand in this growing region, and to investigate options for sustainable supplies for agriculture, industrial, energy, recreation, municipal, and ecosystem needs in the face of projected climate change effects.

- *Singapore.* A holistic approach has diversified and identified key water sources, allowing the city-state to create and begin to implement a long-term water supply strategy. In addition to water supply, other benefits result from employing WPM principles. By 2015, Singapore's water industry is expected to contribute US$ 1.2 billion to the gross domestic product and provide eleven thousand new jobs, creating a global center of water industry expertise.

- *Australia.* Achieving sustainable water management is the major challenge of the 21st century. In response, regions have used WPM (referred to in Australia as Integrated Water Cycle Management) approaches to protect, enhance, and restore water sources and ecosystems while enabling the allocation of water among stakeholders, considering the water cycle from extraction to the natural system. In Queensland, water needs are met through a regional reuse and conveyance system that links agriculture, urban, and environmental uses. In Canberra, the WPM dynamic simulation approach is being used to assess various hydrology, storage, withdrawal, demand, and treatment scenarios for the entire water cycle.

These WPM planning approaches have and will continue to provide the framework for future water management decisions in drought-stricken regions such as Australia as well as for all climates around the world.

A "Cloud-to-Coast" Decision Framework

MICHAEL NORTON, MANAGING DIRECTOR OF THE WATER AND POWER
DIVISION, HALCROW GROUP; AND ROGER FALCONER, HALCROW PROFESSOR OF
WATER MANAGEMENT, CARDIFF UNIVERSITY

The concept of management of water on a river basin basis has long been lauded as the only means of arriving at rational decisions around hard and soft interventions in the water sector. Indeed, in 1973 in the United Kingdom, the concept led to the establishment of river basin–based institutional structures to replace the previous water supply areas and municipal wastewater administrations. The concept was articulated further by the Global Water Partnership (GWP), who coined the term Integrated Water Resources Management (IWRM), and who have done much to disseminate the IWRM approach and associated analysis tools since GWP came into being in 1996. GWP defines IWRM as a process that "promotes the coordinated development and management of water, land, and related resources in order to maximize the resultant economic and social welfare in an equitable manner without compromising the sustainability of vital ecosystems."[3] One of the important concepts of IWRM is the engagement of all stakeholders in the decision-making process.

With increasing appreciation of the vital role of water in the production of food and energy, and in the achievement of economic and national security, there is a need for decision frameworks that allow even more water impacts to be assessed. A strategic collaboration between Halcrow and Cardiff University has developed an innovation in integrated water management, expressed as Cloud-to-Coast, or C2C, solutions. The concept takes IWRM to the next level in its ability to encompass all water systems *and* water use from rainfall at the "upstream" boundary to coastal systems at the "downstream" boundary, and enables trade-offs and water efficiency improvements to be explored. The C2C concept absorbs the categorization of green, blue, and gray water streams, the important distinction between withdrawal and consumptive use, and the effects of flows of virtual water.

The C2C solutions approach embraces the findings of the 2003 US National Science Foundation report titled *Revolutionizing Science and Engineering through Cyber-Infrastructure*, which identified opportunities in integrated approaches linked to new developments in computing and communications technology. Observation of movements and patterns between features in the water environment often suggest an underlying conceptual relationship. Within a C2C system, a component of a complex system is indeterminate until that component can be associated with other features of the system. The starting point for the application of the C2C solutions philosophy is the definition of the C2C boundary and its conceptualization in space and time. Then a framework for predictive simulation associated with the C2C concept takes us from the challenges to the solutions.

The approach has reached proof of concept through its application to derive a sustainable water management strategy for a riverine area of special ecological conservation. With the introduction of C2C solutions, the boundary of the problem was redefined and conceptualized. Application of the C2C solutions approach resulted in development of control rules for upstream groundwater flow augmentation as a replacement water resource, and relocation of the treated wastewater downstream of the raw water intake. Unit wastewater treatment costs were halved as a result. The Cloud-to-Coast concept is a new and powerful decision framework.

An Integrated Sustainability Index for Effective Water Policy

Rabi H. Mohtar, Director, Global Engineering Program; Professor, Agricultural and Biological Engineering Department, Purdue University; Member, Global Agenda Council on Water Security

The interlinkages of the water system with other systems, such as food, energy, climate change, and the economy, must be explicitly defined to enable the exact quantification of those relationships. This will then allow for comprehensive, integrated management systems to emerge. For example, development of a "water value" for all sources of water (sea, surface fresh, deep aquifer, recycled water, etc.) to feed into such a system would include the cost associated with transporting the water to a specific destination for a certain need; it would also consider the environmental quality associated with the use of this specific water, such as long-term soil quality, pollution risk, and so forth.

Even though specific metrics exist that can address the status and progress of water resources, a wider benchmarking tool that can address multidimensional water systems and their interrelations to food, energy, and other closely related systems is yet to be established. Water data attributes identified in relation to these interlinkages and their multi-scale processes are needed. These attributes should include, but not be limited to: water values, water pricing, water laws, environmental impacts, energy impacts, food security, ecological impacts, biodiversity, and air, soil, and water quality.

As we explore the architecture and the implementation possibilities of such an interlinked water system (perhaps better described as an integrated sustainability index for effective water policy), various types of data will help us to connect and define the interface between its separate components. These data types include system *input data*, such as weather/climate with its spatial

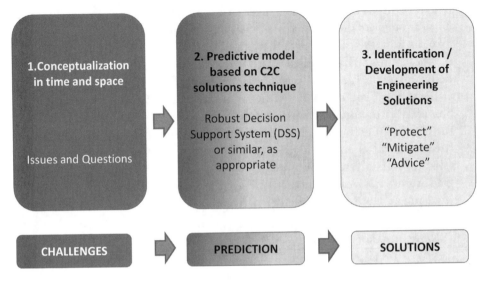

Figure 10.5 Cloud-to-Coast framework

and temporal variability in the short and long term; *system* data, such as soils, land use, geomorphology, socioeconomics, land management and tenure, governance system, social structure, indigenous knowledge, and the like; and system *output data/indicators*, such as the robustness of the system, the well-being of people being served, and the implications on food security, health, energy security, and so forth. Likewise, the development of an early warning system will also require system input and system parameters data; and for system sensitivities and evaluation, system output data are needed. A critical issue here is the quality of data, the standards/format, and their accessibility.

Figure 10.6 is a simplified system for the elements of sustainability and includes explicit interlinkages. This system can be a starting point towards sustainable water-food-energy systems.

It can be seen that a comprehensive, interlinked water security strategy will be complex and difficult to achieve. It can be attempted, however, using the perspective identified above, and based on relatively simple principles that focus on:

- multi-scale dimensions
- metrics that are easily obtained
- achievable benchmarking targets.

To obtain the data to underpin the activities, a *water knowledge virtual hub* that can integrate new and existing knowledge (from research centers, universities,

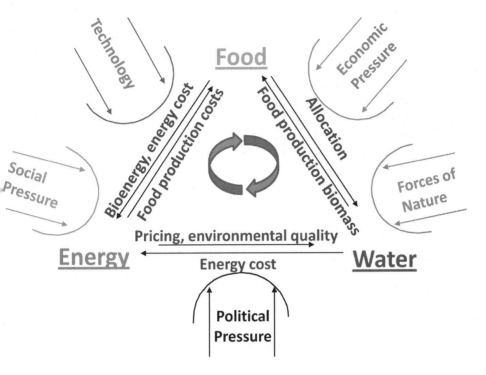

Figure 10.6 Energy-Food-Natural Resources Continuum: System Challenge

industrial and private patents), as well as effective rural community indigenous knowledge, is a good starting place. As well as developing a suite of water
knowledge hubs (domestically or regionally) to help pool and sift interconnected data, a comprehensive state-of-the-art model design exercise should be
explored to identify the various areas in interlinked water-food-energy policy-
making, where these tools/frameworks can be of most help.

*Water Skin: A Global Multi-scale River Basin Decision-Support Framework
for Collaborative Water Resource and Risk Management from the Planetary
Skin Institute*

JUAN CARLOS CASTILLA-RUBIO, PRESIDENT, PLANETARY SKIN INSTITUTE;
MANAGING DIRECTOR, CISCO SYSTEMS SUSTAINABILITY AND RESOURCES
INNOVATION GROUP

Two powerful trends are reshaping the world. The first trend is *resource scarcity*,
the result of explosive demand growth for resources (water, energy, food, land,

etc.) driven by growing populations and economic development. The second trend is *data abundance,* driven by huge but siloed data sets and increasing information processing capabilities, space-to-ground sensor networks, and emerging information and communication technologies.

Planetary Skin Institute (PSI) aims to address the challenge posed by the first trend with the opportunity presented by the second. In March 2009, Cisco and NASA agreed a multiyear R & D public private partnership to pool their capabilities and assets in a partnership based on joint and open innovation. Cisco has embedded the fruits of this partnership in the PSI, which was named one of *Time* magazine's "Top 50 Inventions of 2009."[4] PSI is a unique R&D partnership between leading corporations, government agencies, and research institutions around the world.

PSI's nonprofit status is intended to facilitate cooperation across institutional, disciplinary, and national boundaries and to create a space for flexible pooling of assets, capabilities, and ideas among stakeholders. PSI has recruited a global advisory council consisting of thought leaders in science, technology, economics, and innovation to guide this work.

PSI is currently working with selected corporate, government, and academic partners in the US, EU, India, and Brazil to build working prototypes of resource and risk management *decision-support tools* that have the potential to increase food, water, and energy security and protect ecosystems such as tropical forests. These include the utilization of satellite data to analyse land use change and estimate greenhouse gas emissions; integration of sensor data and analytics to identify cost-effective pathways to significantly increase renewable energy and energy efficiency adoption; and the use of satellite sensors, mobile networks, and analytic models to support smallholder agriculture productivity enhancement and accelerate crop insurance. A water component of this work is also under way.

WATER SKIN

The challenges facing the world's water resources have been addressed in detail in this book. Yet society's ability to manage these challenges is impaired by seemingly intractable informational, political, economic, and institutional challenges. Decision-makers need substantially more data and analytic support to reconcile water demands at local and regional levels and to build consensus among users for adaptive water resource and risk management. But data at appropriate spatial (i.e., subbasin) and temporal (e.g., seasonal) resolution are uncommon. More flexible, adaptable, and integrated decision-support tools are also required to reflect the highly localized and cross-disciplinary challenges of water resource management. Consequently, and recognizing that every watershed faces unique challenges, some subset of the following five capabilities will likely need to be built in order to create an overall supporting "skin" for water resource decision-making in any given location.

1. *Systems modeling.* How does the hydrology of the system work today? What are the major sources and the dynamics of supply and demand across all stock and flow categories, and how do they interact with natural features of the environment?

2. *Change modeling.* How are the mean and variance characteristics of supply and demand likely to change under various economic and climatic scenarios? What are the implications from the increasing frequency of weather extremes in the short term? What are the implications for risk prevention, mitigation, and transfer?

3. *Infrastructure optimization.* What infrastructure choices are available to manage change, and what trade-offs do they imply for the welfare of various stakeholders, including both economic and environmental considerations? What are the right infrastructure build-out linkages and sequencing decisions? What are the optimal demand-side infrastructural choices? How to optimize these choices for a systemic view of the water-food-energy-climate nexus?

4. *Policy optimization.* What policy choices (e.g., adaptive resource allocation) are available to manage change, and what trade-offs do they imply for the welfare of various stakeholders, including both economic and environmental considerations? What is the policy trade-off, for example, for homegrown production versus trade, and in terms of optimal crop choices for the environment?

5. *Ecosystem management.* Where are the different sources of ecosystem damage (pollution) in the water system, and how can policy-makers attribute responsibility to different stakeholders under a regulatory or market-based approach?

Managing Water, Food, and Energy Interdependencies

Unlocking humanity's ability to manage water resources will require, among other things, advanced decision-support capabilities that provide a shared analytic and technical basis for cooperation. The Water Skin R&D program aims to engineer new decision-support capabilities that draw upon innovations in the sensing, the analytic and the collaboration layers to create the groundwork for integrated and adaptive water resource and risk management:

- Innovations in the *sensing layer* are designed to leverage integrated configurations of ground-, people-, airborne-, and satellite-based technologies to monitor the state of land, catchments, rivers, defenses and vulnerable areas in near real time. A common problem in resource management is the absence of data at temporal and spatial resolutions detailed enough to guide decision-making of both surface and underground water levels. Another has to do with data sharing across local and international boundaries. Water Skin will test innovations in targeted low-cost sensor data from a variety of platforms (e.g., *in situ*, wireless water quality sensors, satellite sensing, UAV sensing) to evaluate their potential contribution to better decision-making.

- Innovations in the *analytics layer* are designed to integrate and analyze data in the sensor layer to draw inferences that are useful to end users, enabled by a cloud-based compute and open modeling capability. The analytics layer will include cross-disciplinary analytic and modeling capabilities to support decisions in water resource management that require analyzing issues from a range of perspectives (e.g., decision-support systems to optimize water (re)allocation strategies; reservoir and water transport management; hydropower systems; energy generation strategies; demand-side management for devising short-term crop-planting strategies, for informing crop-choice optimization decisions, and for precision farming in agriculture, among others). Other examples in water risk management include early warning systems for floods and droughts to assess, for example, the reliability of flood infrastructure, to improve evacuation strategies, and to develop model-driven management strategies to predict and minimize the impacts of flooding and drought.

- Innovations in the *collaboration layer* are designed to provide meaningful, value-added and collaborative interfaces with local context for a myriad of end users and decision-makers in the public and private sectors and in local communities. Innovations in this space include advances in user interfaces, immersive geospatial visualization environments, collaboration capabilities, and end uses themselves (i.e., the creation and support of ecosystem market infrastructure).

Assessing the multiple risks that water shortages will create requires information integration across multiple disciplines and domains (e.g., economics, weather, hydrology, energy systems, crop-systems risk modeling), scenario-based and geo-spatially explicit modeling and analysis tools, and the ability to characterize information in terms of risk distributions and mitigation measures. PSI is designed to address these challenges.

Consequently, the Water Skin is just one component of a broader set of sensing, analytic, and collaboration capabilities under the PSI decision-support framework and platform. This allows for the Water Skin to interface natively with other PSI Energy, Agri-food, and Forestry resource decision-support management and risk systems to better understand the complex interactions, particularly the dynamic risk characteristics, and spatial dimensions of this interconnected challenge.

Currently, only rudimentary insights exist on when and where interlinked problems are likely to materialize, and under what assumptions and scenarios. Most analytic approaches to date are static, lack geo-spatial resolution, and do not incorporate effective risk analyses. But these features are precisely the capabilities that policy-makers, communities, businesses, investors, and asset operators need in order to make better resource allocation and risk management decisions.

When fully developed, the Water Skin will provide an immersive information-rich platform to better understand and model the complex interrelationships between energy, water, land, agriculture, and other resources. In particular, the Water Skin decision-support platform, with a focus on the global public good, will be structured to allow open access and interoperability to specific areas of the platform by a broader set of cross-disciplinary experts across the public, private, and research sectors. Open data exchange standards will be published to allow research and development communities globally to integrate and access data and decision-support capabilities through Water Skin user collaboration inter-faces.

The Journey Ahead

The ambition is that a Water Skin R & D consortium of leading corporations, governments, space agencies, NGOs, foundations, and research academic institutions codevelops new technical and institutional capabilities in the next three to five years that will substantially advance the ability of decision-makers in both water resource and risk management to meet changing needs in an environmentally sustainable and equitable fashion. Our plan is to prototype a next-generation set of capabilities for water resource managers and experts that can be replicated and scaled globally. By developing and testing innovations in sensing, analytics, and collaboration layers in several high-priority river basins of the world, Water Skin will demonstrate the art of the possible, yield significant benefits for participating communities, and generate a new set of research and development questions to be addressed iteratively over time.

Notes

1. World Economic Forum Water Initiative, *The Bubble Is Close to Bursting*, 2009.

2. http://www.mckinsey.com/App_Media/Reports/Water/Charting_Our_Water_Future_Full_Report_001.pdf

3. Global Water Partnership/Technical Advisory Committee, "Integrated Water Resources Management—at a Glance." http://www.gwp.org/Global/The%20Challenge/Resource%20material/IWRM%20at%20a%20glance.pdf

4. *Time*, "The 50 Best Inventions of 2009." http://www.time.com/time/specials/packages/completelist/0,29569,1934027,00.html

CHAPTER II

Innovative Water Partnerships

This chapter sets out some findings on how to create public-private coalitions for water sector transformation—the multistakeholder platforms that can bring different stakeholders together to help discuss, design, and implement water reform programmes, projects, and policy suggestions for governments, in reaction to a clear fact base that sets out the challenge. The chapter draws on work undertaken in India, South Africa, and Jordan between 2006 and 2009 by the first phase of the World Economic Forum Water Initiative, with generous support from the Swiss Agency for Development and Cooperation (SDC) and the US Agency for International Development (USAID).

The chapter is drawn from work presented in two World Economic Forum reports (2008, 2010),[1] prepared by Christoph Jakob, SDC Senior Adviser seconded by the SDC to the World Economic Forum from 2007-2009. His work was done in collaboration with Rachel Cardone, Adviser to the Water Initiative, and supported by Alex Wong, a consultant who closely collaborated with the SDC. Substantial commitment and expert input for this analysis also came from an expert team at Halcrow, consisting of Jon Bateman, Richard Harpin, Bryan Harvey, Lauren Mittiga, Michael Norton, and Bill Peacock; and in addition, the analysis draws from the on-the-ground activities of Chandan Chawla in India and Thabani Myeza in South Africa. The reports can be found at http://www.weforum.org/water.

Background

The World Economic Forum's Water Partnership Projects work was launched in 2005 through a public-private partnership between Alcan (now Rio Tinto Alcan) and the Swiss Agency for Development and Cooperation. It was clear between partners that action was urgently needed to address a rapidly emerging issue: that competing demands for water resources across the water-energy-food-climate nexus—particularly in developing or quickly growing economies—would increasingly cause rifts between different users and eventually impede progress on social and economic development goals. The challenge: how to devise ways to identify and devise ways to develop significant public-private projects that could create opportunity rather than conflict from these trade-offs.

It was recognized that a shift in mind-set towards collaboration between stakeholders from differing sectors would be needed. While there existed a number of successful multistakeholder partnerships and pilot projects in water, widespread adoption and replication of such projects was limited. Thus the secondary challenge was how to create scalable public-private collaboration mechanisms. The Initiative's exploratory phase had identified a bottleneck in the development of successful partnership projects, which was the significant time and effort required from parties to engage in such a process.

Consequently, the pilot initiative between 2006 and 2009 became a "learning-by-doing" laboratory, working to create innovative multistakeholder platforms that could unlock the potential of public-private-community partnerships (PPCP) in the water sector. By the time the pilot came to an end, the progress had been significant. Three active and operational collaboration platforms had been created—in India, South Africa, and Jordan—each with its own project pipelines and strategies for growth. Funding to support these processes and networks had been secured through partnerships with two development agencies (SDC and USAID).

The Initiative experienced not only successes but also challenges, which forced stakeholders to reassess, learn, and improve processes. Through these lessons, the pilot process identified that project *brokerage*—measured by the number of projects in a pipeline—is only one aspect of the work that is needed to successfully generate projects. It was found that the collaboration platforms actually play a number of other significant roles, all of which contribute to the advancement of win-win ideas and the shifting of mind-sets that enable stronger collaboration between stakeholders.

The Regional Platforms and Networks

India

The Indian collaborative platform came into focus at the India Economic Summit in November 2005 when the Confederation of Indian Industry (CII) and the Forum joined together to form the Indian Business Alliance on Water (IBAW). IBAW was designed to foster significant public-private-community projects on a range of activities, such as water resources development, watershed management, treatment and recycling of wastewater, and provision of safe drinking water. The IBAW was supported with a USAID grant from November 2005 to November 2007, and subsequently by SDC India. The grants are managed by the United Nations Development Programme with

CII as the implementing agency. By 2006, the Indian state of Rajasthan had emerged as the focal point for the Initiative's work at state level. At the time of this book's publication, the IBAW in Rajasthan has approved six projects that are in various stages of implementation, and more than fifty projects are in the pipeline.

The following is a good example of an IBAW public-private-community project. The Jal Bhagirathi Foundation—an NGO working in Rajasthan—facilitated the development of a community-level desalination plant with the involvement of the private sector within a PPCP construct. The private-sector partner, Environze Global, designed, manufactured, installed, tested, and commissioned the desalination plant at Pachpadra village in the Barmer district at its own cost. With the commissioning of the plant, safe drinking water became available to the villagers at a much lower cost. The villagers are happy to pay for the water, regulated under the auspices of local government regulations, which can then help to pay for the plant. The role of the Foundation was critical in ensuring the project was designed with the local users firmly in mind.

Another project involved the reuse of one thousand cubic meters of municipal wastewater per day for industrial purposes in Beawar. This made available for domestic use the equivalent amount of potable water that industry had previously used, benefiting approximately 370,000 people. The partners involved were Shree Cement, the government of Rajasthan, and the Municipal Corporation of Beawar City, Rajasthan. The ability of the collaboration platform to help these public and private stakeholders codesign a win-win project was central to the project's success.

The Rajasthan model generated significant lessons for working on projects based on multistakeholder participation. While working with a state government as a project partner, for example, several activities were delayed due to changes in the ruling government and the transfer of officials. Despite this, multistakeholder approaches to the development of water projects remain attractive to the state, which maintained interest in the model throughout. Thus, despite a different pace and a change in personnel within government, a sustained commitment to work with and support government in its water transformation process was vital to build trust and develop legitimacy for the platform. Through the support of CII, IBAW also took the proactive step to mobilize resources and expertise to train industry members to design and implement PPCP projects in water and watershed development—that is, to work collaboratively with government and others in the codesign of industry water management solutions. The trainees were identified from a pool of medium- and large-scale water-intensive industries (e.g.., thermal power, food and beverage, textiles, pulp and paper, and iron and steel). A similar exercise has been planned to build capacity within the public sector, so that water-sector officials can be more confident in their ability to work collaboratively with private-sector and NGO representatives on codesigned water project concepts.

South Africa

The process of creating a collaborative water project design platform in South Africa began in 2006, when the Initiative joined with the NEPAD Business Foundation (NBF) to create a partnership at the national level. A network of more than thirty public, private, and civil society organizations was formed at the World Economic Forum Africa Summit in 2006, coordinated by the NBF. The platform focused its activities on two key water projects that were designed to both provide clean water for 750,000 people in some of the poorest areas of northern South Africa and provide a reliable water supply to mining industries to help stimulate economic growth.

Once the projects were conceptualized, both were handed over to project champions to carry forward. Unfortunately, without a trusted broker or "rainmaker" to oversee the projects and shuttle between government, industry and other stakeholders, implementation stalled. Interestingly, however, the stakeholders recognized the value in the concept and remained committed to and engaged in the process, creating a change in its design as a result. The NBF Water Initiative consequently set up a dedicated project management office to coordinate project activities and facilitate collaboration among stakeholders, and recruited a full-time project manager, a well-known and trusted individual from the water sector in South Africa. The African Partnership Programme (APP) within the Ministry of Water Affairs partnered with the NBF to integrate businesses into the process and drive project development, with businesses taking a lead role in one work stream, which focused on joint government-industry partnerships. Aligning with a key initiative and receiving the support of a ministry helped the NBF to consolidate the process. The platform then received a mandate from the South Africa Water Network to align its efforts with national strategic water priorities on wastewater treatment, reuse, and water demand management/conservation projects. The NBF Water Initiative now works with the South Africa Water Network to engage private-sector champions in three significant projects that will help deliver South Africa's Water for Growth and Development strategy, and other potential areas of collaboration are also actively being pursued. These projects support national strategic objectives to diversify water sources and have the potential to change the way South Africa uses its wastewater. The result of the Initiative's work in South Africa has been a streamlined and improved process for integrating private-sector contributions to water projects.

An example of a public-private-community project in the South African context is the NBF platform working with a major coal mining company to codesign a large project that treats and uses excess underground mine water to supplement a local municipal system. The proposal is to treat wastewater to potable standards, with other stakeholders signing long-term purchase agreements. The NBF platform is working with the project owner to secure project financing from potential developers and funders, including identifying purchasers for the treated water. The ability to bring together private, public, and NGO stakeholders (to help design social aspects of the project) would have been impossible for any one of these entities to do without the existence of the platform and its brokerage capabilities.

Jordan

During a meeting held at the World Economic Forum on the Middle East in May 2009, public and private stakeholders recommended creating a Jordan Business Alliance on Water, inspired by the experiences of India and South Africa. The Jordanian Minister of Water and Irrigation and the Minister of Planning and Infrastructure mandated the World Economic Forum to help the government catalyse a major new partnership initiative to develop a stream of new public-private-community water projects that could benefit all aspects of Jordanian society, making best use of scarce water resources and attracting private as well as public financing. The ministers set the new initiative the task of mobilizing more than US$ 50 million in new projects for Jordan by 2012. In October 2009, the World Economic Forum, USAID, and GTZ (German Society for Technical Cooperation) organized a Jordan Business Alliance for Water workshop in Amman. Seventy representatives from Jordan's public, private, and civil society sectors took part in the workshop, which brought representatives together for a day of open dialogue, networking, and brainstorming on encouraging collective action to tackle Jordan's severe water problem. Following this workshop, a task force was established that included USAID, GTZ, the Jordan Chamber of Industry, and the American Chamber of Commerce in Jordan, alongside the two Ministries. A project coordinator has been recruited, a strategy developed, and the Jordan Business Alliance on Water is now working on its first two projects—both on wastewater treatment and reuse for the country's stone and marble cutting sector.

An Evolving Process

From the beginning, the focus of this pilot work was to explore and establish multistakeholder coalitions for water reform by centering on the concept of "brokerage"—an entity that could facilitate deals among relevant stakeholders by matching people, resources, and projects to increase and improve the water initiatives emerging from the process. While the brokerage issue has emerged as an integral element to success, it was found that the platforms themselves also played key roles that contributed to the success of the process. These include the ability of a portion of new local or national water architecture to:

- advocate and support a new public-private-civil approach to problem identification and project codesign
- connect key stakeholders in the water sector, across the public, private and civil society space, within a neutral context to develop relationships, understand different agendas, and share experiences and ideas
- anchor the new process, providing a neutral locus for people to submit their frustrations and questions to (e.g., a "postbox" needed to be created, along with a "phone number" and an entity that would manage workshops and discussion fora).

While these dimensions do not constitute a formula, combined they did play a key role in supporting a new and enhanced collaboration between stakeholders and the delivery of partnership projects over a sustained time frame.

For example, in Jordan during the initiative's inaugural workshop, several participants commented that it was the first time they had ever spoken with and learned of the priorities and activities of stakeholders from other sectors involved in the national water agenda. While in the beginning several of the thematic working groups (e.g., agriculture, food processing, energy, industry) struggled to see ways in which they were connected, further dialogue soon created self-identification of interlinked nexus issues. More than just a courtesy sharing of information, these initial discussions required intensive preparation, a clear fact base of analysis, and robust facilitation to ensure effective dialogue and transfer of knowledge between stakeholders unaccustomed to collaborating across sectors.

In India, training exercises for private-sector representatives on how to codesign PPCP projects showed that they were unused to thinking about water in collaborative terms. Connecting them to others became valuable only once they expanded their perspective of the problem and possible solutions. Only then did they start to recognize the commercial logic of win-win public-private projects such as wastewater reuse.

A further key lesson was the need to translate cultural and sector-based ways of thinking and communicating into a common language. Parties with different backgrounds required a common understanding of the water problem before they could move forward. In South Africa, a key and constant message throughout discussions was the usefulness of framing the water discussion in the context of South Africa's economic growth strategy. This enabled government representatives to view the water challenge as something cutting across portfolios (agriculture, energy, industry, etc.) and not just being relevant to the Department of Water Affairs. Similarly, private-sector representatives increasingly saw the necessity of securing South Africa's water challenge collectively for all, so that the national growth challenge could be met. Consequently, this meant developing company partnership strategies that went beyond meeting minimum legal requirements and towards engaging in activities with other stakeholders to address common problems.

One other important outcome from the process was the ability of these coalition platforms to catalyse financing not only of individual projects but also of the overarching process. In India, the IBAW platform benefited from a US$ 200,000 grant from USAID; and in turn, this stimulated an additional US$ 20 million of project financing support, with the ratio being for every US$ 1 of development grant, US$ 6 of private-sector and US$ 3 of "unblocked" government funding was catalysed for the new project pipeline. This suggests that investing in a public-private process or a collaborative water platform can be an effective use of development aid, and that it can leverage significant amounts of private-sector capital to support the projects and programmes the platform generates.

In contrast, during the first stage of the pilot experience in South Africa, no finances were available to support a full-time coordinator of the process, and that absence of a local coordinator delayed the implementation of the conceptualized projects. Experience showed that if funding can be found to resource a platform and trusted broker up front, the work can catalyse results and therefore stimulate additional project financing. A known and trusted coordinator who can guide the process and motivate stakeholders, who is affiliated to some form of neutral secretariat, can make the difference between success and failure. (The South African platform now has resourcing and such a coordinator, and is working well.)

Another lesson was that "anchoring" work such as this is, without question, the most critical piece of the puzzle. The public-private process that is being advocated requires numerous shifts in thinking about the problem, potential solutions, contributions, relationships, and roles, both for governments, business, and NGOs and for development agency partners. Without constant upkeep, it is all too easy for people to have an "existential crisis" and return to former habits and patterns of thinking; as a result, the new platform can serve as the anchor to secure the process, set a north star, and ensure progress. Creating lasting change requires this anchor that can partner with all the stakeholders, help in the transfer of knowledge, build trust, oversee project activities, assist with implementation, and follow up with stakeholders to ensure continued commitment.

The Way Forward

Clearly, as previous chapters in this book have shown, there is no single solution to the water challenge: the right solution is highly dependent on political and cultural contexts at subnational, national, regional, and global levels. Because of this, it is widely acknowledged that governments, industry (including agriculture/agribusiness), communities, and nongovernmental organizations must work together to mobilize the resources and unique strengths of each.

Yet finding common ground among these diverse stakeholders is challenging, frustrating, and time-consuming, and therefore it is often neglected. The pilot work described above has had some success in creating coalitions and platforms to develop multistakeholder solutions to water scarcity challenges in the context of economic growth.

Although the implications of water scarcity are daunting, the challenge also presents an incredible opportunity to rethink how to meet the needs of multiple water users with fewer water resources. A long-term approach is required to fully achieve this vision, but practical steps can be taken by individuals and organizations today to initiate the transformation. Based on the experience of this pilot work, the following strategic elements could be viewed as a basis for action:

1. Create an institutional commons—the shared resource or "space" formed by individuals and organizations that are linked by mutual needs and interests, where ideas are shared, challenges are tackled, and innovation can emerge.
2. Provide funding to support these networks and processes—experience shows that creating institutional commons at different scales (project, local, national, regional, global) is fairly cheap and can result in better-designed projects that leverage private capital and meet social needs; despite these benefits, it remains difficult to attract public or donor funds to support these efforts.
3. Develop innovation vectors—individuals with the skills and motivation to collaborate with counterparts in other sectors for

sustainable water management and use at local, regional, and global levels; such innovation vectors can be engineers, businesspeople, financiers, government bureaucrats, grassroots organizers, or others who are working on water-related issues in their respective organizations, companies, and fields.

4. Focus on *integrated* water management and service delivery—diversify away from traditional solutions of ad hoc water storage and supply projects, and emphasize investment in integrated solutions (e.g. wastewater reuse between industry, municipality, and agriculture) that are capable of meeting the needs of multiple water consumers in a watershed.

5. Base all of these discussions and activities on a sound fact base regarding the water resource situation of the country now and under business-as-usual trends into the near future (e.g., through 2030)—ensure that all key stakeholders debate and agree on the core dimensions of the water resource "situation analysis"; from a common starting point, a transformation discussion can begin.

At the World Economic Forum Annual Meeting in 2010, the potential for a leader group of countries to engage in informal multi-country platforms to drive forward water resource management reform was discussed. It was agreed that the combination of using the economic analysis developed by the first phase of the 2030 Water Resources Group (as discussed in the previous chapter) as a starting point to develop a fact base on which to secure reform discussions, together with the formation of multistakeholder coalitions and platforms that governments would need to work with in order to catalyse a comprehensive water-sector reform process, was a compelling combination.

The challenge was then set out: how to create a mechanism to *ACT*. Could a next stage of the Forum's Water Initiative be combined with the WRG approach, such that a marriage of fact-based *A*nalysis and multistakeholder *C*oalition building could lead to a water-sector *T*ransformation process in a country that was keen to engage in such novel cross-sector, public-private-civil activity?

Conclusion

The previous chapters have shown that water security (whether it be the challenge of too little water over long periods of time, or too much water all at once) is one of the most tangible and fastest growing social, political, and economic challenges we face. It is also a fast unfolding environmental crisis.

Analysis in this book suggests that the world will face a 40% global shortfall between forecast demand and available supply by 2030. Further, and because of our interlinked economy, accelerating stress on the world's water will affect food and energy systems around the world. For example, within the next fifteen to twenty years, the worsening water security situation risks triggering a global food crisis, with shortfalls of up to 30% in cereal production. At the same time, fast-growing regions such as Asia will also need to access much more freshwater for their energy and industrials sector (close to a 70% increase by 2030). Without a step change in how available water resources are managed, these trade-offs create an impossible demand-supply conundrum for governments to resolve.

The public-good and common-property characteristics of water (unlike energy), and the close and intricate links between water security and food security, energy, trade, national security, health and livelihoods, business strategy, financial markets, and an increasingly variable climate, have been highlighted in various chapters throughout this book. These characteristics and interlinkages, however, make finding solutions to the water challenge that much more difficult. While government might be the ultimate custodian of the national water resource, and can play a role in setting frameworks, it is clear that many stakeholders across different government departments and across the business, academic, and civil society communities have to also play a role in designing and delivering these national or local solutions. This multi-stakeholder challenge means that *coalitions* are required—public-private-civil coalitions focused collectively on meeting the water security challenge, each leveraging their own comparative advantage towards meeting this challenge, within a common policy framework. This has been a core finding from many recent business and water reports and initiatives, as discussed in chapter 8, and from the pilot work undertaken to explore new water partnerships, discussed in chapter 11.

Yet coalition building is not easy. It is beyond the ability of an international agency, an NGO, a think tank, a farmers' association, a trade union, or a company to create a "neutral convening" process to build a multistakeholder coalition to address the water security challenge in a properly holistic manner. Even governments find it sometimes difficult to do.

Nevertheless, three years of awareness raising about the water-food-energy-climate nexus, including by the World Economic Forum's Water Initiative, the Global Agenda on Water Security and more latterly the Water Resources Group, has helped to shift the global, regional, and industry agenda on water security. Over this time period, the desire among many officials, business leaders, experts, and civil society representatives has grown from raising awareness to taking action. This desire has been fueled by the arrival of new economic analysis, such as that described in chapter 10, that creates a clear fact base on which to design reform actions and implement some of the innovative decision-support system ideas available. The interest from some governments facing water security challenges to engage with such a coalition of expertise to help them with their water challenge has also been growing.

In a session at the time of the World Economic Forum Annual Meeting in Davos-Klosters in January 2010, the desire to move from dialogue to action, to build from economic analysis to coalition building, to work with and support governments in the water reform agenda, formed the core of the "Davos Initiative." This was a concept developed by a combination of business leaders and water experts who formed part of the Forum's network active in water across the Water Initiative and the Global Agenda Council, as well as representatives from the Water Resources Group. It sets out a proposition for a significant new initiative on water, based on the best available knowledge about how to offer a platform to work with governments to support a change process in water. This Proposition is summarized below.

"The Davos Proposition"

There is a need to move from dialogue to accelerating change. Using the World Economic Forum's neutral platforms and convening strength, a "Davos Initiative" is proposed. The initiative will create an unparalleled network of public, civil society, and private expertise on offer as a supporting partner for those countries seeking to transform the management of their water resources.

Building on analytical approaches from the 2030 Water Resources Group (http://2030waterresourcesgroup.com/), the Davos Initiative will engage with countries in their path towards water reform by helping them to obtain efficient access to the best available tools, practices, partnership models, and policies; build management capabilities; mobilize financial resources; and develop peer relationships across countries.

The Davos Initiative will work in collaboration with a set of countries for whom water is a high priority and who invite the Initiative to partner with them on the journey towards water security. The intention is to draw on knowledge from the public, the research, the nonprofit, and the private sectors, and to ensure that what is learned in those experiences can then become the basis for similar support in other countries.

The Davos Initiative will follow six principles:

- Create supportive country-level coalitions and networks, catalysed through partnerships involving members of the World Economic Forum's Water Initiative
- Accelerate change by using these networks to leverage and amplify existing efforts (rather than creating a parallel entity) and to disseminate knowledge widely
- Recognize the links between energy, food, and water security, and that smart management of these linkages can create win-win alignments with positive implications for growth, development, and sustainability
- Incorporate breakthrough ideas from all sources: technology and engineering companies, financial services partners, social entrepreneurs, aid agencies, international organizations, development finance institutions, civil society, NGOs, community organizations, farmers, think tanks, and research centers
- Leverage deep content experts, including networks of national and international expertise as well as those who form the World Economic Forum's Global Agenda Council on Water Security and other Forum Agenda Councils
- Enable countries to highlight collective and individual leadership in the water space, lessen political risks of action, and leverage shared intellectual resources across countries.

Those meeting at Davos agree to form a working group to develop the frame, content, specific reform activities, governance, partnership, and financing arrangements for the new Davos Initiative vehicle. The aim is to launch the new vehicle in 2010.

The scope of such an initiative is ambitious. It would aim to bring a sense of coordination across contemporary areas of work in the water space, helping to channel resources and maximize impact. A snowball effect is aspired to, whereby if many of the key water activities and tools being explored today were to form part of a broader coalition for change (each being able to offer services fitting their particular comparative advantage and the bespoke needs of the government in question), this alignment would make it easier for governments to gain a truly demand-driven set of services and resources to fit their various needs. A critical-mass public-private coalition for change in water could emerge to support governments, setting in play the required transformation.

The sentiment to move from analysis to collaborative action, as laid out in the Davos Initiative, is echoed by senior business figures. "To make a difference on the water challenges we all face, governments, civil society and businesses must work together as never before. For business leaders in particular, we need to speak up, stand up and scale up our efforts on water sustainability," says Muhtar Kent, Chairman and CEO, The Coca-Cola Company, United States.[1] The ministers, government officials, international organization, CEO and NGO leaders, and other experts who discussed the Davos Initiative that day in January 2010 agreed that it was a good idea, the right idea, and that the work should go ahead—that a significant new public-private expert coalition to work with governments on water should be developed.

As a result of that discussion, and through further conversations through spring and summer 2010, several governments facing severe water challenges are now involved in more substantive public-private expert dialogue on water security and water resource reform by engaging with this new initiative. These include the Government of Jordan, the State Government of Karnataka in India and the Government of Mexico, through its national water authority Conagua. Below is the viewpoint from one of those governments, Jordan, who arguably faces one of the severest water security challenges of any fast-growing middle-income country.

A Viewpoint from Jordan

Ministry of Planning and International Cooperation of Jordan

Realizing that water scarcity is becoming more and more of a pressing issue in many parts of the world, and a key challenge to our country's economic and social development as well as political stability, our priority should continue to focus towards affording the right weight to this issue in our planning process, as an underlining condition for livelihood, development, and growth. Therefore, we welcome and support the idea of establishing a multistakeholder and trans-sectoral water platform to help us tackle water challenges and develop a set of practical water reform pathways applicable to our country's specific needs. In this context, bringing together efforts of governments, donors, and industries, in addition to creating business alliances by building public-private partnerships to tackle challenges in this sector, continue to be of prime importance.

In Jordan, the issue of water scarcity is of utmost importance to the country's future development and growth, as Jordan is one of the ten most water-deprived countries in the world. The average Jordanian's share of fresh water is 145 cubic meters per annum, critically below the international water poverty line of 1,000 cubic meters per capita annually. This reality has been at the center of our development plans, where we have been committed to developing comprehensive and integrated water strategies, taking into account that the projected water deficit in Jordan by 2022 is 284 MCM (million cubic meters).[2]

Jordan has invested heavily in the water sector, having designed and implemented numerous projects in the field of treatment plants, water networks, and desalination plants, all with the objective of achieving water security to Jordanians. The government of Jordan, with the support of its partners, has heavily invested in improving water supply throughout the Kingdom, enhancing water loss reduction, as well as upgrading and rehabilitating water networks and wastewater treatment plants. The government's investments in the water sector over the past three years amounted to 17% of our total investments in all sectors. Envisaged investments between 2011 and 2013 in the water sector is expected to reach around 21% of the government's total investments, which is the highest investment among all priority sectors.

As part of our medium- to long-term planning, Jordan is working on a number of mega-projects in the water sector that are based on partnerships with the private sector, and are particularly essential in overcoming the chronic natural resource and development constraints in this vital sector, as well as significant environmental challenges. In the medium term, Jordan has embarked on the implementation of the Disi Water Conveyance project to help alleviate a severe water shortage in Jordan's capital and surrounding areas. In the longer term, efforts are also undergoing to move forward with the launch of the Jordan Red Sea–Dead Sea Conveyance project. The project consists of constructing a tunnel to transport water from the Red Sea to the Dead Sea, a desalination plant to provide drinking water for the region, and a hydropower plant to take advantage of the more than four-hundred-meter difference in elevation between the two seas. The aim of this project is to halt the decline of the Dead Sea level and also to provide drinking water for the people of Jordan, Israel, and the Palestinian Authority.

But hard water infrastructure alone won't close the looming water deficit. Jordan's water deficit would occur despite new water collection, distribution, and treatment plants. Water investments are expensive and yield low economic dividends. Extreme water scarcity and increasing cost of supply will suppress Jordan's potential for economic growth until and unless it can do more with less. That is why the government's water strategy for 2008–2022 is based on the premise of "Water for Life." It is based on a vision-driven aim of reducing water demand, boosting efficiency, increasing the number of stakeholders involved in water decision-making, reaching innovative solutions for water shortages, and realizing alternatives. All of this requires an inter-sectoral approach to managing Jordan's future water needs. Indeed, the initiative on the water sector undertaken by the World Economic Forum/Water Resources Group is of prime importance, particularly in bringing together governments, business leaders, civil society, and global water experts to further raise awareness about the structural challenges in this vital sector, and build alliances with businesses and civil society to help address the water challenge.

Building on Jordan's experience to date with the Business Alliance on Water, catalysed at the World Economic Forum on the Middle East in 2009, the World Economic Forum Water Initiative with WRG is crucial for Jordan. In particular, its objective aligns with our commitment to engage in multistakeholder dialogue and create a platform in order to explore new possibilities and to benefit from international experience to address the water challenge, in addition to encouraging cross-territorial water projects. We hope that successful experiences elsewhere could be duplicated in Jordan with the initiation of numerous public-private-community partnerships for water projects. This effective international platform will help us develop a common language with nations who face water security challenges, and it will help in exchanging ideas to develop and implement water reform pathways to reach the common objective of reaching global water security and synergizing water-sector development.

So, How Will This Initiative Work?

An alignment has been devised between the Forum's Water Initiative and the Water Resources Group. The combination of high-class analytical capacity, as demonstrated by the Water Resources Group in chapter 10, and the multistakeholder convening capabilities of the World Economic Forum, as discussed in chapter 11, offers great potential to develop a high-impact public-private platform for fast action on water issues. Its work would be placed within the context of the water nexus for economic growth set out across the preceding chapters, such that an integrated approach to water resource management and reform is taken, one that views the nation's water endowment as an integral part of the political, social, and economic fabric of the country and its contribution to the world.

The goal of this alignment is to build a demand-driven platform of world-class expertise that can support governments to *ACT*: to engage in fact-based *A*nalysis, to *C*onvene multistakeholder discussions, and to build coalitions so as to undertake public-private *Transformations* in the water space. It is based squarely on the concept of the Davos Initiative.

The project will work for a specific period of time, autumn 2010 through spring 2012, in a few example countries, such as India (particularly at the state as well as potentially the national level), Jordan and Mexico. The objective is to show "proof of concept" that a public-private-expert platform can work with—and in support of—governments to help design and action a very practical national water reform agenda within the context of economic growth strategies. It is possible that a chapter in China and potentially South Africa may also be pursued, too. A network of companies, including many of those mentioned in this book, is helping to support and spearhead the work. A range of development agencies, international finance institutions, NGOs, and other expert organizations are also involved, particularly at the country level.

In general the work will follow two steps.

1. The first step will support the development of national and regional fact-based analysis on gaps between water supply and demand, which will lead to prioritized recommendations/sector strategies, developing analysis similar to the approach set out in chapter 10. The work will build on and deepen these existing analytical approaches. It will draw particularly on the ability of international finance institutions such as the International Finance Corporation (IFC) and the Asian Development Bank (ADB) to help establish a request for a water dialogue from governments, and then use the fact base that these governments request as the basis for detailed discussion and action planning. This work can be viewed as a series of time-bound developments of analytic tools (up to four to six months) in each country, region, or river basin, supported by expert consultancies.

2. In these example countries, and working from the first-step analytics, the work will then help in the building of local public-private coalitions to identify potential reform projects, programmes, and policies, and to help leverage expertise from the expert, civil society, and private sector (technology, expertise, and advice) to assist the public sector in their water planning and management activities. This will be done through cataloguing best practices domestically and internationally, and by holding workshops, dialogues, and stakeholder engagement and awareness raising activities. The analysis created in the first step will help provide the frame and context for these catalogues and discussions, helping to focus stakeholders to design ways to implement the most cost effective levers for improved water management. Government, business, NGO, farmers, domestic users and international community representatives will all be engaged in these discussions, so that the specific actions (projects, policies,

partnering arrangements, etc.) that emerge are understood and generally supported by all. In essence, this work can be viewed as establishing a substantive public-private-expert interaction in-country, which leverages domestic and international networks of industry and civil society expertise to work alongside public-sector representatives and expert staff from the international financial institutions, regional development banks, and bilateral development agencies. It will entail a series of longer-term partnership activities with the government and country in question, especially to monitor and track the impact of the reforms and projects that are implemented. It may well draw on expert domestic or international consultancy expertise to assist in specific matters or structural analyses, as required. It will operationalize the idea of a public-private-expert platform to help countries undertake water reform journeys that the experiences set out in chapter 11 have conceptualized.

While the primary focus of this work is to create impact and a "proof of concept" for this new public-private approach in some key regions, the project will also design a new global entity, in collaboration with the IFC and other international organizations, that can drive such work forward on a permanent basis for any other government who may want help with their water strategy in the future. In this way, the work itself becomes an incubator that will grow and launch a new piece of global architecture in water. The IFC is an important stakeholder, as it bridges the public and private sector. It can develop many of the innovative financing mechanisms that have been identified as important to be able to leverage domestic and international investment into countries for water, on the back of a reform strategy.

In addition to the generous support the World Economic Forum Water Initiative receives from its Industry Partners to deliver its work on water, this particular initiative also benefits from further sponsorship, from both the public and the private sector.[3] Uniquely, the work also asks the participating government or related domestic agencies to co-sponsor activities, such that all stakeholders are working within a "shoulder to shoulder" collaboration.

The project concept was developed in conjunction with the Forum's Water Initiative Project Board companies, the Forum's Water Security Global Agenda Council and the Water Resources Group, within the context of the Forum's recent Global Redesign Initiative (GRI). This sort of short-term, high-impact initiative that can create both country impact and a new piece of public-private architecture for the world system is very much in line with what the findings of the GRI suggested the World Economic Forum can helpfully do. The work will offer those involved a unique opportunity to advance the global, regional, and industry agenda on water security; further, it will provide a tangible benefit to the pilot governments, supporting them as they address one of their most pressing development problems.

The story of the water security nexus that public figures, experts, NGOs, and business leaders have put together over the previous chapters is compelling. A deeper understanding of our future water needs has been achieved through this work and others. With renewed urgency and greater political appetite, leaders from across the government, expert, and business communities are now embarking on a tangible public-private-expert reform agenda.

You can find out more about where the first reforms will be taking place and how to get involved by going to http://www.weforum.org/water.

Notes

1. World Economic Forum Water Initiative, *The Bubble Is Close to Bursting*, 2009.

2. Royal Commission for Water/Ministry of Water and Irrigation, Water for Life. Jordan's Water Strategy 2008–2022, 1999. http://www.idrc.ca/uploads/user-S/12431464431JO_Water-Strategy09.pdf

3. At the publication of this book, additional sponsors included The Coca-Cola Company, the IFC, Nestlé, PepsiCo, the Swiss Development Agency SDC and USAID.

Acknowledgments

Many people have contributed to the work set out in the previous pages.

At the World Economic Forum Annual Meeting 2008 in Davos-Klosters, a special focus was given to water. The intent was to reframe how we think about this unique natural resource. Thanks to the sustained leadership of the CEOs and senior executives of a core group of World Economic Forum Industry and Strategic Partner Companies, the debate has been sustained and deepened through 2008, 2009, and 2010.

This book encapsulates the progression of the debate, through three Annual Meetings and many World Economic Forum regional meeting workshops, private discussions, and public events linked to the wider official calendar. Forum Industry Partners and Global Agenda Council Experts said in 2008 that they wanted a publication that could pull together the best global thinking there is on water as a key strategic asset, and to describe where we might be in an economic and geopolitical sense by 2030 if we don't deflect from a business-as-usual management path.

This publication is the fruit of those labors.

Looking back over the records of meetings over the last three or four years, close to 350 representatives from business, government, NGOs, the scientific community, and international agencies from all around the world have taken part in the Forum's series of water discussions to help contribute to the debate and to this publication. If you were one of them, our sincere thanks. You may well recognize your contributions to a session reflected somewhere in this publication.

The Forum Water Initiative has benefited from an exemplary Project Board of CEOs and designated content professionals, listed below, to whom we extend our deepest gratitude for their leadership and commitment. You will find many of their contributions highlighted in the previous pages.

- *CH2M HILL:* Lee A. McIntire, Chairman and CEO; Robert Bailey, President, Water Group; and the late Ralph Peterson, former Chairman and CEO.
- *Cisco Systems, Inc.:* John Chambers, Chairman of the Board and CEO; and Juan Carlos Castilla-Rubio, Managing Director, Sustainability and Resources Innovation Group.
- *The Coca-Cola Company:* Muhtar Kent, Chairman and CEO; Jeff Seabright, Vice-President, Environment and Water; Greg Koch, Managing Director, Global Water Stewardship; Lisa Manley, Director,

Sustainability Communications; and Neville Isdell, former Chairman and CEO.

- *The Dow Chemical Company:* Andrew Liveris, President, CEO, and Chairman of the Board; and Lisa Schroeter, Director of International Policy.
- *Halcrow Group Ltd.*: Tony Pryor, Non-executive Chairman; Michael Norton, Managing Director, Water and Power Group; Richard Harpin, Head of Water Scarcity; Bryan Harvey, Strategy and Development Director for Water and Power Group; and Bill Peacock, Regional Managing Director, India.
- *Hindustan Construction Company Ltd.*: Ajit Gulabchand, Chairman; and Niyati Sareen, General Manager of Corporate Social Responsibility.
- *International Finance Corporation:* Lars Thunell, Vice-President and CEO; and Usha Rao-Monari, Global Head of Water, Global Infrastructure and Natural Resources Department.
- *Nestlé SA:* Peter Brabeck-Letmathe, Chairman of the Board and Foundation Board Member of World Economic Forum; Paul Bulcke, CEO; Frits van Dyke, Zone Director for Asia, Oceania, Africa, and Middle East; and Herbert Oberhänsli, Head of Economics and International Relations.
- *PepsiCo, Inc.*: Indra Nooyi, Chairman and CEO; and Daniel Bena, Director of Sustainable Development.
- *Rio Tinto Group:* Tom Albanese, CEO; Paul Skinner, former Chairman; and Kristina Ringwood, Principal Adviser, Environment.
- *SABMiller plc*: Graham Mackay, CEO; and Andrew Wales, Global Head of Sustainable Development.
- *Standard Chartered Bank*: Peter Sands, Group Chief Executive; and Alex Barrett, Global Head of Client Research.
- *Syngenta AG*: Mike Mack, CEO; Juan Gonzalez-Valero, Head of Public Policy and Partnerships; and Peleg Chevion, Head of Business Development Water.
- *Unilever NV and plc*: Paul Polman, CEO; Miguel Pestana, Vice-President of Global External Affairs; and Rebecca Marmot, Global External Affairs Director.

The foreword has acknowledged the extraordinary level of leadership and commitment this project has received from senior business leaders, and I echo fully those sentiments.

Acknowledgement also to Martin Stuchtey, Giulio Boccaletti and the rest of the Water Resources Group team at McKinsey & Company, both for their outstanding work with the Water Resources Group and their expert support and insight as project advisers to the Forum's Water Initiative.

As is the multistakeholder nature of the World Economic Forum, the Project Board is supported by a Council of Experts (the Forum's Global Agenda Council on Water Security) and also by other sponsoring agencies and observers to the board. Our grateful thanks are extended to all of the Water Agenda Council members past and present, with particular appreciation to the Chair of the Council 2008–2010, Margaret Catley-Carlson, for the personal leadership she has brought to this issue. We are extremely grateful for the hard work and commitment she has shown both to this topic, the Water Security Council, and to the Forum's wider mission, and we are delighted she has provided such a compelling foreword to this book. Insight and thought from many other members of the Council are also provided throughout the publication and we are grateful to them all.

Past and present Members of the World Economic Forum Global Agenda Council on Water Security between 2007 and 2010 include:

- *Arjun Thapan,* Chair of Council; Director-General, South-East Asia Department, Asian Development Bank, Manila
- *Margaret Catley-Carlson,* Vice-Chair of Council; Member, UN Secretary-General's Advisory Council on Water
- *Tony Allan,* Professor, and Head of KCL Water Research Group, King's College, United Kingdom
- *Don Blackmore,* Chair, eWater, Australia
- *Peter Brabeck-Letmathe,* Chairman of the Board, Nestlé SA, Switzerland; Member of the Foundation Board of the World Economic Forum
- *John Briscoe,* Gordon McKay Professor of the Practice of Environmental Engineering, Harvard University Schools of: Engineering and Applied Sciences; Public Health; and Kennedy School of Government
- *Daniel C. Esty,* Director, Yale Center for Environmental Law and Policy, United States
- *Franklin Fisher,* Emeritus Professor, Massachusetts Institute of Technology, United States
- *Gao Shiji,* Director, Institute for Economic System and Management, State Council Office for Restructuring the Economic Systems, People's Republic of China
- *Peter Gleick,* President and Cofounder, Pacific Institute, United States
- *Angel Gurria,* Secretary-General, Organisation for Economic Co-operation and Development, Paris

- *CS Kiang,* Chairman, Environmental Fund, Peking University People's Republic of China
- *Upmanu Lall,* Professor, Department of Earth and Environmental Engineering, Columbia University, United States
- *Joe Madiath,* Executive Director, Gram Vikas, India
- *Francis Matthew,* Editor-at-Large, Gulf News, United Arab Emirates
- *Rabi Mohtar,* Director, Global Engineering Program, and Professor, Environmental and Natural Resources Engineering, Agricultural and Biological Engineering Department, Purdue University, United States
- *Maria Mutagamba,* Minister of State for Water of Uganda; President, Africa Ministerial Conference on Water
- *Jacqueline Novogratz,* Founder and CEO, Acumen Fund, United States
- *Herbert Oberhänsli,* Head of Economics and International Relations, Nestlé SA, Switzerland
- *Stuart Orr,* Freshwater Manager, World Wide Fund for Nature International, Switzerland
- *Usha Rao-Monari,* Global Head of Water, Global Infrastructure and Natural Resources Department, International Finance Corporation
- *Amitabha Sadangi,* Executive Director, International Development Enterprises, India
- *Claudia Sadoff,* Lead Economist, South Asia Water Resources Group, World Bank, Kathmandu, Nepal
- *Jeff Seabright,* Vice-President of Environment and Water Resources, The Coca-Cola Company, United States
- *Ismail Serageldin,* Director, Bibliotheca Alexandrina, Egypt
- *Jack Sim,* Founder and Director, World Toilet Organization, Singapore
- *Pasquale Steduto,* Chief of Water Development and Management Unit, Food and Agriculture Organization, United Nations, Rome
- *Alberto Székely,* Ambassador, Border Resources Division, Ministry of Foreign Affairs, Mexico
- *Dr. Patricia Wouters,* Director, UNESCO Centre for Water Law, Policy, and Science, University of Dundee, Scotland

Thanks are also due to the Swiss Development Agency, particularly François Münger, Christoph Jakob, and Director-General Martin Dahinden; and the US Agency for International Development, particularly Sharon Murray and Rebecca Black, who have provided invaluable support and guidance to the Forum's water work over the past several years. Additional thanks for thoughts and contributions over the years to the water initiative are also due to Mohamed Ait-Kadi, President, General Council of Agricultural Development, Morocco; and David Molden, overall coordinator for the

Comprehensive Assessment of Water Management for Agriculture (*Water for Food, Water for Life*).

The production of this book, nor indeed the Water Initiative itself at the Forum, would not have been possible without an outstanding and hard-working team. Deepest thanks to all past and present Water Initiative team members and all associated staff at the World Economic Forum. You do a tremendous job. I hope you enjoy this book and see your influence within its pages. Maybe it goes some way to repaying all the effort you put in over the years. Thanks in particular to:

Alexandre Dauphin
Alex Wong
Arun Eapen
Darren Wachtler
Helena Leurent
Katherina Kumar
Melanie Duval
Peter Beez
Ramya Krishnaswamy
Sylvia Lee
Valerie Aillaud
Valerie Weinzierl

A special thanks to Robert Greenhill, Managing Director and Chief Business Officer of the World Economic Forum, and to Sarita Nayyar, Senior Director at the World Economic Forum, for their guidance and strategic insight in managing this process. A special acknowledgement is also due to Dan Gagnier, former Senior Vice-President of Corporate Affairs, Alcan; and Jürg Gerber, former head of Global Projects, Alcan, who together with their colleague François Münger, Senior Water Adviser at the Swiss Development Agency, and Forum Managing Director Rick Samans, had the remarkable foresight back in 2005 to first establish a Water Initiative at the World Economic Forum.

There are, of course, countless others we acknowledge who have contributed to this work. Please accept our apologies that we couldn't fit all your names into these few pages.

To create the book itself, acknowledgement is due to James Workman, who helped edit various first draft inputs, and to the publishing team (past and present) at Island Press, the very patient editors Emily Davis and Todd Baldwin, and the steady hand of President of Island Press Chuck Savitt.

It has been a privilege to lead this work at the World Economic Forum, and to be able to serve such an auspicious public, private, and expert network.

I am looking forward immensely to the next stage of the work as the Water Resources Group collaboration moves from insight to action.

Finally, please accept my apologies for any mistakes or misrepresentations that might be found in the preceding text. As the editor for this project, the responsibility for any errors that may have crept in rests with me.

—Dominic Waughray
Senior Director, Head Environmental Initiatives
World Economic Forum, Geneva, October 2010